The **LIFE** of
I

Anne Manne is a Melbourne writer. She has been a regular columnist for the *Australian* and the *Age*. More recently her essays on contemporary culture such as child abuse, pornography, gendercide and disability have all appeared in *The Monthly* magazine. Her essay 'Ebony: The Girl in the Room', was included in *The Best Australian Essays: A Ten-Year Collection*. Her book, *Motherhood: How Should We Care for Our Children*, was a finalist in the Walkley Award for Best Non-Fiction Book of 2006. She has written a *Quarterly Essay*, 'Love and Money; The Family and the Free Market', and a memoir, *So This is Life: Scenes from a Country Childhood*.

The LIFE of
I

THE NEW CULTURE
OF NARCISSISM

ANNE MANNE

MELBOURNE
UNIVERSITY
PRESS

MELBOURNE UNIVERSITY PRESS
An imprint of Melbourne University Publishing Limited
11–15 Argyle Place South, Carlton, Victoria 3053, Australia
mup-info@unimelb.edu.au
www.mup.com.au

First published 2014
Reprinted twice, 2014
Text ©Anne Manne, 2014
Design and typography © Melbourne University Publishing Limited, 2014

Cover design by Jenny Grigg
Typeset in Berthold Baskerville 12/16pt by Cannon Typesetting
Printed in Australia by McPherson's Printing Group

National Library of Australia Cataloguing-in-Publication entry

Manne, Anne, author.

The life of I : the new culture of narcissim / Anne Manne.

9780522861082 (paperback)
9780522861099 (ebook)

Narcissism.
Self.
Personality and culture.
Moral development.

616.85854

Australian Government

Australia Council
for the Arts

MIX
Paper from
responsible sources
FSC® C001695

Contents

Acknowledgements

WRITING SEEMS A solitary task—yet it is also a deeply collaborative process. One is surrounded by companions, even while alone at one's desk. In a book ranging across so many subjects, there are all the wonderful writers, scholars, thinkers and courageous journalists whose work one engages with and benefits from on a daily basis. It is not always possible in to pay tribute to each one, but all those I have talked to or read have made important contributions to the book.

Thanks to Frances Salo Thompson and The Melbourne Psychoanalytic Society, and Ron Spielman from the Sydney Psychoanalytic Societies who invited me to write a lecture on the 150th anniversary of Freud's birth, which formed the kernel of Chapter 4. Frances and Vivienne Elton also generously shared their ideas on narcissism, as did Ron Spielman. I have received so much encouragement from friends in the writing of this book it is impossible to mention them all, so I will just mention a few. To Naomi Stadlen and Lauren Porter, the strength of our friendship and our long-standing conversation about what matters means more to me than I can say. Tom Pataki has always been a wonderful interlocutor on psychoanalysis, and to Rai Gaita, whose every word is antithetical to narcissism and his lovely wife Yael, you are precious to me.

A book is also a collaborative enterprise with the publisher. Sadly, few readers would know that behind the author's name is a small army of contributors, without whom the book would never come to fruition. I am grateful to the many people at Melbourne University Publishing who have given energy and attention to this project. Many thanks to my publisher Louise Adler for sparkling lunches and her exuberant enthusiasm, as the ideas were first sketched out. To my editor Sally Heath, thanks for your encouragement, perceptive eye for what interests readers, patience and unfailing good humour as we worked to a tight deadline. Copy-editor Emma Schwartz was a rigorous and careful first reader, while a cool-headed Penelope White did a wonderful job pulling together the manuscript over the final stages. I am very grateful to both of them for the high standard of their work. Many thanks also to designer Jenny Grigg for her stunning cover and to publicist Terri King for her indefatigable efforts.

The book's gestation also coincided with my mother's growing frailty. Thank you for your pride in this book. I hope I have your courage and stoicism in the face of ageing, yet at the same time the willingness to enjoy life and reach out to new friends when I am ninety! My daughters Kate and Lucy and my son-in-law Daniel, remain an inspiration with their piercing wit, high intelligence, moral seriousness, and deep capacity for empathy and care.

The deepest debt, of this book and my life, is to my husband Robert Manne. He has been the great encourager of my work. No one could have done more than he did in the course of writing and during the final stages. Typical of his generosity and capacity for attentiveness, he took over all domestic tasks and responsibility for our many animals, looked after me tenderly, yet still gave his formidable intelligence to reading and editing every draft. Not a day goes past without me feeling an astonished gratitude for the goodness of his character, and the happiness in our marriage. He is my truest friend and the very great love of my life. It is to him that the book is dedicated.

Part One

Narcissism and the Individual

Chapter 1

The Chosen One

Paranoia is the self-cure for insignificance ... the para-
noiac is at the centre of a world which has no centre ... to
be hated makes him feel real: he has made his presence
felt. To be unforgivable is to be unforgettable.

Adam Phillips, psychoanalyst

THE FIRST DAY of the holiday season in Norway dawned
sunny and calm. The promise of the summer drifted in on
the gentle breeze. On the idyllic island of Utøya, in the great tradition of the Norwegian labour movement, young idealists gathered
for their annual camp. In a tent city sprawled cosily among the
trees, the teenagers could meet, passionately discuss politics, talk
and sing around the campfires, go hiking and fall in love. In the
tiny coves beneath the rocks, the water from the lake, deep and
cold, lapped quietly on the shore.

Just then news of a bomb blast came across the radio, shatter-
ing the calm of the day. Terrorists, it seemed, had struck at the very
centre of the peaceful Scandinavian nation. Eight were dead,
many more injured. Frightened parents texted their children,
telling them how glad they were that they were safe at Utøya.

3

A handsome blond man, heavily armed and dressed in police garb, walked calmly towards the youngsters, beckoning them to come closer, telling them, 'You will be safe with me. I'm a cop.' Alarmed by news of the bomb, and reassured by the fact of his uniform, many of them began to move towards him. Then he shouted, 'You all must die!' And opened fire.

As their friends fell dead around them, the survivors took flight and ran, screaming in terror as the uniformed figure whooped with joy, laughing and cheering, as he picked them off one by one. They ran onto beaches and sheltered anywhere they could find: in tents, in buildings and under rocks. Some hid beneath corpses of the fallen. They dived into the icy lake, trying to swim away. Some could not bear the cold and turned back, only to find him standing above them, spraying bullets into the swimmers. As the water in the small coves turned red, they begged for their lives. Then the killer turned and pursued the others, who had fled through the trees before realising that, on the island, there was nowhere to run to. They hugged each other, sent text messages to parents saying they loved them, then turned off their mobile phones lest any noise—a tell-tale beep or even the sound of their ragged breathing—give away their hiding place. Few of those shot survived; the killer had chosen his weapon with care, using special dum-dum bullets that explode inside the body, causing maximum internal damage. And he shot each person multiple times.

The bomb and the holiday combined meant that police were horribly slow to arrive, allowing the killer over an hour to continue his rampage unimpeded. By the time they arrived, the gunman surrendered easily, showing the same calmness as when he had pulled the trigger. He stood with his hands above his head, his weapons lying a little way off behind him. At the end of his killing spree, sixty-nine young people lay dead on the island and eight by the bomb blast downtown. In a photograph appearing around the world, the gunman was shown being driven away, wearing a bright red sweater, unshaven, flanked by two heavily armed policemen. His expression was serene; he looked pleased, satisfied with a job well done.

The political Right around the world quickly declared, in advance of the evidence, that it was Islamic fundamentalist terrorists who were behind the attacks. However, the killer, Anders Behring Breivik, was no Islamist. Rather he was a 32-year-old Norwegian with a reasonably privileged and conventional background. His parents, a diplomat father and a mother who was a nurse, were divorced. In fact, he was much more sympathetic to the Right's own attacks on 'political correctness' than anything else.

All this was clear from Breivik's own words. Just before his crimes, he had posted on the internet a bizarre, rambling but coherent 1500-page manifesto he entitled *2083: A European Declaration of Independence*. Far from being an Islamic fundamentalist, Breivik quoted copiously from the Right's own ideological and populist rants—from the US Tea Party to the German-speaking *PI-News* blog, a European website devoted to 'politically incorrect' views. As one of the bloggers on *PI-News* admitted after the killing, everything in Breivik's manifesto could largely be found on this forum: virulent anti-Muslim sentiment; the desire to purge not just Norway but all of Europe of its Muslim invaders and their treasonous allies; a hatred of all those progressives and multiculturalists Breivik called 'Cultural Marxists', who supported immigration, feminism, sexual liberalism and the European Union.

In a curious echo of the Islamic fundamentalists he opposed, Breivik saw his massacre as a pivotal historic moment in the clash of civilisations: between Christian Europe and the invading Muslims; between the old patriarchal order and modern sexual depravity and promiscuity; between male domination and supremacy and what he saw as the disorder of the 'matriarchal, feminized' world that he had endured growing up, a civilisation brought undone by feminism.

The massacre on Utøya, Breivik declared, was no less than the opening salvo in a war in defence of Western civilisation, on behalf of a group he called the Knights Templar. Breivik claimed he had travelled to the United Kingdom, where the group had recently reactivated the medieval order of knights to fight the modern scourge, the conspiracy of global Muslims and their treacherous allies, Cultural Marxists. Breivik had, he claimed, been 'ordinated as the 8th justicar knight for the PCCTS, Knights Templar Europe'. It was this name that Breivik used to sign off his last diary entry before carrying out his attacks.

The Knights Templar, an elect group of fighters and assassins drawing their identity and inspiration from medieval times—one called himself Richard, after Christian crusading king Richard the Lionheart—would fight against European treason, depravity and disorder, against sexual licentiousness and the usurping Islamic infidel. 'God will anoint you with his power to go into battle,' Breivik told his fellow knights. Breivik, then, was a political assassin who had wanted, for political reasons, to execute the flower of Norway's leftist youth.

All political assassins, however, have a cradle. The first real clues to Breivik's family background emerged in the passages of his manifesto concerning women. Feminism was a central modern evil for Breivik. European women, he argued, had been ruined by it. They no longer had enough children to keep at bay the threat from the faster breeding Muslims. To this end, in his future utopia they would be discouraged from having anything above a bachelor's degree. They would have just three options: 'be a nun, be a prostitute, or marry men and bear children'.

His most vindictive chapters were aimed at his mother and sister. He derided the materialism of his half-sister, who now resided in the United States: 'The acquisition of wealth is the driving force in her life.' He railed against them both as 'promiscuous' and representatives of a degraded, degenerate modern humanity. He condemned his half-sister Elisabeth for contracting chlamydia 'after having more than 40 sexual partners (more than 15 of them Chippendale strippers who are known to be bearers of various diseases)'.

His mother, he claimed, had multiple sexual partners before developing meningitis from a venereal disease, contracted from his stepfather, who was a 'sexual beast with over 500 partners'. This had left her with 'the mind of a ten-year-old' and a stent in the brain. Rather than express compassion for his mother's predicament, Breivik was concerned only with male family dishonour: 'Both my sister and mother have not only shamed me, but they have shamed themselves and our family, a family that was broken in the first place due to the secondary effects of the feministic/sexual revolution.'

Despite borrowing from Far Right thinking, the gun-toting Breivik did not appear familiar with the conservative body of thought that argues that one response to a father-absent childhood may be a hyper-masculinity marked by misogyny and violence: 'I do not approve of the super-liberal, matriarchal upbringing as it completely lacked discipline and contributed to feminise me to a certain degree.'

Perhaps this fear of being feminised can account for Breivik's hyper-masculine photos at the end of his manifesto. He smiles and poses in profile shots, wearing a self-designed Knights Templar uniform or military garb festooned with medals, or, perhaps weirdest of all, a tight wetsuit, as he brandishes a sniper's rifle, with a caption on one sleeve, 'Marxist Hunter'. Presumably the wetsuit was designed to give him extra muscle definition. These carefully stage-managed photos were also posted on Facebook.

Soon other facts about Breivik's life began to emerge. The word 'ordinary' occurs again and again. Yet although he seemed to be a quiet, mild and undistinguished product of the Norwegian middle class, from an affluent area of Oslo, his background was not quite as placid as the oft-mentioned manicured window boxes and neat apartment buildings implied. It transpired that his father, Jens, had deserted Anders and his mother when he was about one year old. Jens then fought Anders' mother, Wenche, in an ugly custody battle for the son he hardly saw.

The custody bid failed. Over the years, Breivik saw his father off and on, before Jens abruptly severed all contact with him—and indeed all his children—after Breivik became a teenage graffiti artist. The young man expressed resentment of his father and the severance of the relationship: 'I have not spoken to my father since he isolated himself when I was fifteen—he was not very happy about my graffiti phase.' Commenting on the fact that his father had also cut off contact with his other children, Breivik remarked, 'So you can see whose fault that was.'

Evidence emerged of rejection, of failure and of extreme sensitivity to slights. Breivik left higher education before finishing a degree, preferring to self-educate. In his teens he was rejected by the army as 'unfit', for undisclosed reasons. While in his manifesto he claimed his business ventures were a success, it is abundantly clear they were a disaster. By his early twenties he had gambled in the stock market, invested in a bogus Nigerian internet scam for 'blood diamonds', lost a lot of money (more than a million kroner) and been declared bankrupt. It was at this point, the psychiatrists evaluating him said, that Breivik became increasingly isolated. He had few relationships with women although mentioned using the services of prostitutes just before the massacre. The only evidence of a girlfriend was an internet date he brought to Oslo from Belarus; he treated her so badly that the relationship went nowhere. She decried his 'male chauvinism'. He had no idea, she said, how to treat women except as inferiors. After this rejection, Breivik made no more attempts to have any relationships with women. Friends referred to his large ego, and his anger when women at his workplace preferred men of Asian descent. He wore makeup, and wanted to look like the British soccer star David Beckham. He feared he was 'ugly', and had undergone plastic surgery in his early twenties, producing an Aryan nose and a perfectly cleft chin. He was obsessed with bodybuilding, took testosterone and steroids to build muscle, and moved in social circles of gym buddies equally obsessed. At the time of his crime, however, he had lost touch with all friends. He had moved back to live with his mother, was rarely able to be prised out for even a coffee, and devoted a year of his life to playing the violent video game *World of Warcraft* night and day. His friends were worried about him, and about his increasingly extreme anti-Muslim ideas. By the time of the attacks, he was an isolated loner.

Once in jail, when he was asked by psychiatrists what he thought his victims might have felt, Breivik spoke only about his *own* suffering. Enacting all that carnage had been traumatic: 'On this day, I was waging a one-man war against all the regimes of Western Europe. I felt traumatised every second that blood and brains were spurting out. War is hell.' His greater interest was in how his death toll stacked up against similar mass shootings. And Breivik had other preoccupations. He was extremely sensitive about his appearance, and was highly disturbed by being unshaven while interviewed. His one moment of regret was over his earlier decision to have plastic surgery, which resulted in the 'loss of his great Nordic nose'.

When the first team of psychiatric experts gave their verdict, they declared that Anders Behring Breivik suffered from paranoid schizophrenia. They argued he was in a state of psychosis when he committed the crimes. He was of unsound mind and therefore unable to stand trial. Rather than being imprisoned, he should be detained in a closed, purpose-built psychiatric facility. The prosecutor concurred, offering no opposition.

Their report caused an immediate controversy. The opposition fell into three categories. For the victims' grieving families, it seemed—after all they had suffered—a monumental cop-out. How could justice be done unless Breivik faced trial, judgement, and punishment for his crime? It seemed as if he was escaping responsibility through the ruse of mental illness. Indeed, some argued, this was the intention. No trial meant no publicity or grandstanding; it denied the oxygen of attention not just to Breivik but also to other right-wing extremists and copycat psychopaths. The Norwegian justice system, which provided for a maximum sentence of only twenty-one years—too humane to deal with a crime of Breivik's enormity—could be sidestepped. In permanent psychiatric detention he would not be eligible for release—perhaps ever. Very quickly there were reports of a new, specialist, purpose-built psychiatric facility to house him. He could be detained indefinitely. The conclusion that he was a paranoid schizophrenic was likely a profoundly political one.

Others felt the diagnosis robbed the crime of its clear political dimension. This argument was perhaps best expressed in the e-book *On Utøya*, published shortly after the event, edited by Guy Rundle, Tad Tietze and Elizabeth Humphrys. Breivik's purpose, the book argued, was a mass assassination of the young political Left. It was a clear, unequivocal *political* act. To treat it as a matter of 'madness', as if it had no meaning beyond his individual psychoses, was to rob the culture of an opportunity to understand its significance. For decades, the conservative political class, from conventional politicians to Far Right extremists, had been upping the ante with increasingly virulent anti-Muslim and anti-political correctness rhetoric. Breivik's ideology was a horrifying end point of a veritable hate fest occurring in blogs, magazines and even mainstream publications.

Across the internet for decades, extremists on the Right had given nourishment and succour to each other, raging against Islam, multiculturalism, tolerance, openness, feminism and other values emerging from the great cultural revolution of the 1960s.

This toxic political phlegm, which had spread across the globe via the internet, was characterised by similar arguments to those in Breivik's manifesto, which he used to legitimate mass murder. But this was not just any mass murder of random people, as in a school shooting. Rather this was a mass assassination attempt of a highly political nature, a deliberate act to wipe out the flower of Norway's young leftists, a future progressive leadership.

The third strand of objections to the diagnosis of paranoid schizophrenia came from psychological experts. Leading forensic psychiatrists and psychologists maintained that his behaviour was not consistent with schizophrenia and argued for a reassessment. At the point of psychotic breakdown, paranoid schizophrenia is rarely consistent with the high-functioning behaviour Breivik needed to demonstrate in order to plan and execute the bombing and mass murder. His manifesto is weird but cogent, researched and logical. Its 1500 pages show a real ability for mental organisation and order, however diabolical its premises and conclusions. The manifesto shows intelligence, a capacity for marshalling evidence, and sophisticated cognitive skills. It does not exhibit the kind of 'word salad' typical of schizophrenia—odd pairings and parsings of words and phrases that are connected only by associations known to the sufferer rather than by logic. The executive function in people suffering from schizophrenia, when in acute psychosis and confronted with significant organisational demands, is often disintegrative, whereas Breivik was meticulous, thorough, exhaustive, obsessive, even compulsive in his attention to detail—all adding to his capacity to execute a complex, highly coordinated plan. He had no auditory or visual hallucinations. Most schizophrenics, contrary to popular belief, are not violent. Nor did Breivik show the ambulatory restlessness or the elevated mood common to the acute psychotic phase of schizophrenia. Despite the argument that he was in a state of acute schizophrenic psychosis, which almost always needs medication to bring under

11

control, Breivik was given no medication in jail. The psychiatrists admitted that at that time he was 'not in a psychotic state'. Psychotic states in schizophrenia do not simply switch on and off without treatment.

According to Norway's most famous forensic psychiatrist, Randi Rosenquist, the diagnosis was a political decision. In an interview with *Der Spiegel*, she likened it to the former Soviet Union's use of paranoid schizophrenia for political ends. There were grave implications of such a 'diagnosis'. 'As far as I am concerned,' she said emphatically, 'this diagnosis doesn't follow the facts.' There was a much better case, she said, for diagnosing an extreme narcissistic personality disorder—perhaps the most extreme ever seen. One of the leading aspects of this disorder is a lack of empathy for others. Others include grandiosity, obsession with personal appearance, willingness to exploit others for one's own needs, a sense of entitlement, a belief in the importance and superiority of self over others, a determination to use any means for self-aggrandisement, and a destructive rage when thwarted.

Rosenquist highlighted Breivik's response when he had been asked to feel empathy for his victims. Breivik's reply was straight from the all-about-me handbook. It was all about *his* trauma. This bespoke the radical lack of empathy of someone at the extreme end of the narcissistic continuum, the malignant narcissist.

This opinion—that he suffered from an extreme narcissistic personality disorder, of the kind that has overlaps with psychopathy—was echoed by other leading Norwegian psychologists and psychiatrists. Svenn Torgensen, professor of psychology at Oslo University, agreed. He highlighted especially Breivik's 'delusions of grandeur and his belief that he was singled out to be a knight in the crusade against Islam'. Torgensen said that Breivik 'found an ideal place to nourish his delusions of grandeur' in his 'messianic purpose of the Knights Templar'. All the staged photos at the end of the manifesto, in grandiose poses with weapons and medals and bogus uniforms, left Torgensen in no doubt: 'Breivik must be a narcissist.'

A narcissistic personality is not simply selfishness or vanity. Rather it is a distinct pathological syndrome where so much of the narcissist's life—events, conversations, actions and relationships—is conscripted into the maintenance and bolstering of the grandiose self. One test that psychologists have developed for narcissistic traits is the Narcissistic Personality Inventory (NPI). It offers forced choices between items. The first item asks respondents to choose between 'The thought of ruling the world frightens the hell out of me' and 'If I ruled the world it would be a much better place'. Another is 'I am much like everybody else' versus 'I am an extraordinary person'. Breivik was intending, through his revolution, to rule the world, even describing himself as 'Europe's most perfect Knight since WWII' and future 'Regent' of Norway. Another trait identified by the measure is an inordinately high sense of entitlement. Breivik felt entitled to be the solitary, self-appointed judge and jury, to execute 'Cultural Marxists'.

Narcissism at the extremes, argues Otto Kernberg, the famous American psychoanalyst, becomes 'malignant', resulting in behaviour similar to psychopathy. Both states share a profound lack of empathy, a willingness to exploit and destroy others for the benefit of the self. A narcissist, however, is preoccupied with how they are seen in the eyes of others; their dastardly acts are performed before a fantasised, admiring audience. Slinking off to ruthlessly kill again after a quiet, anonymous crime is not for them. Hence Breivik's video of his manifesto, his Facebook postings, and his anxious, vigilant attention to how he compared with other mass killers. He wanted the number one spot, to be the worst in history.

One of the most interesting aspects of the narcissist is their susceptibility to feelings of humiliation, their desire to retaliate after suffering a narcissistic wound. Psychologists have found that subjects scoring high in narcissism were far more willing to give electric shocks (simulated) to those who had judged their performance harshly on a test than were those who scored lower. This rage after a wound or blow to self-esteem is natural to the narcissist—if things don't go their way, the world will pay. One NPI item says 'I will never be satisfied until I get all that I deserve' versus 'I will take my satisfactions as they come'. Demanding that respect and fame—or infamy—has also been evident in other mass killers such as Eric Harris and Dylan Klebold, who committed the Columbine High School massacre. In videotapes filmed before the attack, Harris made several statements horrifyingly similar to items on the NPI. 'Isn't it fun to get the respect we're going to deserve?' he asked, as he picked up a gun and made shooting noises.

Likewise, Breivik demanded at his trial that he be granted the respect he deserved—indeed 'hero' status—for what he had done to save Norway and Europe. He was more terrified of the humiliation of being declared insane than of being a mass murderer, despite the fact that such a psychiatric evaluation would lead to a much easier life in a hospital, rather than prison, after sentencing. He wrote a letter to several Norwegian newspapers: 'I must admit this is the worst thing that could have happened to me as it is the ultimate humiliation.'

The second and final psychiatric evaluation, published in April 2012, concluded he was not psychotic and diagnosed him with concurrent narcissistic personality disorder and anti-social personality disorder. Expert witness Ulrik Fredrik Malt, a professor of psychiatry, also declared to the court that Breivik was suffering from narcissistic personality disorder and possibly paranoid psychosis.

We need to talk about Anders

How did no one know what was coming? There seem to have been a number of *We Need to Talk about Kevin* moments among those close to Breivik. His half-sister Elisabeth and his mother's best friend tried to alert his mother, Wenche, to the danger of Breivik's deteriorating state of mind. Wenche's friend expressed her concern over his isolation and lack of friends and girlfriends. It seemed abnormal at that age. He had no sexual or romantic relationships of a lasting kind. Wenche dismissed her friend's comments, preferring to see him as just a little shy, something he would grow out of and a sign of his high intelligence. Elisabeth was more blunt, writing an email to her mother about Anders' weird, paranoid political views and warning her about his erratic behaviour, observing that he was obsessed with the violent video game *World of Warcraft*, playing online for sixteen hours a day, living in his own fantasy world.

Breivik's relationship with his mother, it soon became evident, was far from the simple case of a spoiled 'Mummy's boy' first suggested by the British press. From prison, Breivik expressed a profound ambivalence towards her, saying she was his 'Achilles heel' and would undo him, and that she was the one person whose presence he could not tolerate at the trial. 'She is the only one who can make me unstable.'

It is in his relationship with his mother that we find clues to his radical aggression towards women and his misogyny. As his mental state had got worse, he had returned home to live with his mother. He was highly dependent on her; she said he was 'uncomfortably intense … I felt like I was in prison with him.' He wanted to be so close physically to his mother that he would 'sit on top of her on the sofa', while trying to kiss her on the face. Yet Breivik also feared contamination by his mother, and wore an antiseptic mask at home to prevent her from infecting his sinuses. He even rang a local doctor to complain of it. He refused to eat anything she cooked.

The early reports of his happy, 'normal' upbringing in an affluent Oslo suburb, of the 'quiet but normal' little boy, began to give way to a very different picture. In 2012, the novelist Aage

Borchgrevink published a new book, *A Norwegian Tragedy*, causing considerable controversy when it revealed new and very personal information about his childhood. Borchgrevink drew on the expert assessment of Wenche Behring and Anders Breivik by the state Centre for Child Health and Youth Psychiatry (SSBU) in 1983. It turned out he had almost been removed from his mother twice by the age of four, at social workers' requests, for severe neglect and suspected sexual abuse and because of a highly 'sexualised atmosphere'. The psychological assessment of her at that time described a deeply unstable and vulnerable woman, with an 'extremely difficult upbringing', a borderline personality disorder, and an 'all-encompassing' depression, who 'projects her primitive and aggressive fantasies onto him'. She was on an 'extreme emotional roller coaster', constantly changing her mind about Anders going into care. She had little self-insight: 'everything was someone else's fault.' Borderline personality disorder is a condition marked by extreme emotional reactivity, mood swings, wild anger, a lack of empathy and, most significantly, fear of abandonment. At this point in her life, Wenche had actually been abandoned by Jens and left to rear Anders alone as a sole parent. Even before that though, she'd had a relationship with her son marked by ambivalence and hostility, with severe attachment problems.

While we can never know the precise contribution of nature and nurture, the psychologists wanting to remove him had reported that Wenche had had difficulties from the time he was a breast-feeding baby. By the time he was two, he was violently jealous of his older sister. By four, his mother was frightened of the hyper-active and aggressive boy, who actively avoided physical contact with others. He was defiant and unmoved by discipline, laughing in his mother's face when she tried to impose limits. Unusually for a small child of this age, he was 'without pleasure or joy'. Wenche would speak to him in 'a sugary voice' one moment, only to tell him the next she wished he were dead, something she said often.

She also took him to bed with her in what is described coyly as inappropriately 'close physical' contact. There were reports from social workers and neighbours of 'a lot of fighting', and that the children were left alone in the apartment. He was sufficiently neglected that social welfare workers wanted him removed into foster care—something that rarely occurs in Norway—but their intention was never carried out.

His father might have offered a nurturing alternative relationship, but he cut off all contact with Breivik when he was a teenager, over a relatively minor misdemeanour. When interviewed about the massacre, his father gave a grotesquely insensitive interview that resonated with Breivik's narcissism. Jens disowned his son and spoke of wanting to 'move on' and to 'turn the page'. He did not comment on or show empathy for the victims or their families. He spoke only of the sorrow he felt: 'He should have taken his own life, too. That's what he should have done ... *I* will have to live with the shame for the rest of *my* life. People will always link *me* with him.' Breivik, then, had a far more troubled childhood than it had first appeared.

Freud thought the answer to the maladies of the soul that threaten every individual was to immerse oneself in love and work, to find therein a reality principle, which enables the individual to overcome the solipsism of self. By his early thirties, Breivik had failed at both love and work. Rather than face those defeats and consider the imperfections of judgement and character that had led him there, Breivik took flight from reality and sought refuge in the ether of the internet and, in the rage he found there, located blame for his world going awry outside of himself: in Muslims, feminists and Cultural Marxists. Rather than begin again, responding to life's blows with the hard slog of building a life based in reality, he sought solace in a grandiose fantasy that removed him from the sites of his failures and humiliations—and into the grand and glorious delusional world of the crusading

Knights Templar and their mission, of which he was a leader, a 'Judiciar Knights Commander'.

This insignificant young man—people who knew him characterised him as 'a nondescript individual who people quickly forgot'—believed his crimes would bestow not just significance but immortality. His self-designed gravestone was to laud him as a great martyr, reading: 'Born into Marxist Slavery on xx.xx.19xx. Died as a Martyr. All Free Europeans in your Eternal Debt.' Rather than being insignificant, unable to leave home or separate from his mother, rejected by his father, scorned by women, a flop at business, he would stand as a Heroic Being, a brave knight, a man so powerful he could live as a god, with the capacity to give life or death to the young Norwegian progressives who had come to Utøya to share comradeship and love, full of hope, promise and plans for the future. They would never fulfil that promise for he had killed them. *They* were not the Chosen Ones. He, Anders Behring Breivik, was.

* * *

Christopher Lasch, in an afterword to his classic work first published in 1979, *The Culture of Narcissism*, remarked that his book had often been misunderstood. It was not merely about the 'Me Decade'. 'Narcissism,' he said, 'was not just another name for selfishness.' Childrearing patterns and the structure of authority had been changed so profoundly by consumer capitalism over the twentieth century, intensifying in the 1960s, with 'far-reaching psychological repercussions'. Our very character had changed. While my account differs from his defence of the patriarchal family, Lasch located his early study on the precise ground of my own inquiry: the effect of culture upon personality. Lasch pointed to the new character traits of shallowness, self-preoccupation, an incapacity to make commitments, a willingness to pull up roots whenever the need arose, a dislike of depending on anyone, and an incapacity for loyalty or gratitude. All this was combined not with a strong sense of self, but with what Lasch described as the problem at the heart of Werner Herzog's film *The Enigma of Kasper Hauser*—an absence at the core, a 'hollowness', an 'inner emptiness' and feeling of inauthenticity so profound it left one feeling utterly at life's mercy. There was something else, perhaps most important of all, emerging: 'the theatre of everyday life'. In a prophetic passage—long before the world of the internet, blogs, Facebook, Twitter and the rest—Lasch wrote:

> The proliferation of visual and auditory images in a 'Society of the Spectacle' as it has been described, encouraged a similar kind of preoccupation with the self. People now responded to others as if their actions were being recorded and simultaneously transmitted to an unseen audience or stored up for close scrutiny at some later time. The prevailing conditions thus brought out narcissistic personality traits that were present in everyone ...

During the course of the last century, the old hysterias, the classic neuroses analysed by Freud, were giving way to new disorders of the self. 'You used to see people coming in with hand-washing compulsions, phobias and familiar neuroses,' the New York psychoanalyst Sheldon Bach said in 1976. 'Now you see mostly narcissists.' By the early 2000s the celebrated British psychoanalyst Peter Fonagy observed, 'In recent years issues of narcissism have taken centre stage.' While Breivik is undoubtedly an extreme case, narcissism has become the go-to diagnosis for a host of modern ills. It is our modern 'hysteria'. As well as the more serious work by psychologists and psychoanalysts, there is an emerging genre of self-help books for those suffering at the hands of the narcissist—bosses, co-workers, parents, lovers, husbands, wives, teenagers and children. The titles have a plaintive wail. Psychotherapist Eleanor Payson's *The Wizard of Oz and Other Narcissists: Coping with the One-Way Relationship in Work, Love and Family* promises to be a 'source of relief, hope and understanding to the countless adults living with the pain and confusion that occurs when dealing with the narcissistic individual'. In *Why Is It Always About You? The Seven Deadly Sins of Narcissism*, Sandy Hotchkiss offers insight into 'one of the most prevalent personality disorders of our time'. Such people are chronically self-focused; they monopolise conversation, put their own needs first, and exhibit a childlike quality of tyrannical rage when thwarted. A narcissist may seem confident and attractive, until some apparently minor offence triggers a fleecing, annihilating rage like no other. Empathy—that recognition of another's pain—is missing. So too is the capacity for reciprocity—giving as well as receiving. Relationships tend to be one-way streets.

The narcissist must be the centre of attention. They soak up admiration like a sponge, need and use others as a narcissistic line of supply. Whatever is good for the self is good. They are prone to magical, grandiose thinking about their life: it is all or nothing. Greatness is what is desired; to be average is despised. Part of this derives from an exceptional sense of entitlement, of being uniquely special. And, being so 'special', it is hardly surprising they usually feel superior to other people. They can only be up if the people around them are down. They are the 'captain on a ship of fools'. But they are also prone to savage envy. Their arrogance means that apologising, taking responsibility for a wrong, is impossible, for the narcissist is *never* wrong. At the end of any argument, the narcissist will see only that *you* have injured *them*. The capacity to place themselves in another person's shoes is limited or missing. Often people around them give in to them, always walking on eggshells, as offence is taken so easily. They are Arthur Koestler's 'mimophant'—the term he coined for those who are as delicate as mimosa about their own feelings but display an elephantine hide of insensitivity towards the feelings of others.

Narcissists wreak havoc in other people's lives. All of us have our moments, of course, where we might be self-centred, or vain, or envious, or give way to temper, without having a full-blown narcissistic personality disorder. Narcissism exists along a continuum: from the self-important nuisance at work to a psychopath like Breivik. But it is not simply a matter of the individual psyche. This is a problem of cultural significance.

There is very good evidence that the problem of narcissism is growing worse. Changes in our culture have created an economic, social and relational world that not only supports but actually celebrates narcissism, cultivating and embedding it as a character trait. While a malignant narcissist like Breivik is undoubtedly an extreme case, there is also an increasingly common syndrome, the ordinary, everyday narcissists who have their very own cult of personality. Scholars have found that narcissism is rising with each succeeding generation of American college students. Ordinary folk have been affected too. From the explosion in cosmetic surgery around the world, through the egos on display in the blogosphere and Twitterverse, to popular music lyrics, or the crazy world of celebrities and their imitators—where ordinary people hire paparazzi to give their life significance it doesn't have—more people now expect red carpet treatment at home and work, and fume over slights and frustrations, even to the point of physically assaulting or killing fellow motorists in outbursts of the new phenomenon of road rage. In short, too many people behave like princes and princesses without the noblesse oblige.

But why? Are they born that way? Or is it the way they are raised? Is there something in contemporary childhood that might predispose them to such a tendency? What about the wider culture that shapes family life? What are the larger implications for our society of increasing narcissism, and how will it affect our response to the great challenges of our time, like climate change? Some are arguing that we spoil children, that the cult of self-esteem and parents over-involved in their children's lives are at fault for producing an over-entitled generation. Yet no examination of the real facts of Breivik's life really adds up, in any uncomplicated way, to a life of simple spoiling or too much attention. Rather his life was marked by the dark elements of contemporary life that few want to consider: family fragmentation, troubled early relationships, absent fathers, a strange admixture of permissiveness and neglect, combined with a high degree of material affluence.

* * *

When Breivik was arrested he held up a finger. It had a small cut on it. He stood on an island littered with sixty-nine shattered and bloodied corpses, yet as the policemen handcuffed him, he held up that finger. He wanted a Band-Aid. 'He was really intent,' said the policeman later, 'on getting himself that Band-Aid.'

When the second team of psychiatrists ruled that Anders Breivik suffered from an extreme narcissistic personality disorder and *was* responsible for his actions and should stand trial, Breivik was triumphant. Here was the chance he hoped for: standing centre stage in front of the world's cameras, avoiding what he called the 'humiliation' of being dismissed as mad.

Breivik arrived at the court handcuffed and smiling. He raised his fist in the Far Right salute. At first he displayed no emotion apart from that smirk. He was indifferent to the descriptions of his victims' last calls to their loved ones, and to the detailed descriptions of their mutilated bodies. He did not weep at the memory of the sound of the victims' screams, or at the gasps from their grief-stricken families as they heard him coldly relate the circumstances of his killings, nor did he flinch at the enormity of what he had done. The deaths of all those young people were merely 'collateral damage' in the war of his imagining. Describing his act as 'spectacular'—the embedding of spectators in that phrase is revealing—he bragged he 'would do that all over again'.

Yet there *was* something at the trial that made him tremble with emotion: his face fell, the tears welled up and rolled down his cheeks. What made Breivik weep was his own rhetoric, as his video manifesto was played in court. What moved him was the sound of his own words.

As Breivik began his 21-year sentence, he complained about his 'cruel and inhuman treatment'. In one of the most humane prison systems in the world, Breivik did not take long to feel aggrieved. He was not getting the treatment he felt entitled to. His cell lacked a good view. The version of PlayStation given to him was too old. The heating wasn't turned up high enough. And his coffee was served too cold.

Chapter 2

Just a Jerk?

Social Psychology and the Narcissism Epidemic

The narcissistic self is perpetually 'under construction', as
if the construction site were on quicksand.

Carolyn Morf and Frederick Rhodewalt

IN 1999, IN a basement office at Case Western Reserve University in Cleveland, two graduate students were procrastinating. Before doing the next bit of hard grind on their postdoctoral work, they joked and chatted about what they were studying. Keith Campbell was studying the behaviour of narcissistic people. Jean Twenge was examining cultural trends in personality traits. As they talked, they realised how much overlap there was in their projects. And they realised that the really pressing question was what kind of trends existed in narcissism over time. Yet the empirical data simply wasn't available back then.

By 2007 it was. Now young academics, Twenge and Campbell published the results of a study that showed rises in narcissism over the generations. The story quickly went viral. It was covered by Associated Press and appeared in more than a hundred newspapers, as well as numerous other media outlets such as

NBC Nightly News, Fox News Channel and National Public Radio. 'It was then we realised we had hit a nerve.'

And no wonder. By the mid-2000s narcissism as an explanation of bad behaviour was everywhere. The *New York Times* declared that narcissism was not only an academic 'growth industry', but also the explanation favoured 'by columnists, bloggers and television psychologists. We love to label the offensive behaviour of others to separate them from us. "Narcissist" is among our current favourites.' Even allowing for more than a few false diagnoses, judging by the sheer volume of words on the subject, narcissism had become a central problem of our time. Former spouses, rejected suitors and ex-lovers, adult children and parents—all seeing themselves as victims of alleged narcissists—held forth in blogs, newspaper articles, pop-psychology columns and books. Soon there was even shorthand: bloggers talked cosily about their Narc, or N.

Twenge and Campbell argued it was much more than a common diagnosis. They termed it an 'epidemic', in the standard sense of something afflicting 'a disproportionately large number of individuals within a population'. If narcissism was famously analysed first in the 1970s by Tom Wolfe in *The Me Decade*, and Christopher Lasch in *The Culture of Narcissism*, it 'had grown in ways these authors never imagined'. Parenting became indulgent; the struggle for civil rights had given way to 'looking out for number one in the 1980s'.

It is easy to see the phenomenon they were talking about. Celebrity worship and reality TV, and the ever-growing blogosphere and social media's attempts to record our every move ensured the look-at-me mentality. Any action, thought or picture, however banal, can be recorded for posterity on Facebook, Instagram, or Twitter, in a new theatre of the everyday. The new terror is to be invisible; as playwright Preston Sturges once quipped, 'He was forgotten before he was remembered!' Lena Dunham, the clever and creative writer behind the hit show

Girls, put the new sensibility this way: 'My dad finds Twitter just infinitely unrelatable. He's like, "Why would you want to tell anybody what I had for a snack, it's private!?" And I'm like, "Why would you even have a snack if you didn't tell anybody?" Why bother eating?'

Cosmetic surgery rates skyrocketed; breast augmentation for teenagers jumped 55 per cent in one year alone from 2006 to 2007. Some US parents gave it as a graduation gift. Pop songs reflected the trend towards narcissism. One popular dance track repeated over and over the words 'money, success, fame, glamour'. Another yodelled, 'I believe the world should revolve around me!' Even some evangelical Christians accepted that premise: 'Love God, love yourself, love others in that order,' advised one megachurch pastor. Kim Kardashian is famous for starring in a reality TV show ... about herself! Her equally famous partner, rapper Kanye West, declared himself a 'creative genius'.

To properly appreciate Twenge and Campbell's position, we need to understand that back in that basement, they were working under the well-known psychologist Roy Baumeister. Baumeister had punctured the prevailing assumptions about the connection of crime to low self-esteem. In a series of landmark studies, he had found that criminals had higher self-esteem than people who weren't in trouble with the law. In a seminal article, 'Relation of Threatened Egotism to Violence and Aggression: The Dark Side of High Self-Esteem', he and his co-authors argued that violence was the result of threatened egotism, not low self-esteem. The real key to understanding aggression and violence, Baumeister argued, was the 'inflated, unstable or tentative views of the self's superiority that are disputed by some person or circumstance'. Think of a gang leader who feels someone has treated him with disrespect, so pulls out a gun and kills them.

What happens, Baumeister asserted through a careful examination of the evidence, is that the person with the threatened ego directs 'anger outward as a way of avoiding a downward revision of the self-concept'. Rage-filled attacks, so typical of the narcissist, whether verbal or physically violent, are more likely to come from someone with high but unstable (that is, vulnerable to threat) self-esteem. People with low self-esteem, in contrast, tend to be depressed, withdrawn and less aggressive, even submissive. As Baumeister concluded acidly, 'Favourable impressions of oneself may not be an unmitigated good from the perspective of a society if they lead to violence. In our view, the benefits of favourable self-opinions accrue *primarily to the self*, and they are a burden and potential problem to everyone else.'

If this is true, then the self-esteem movement—the effort to boost children's and adults' self-esteem as a social panacea—is fundamentally wrong-headed. Twenge and Campbell's work can be seen as continuing, at a more general level of cultural analysis, the Baumeister tradition of interrogating and debunking prevailing cultural assumptions that many social problems are caused by *low* self-esteem. They want to show that excessive pride, self-esteem that is too *high*—in the form of narcissism—has hazardous social consequences.

For a long time, psychotherapists have argued that there is more to the narcissist's bragging, self-enhancing, self-aggrandisement and self-centredness than meets the eye. It is a mask: a puffed-up exterior to hide a vulnerable inner sense of self. Think of the Wizard of Oz, projecting his blown-up image to create an illusion of an all-powerful wizard on the screen, when in reality he is a puny, weak little man, frightened of life. Pop psychology especially, often distills the work of more complex thinkers to a simple message that the narcissist is really insecure deep down. The heiress Paris Hilton came to fame by posting a sex video of herself on the internet. For a *Los Angeles Times* interview in 2011, Hilton posed on gold-trimmed sofas beneath a huge nude photo of herself. On the opposite wall was another, equally large, naked photo of herself. All the couch pillows were decorated with her photo. The response of celebrity life coach Patrick Wanis captured the view that there is more to narcissism than meets the eye: 'Paris Hilton is suffering from narcissism. Although she seems confident she is in fact insecure, arrogant and has low self-esteem.'

Twenge and Campbell's argument is the exact opposite: Paris Hilton and Kanye West are every bit as vain, arrogant and conceited as they sound! They really *do* admire themselves that much. As for any mask, they found there was *less* than meets the eye. They base their argument on a flurry of empirical studies beginning in the late 1990s. Despite some powerful scholarly contributions that used case studies of psychoanalysis patients, there was little actual empirical research done on narcissism in the general population. All that changed with the development of the Narcissistic Personality Inventory (NPI). It has now been used on thousands of college students in the US and elsewhere to measure narcissism and its behavioural consequences.

Twenge and Campbell argue that what makes a child grow into a narcissist is spoiling, indulgence, an absence of moral discipline in building character, and a culture of excessive praise, of telling children they are special. The 'mask' theory is 'seductive in its convenience, allowing us to write-off narcissistic people as flawed people who just need to learn to love themselves enough—our culture's cure-all'. The narcissist is not 'hurt deep down inside'. The narcissist is just a jerk.

They are especially concerned with the rise in *cultural* narcissism—widespread changes 'in behaviour and attitudes that reflect narcissistic cultural values' and 'a flight from reality into the land of grandiose fantasy'. They also find a growing rate of individual narcissism, especially among college students. They concentrate on obnoxious but functioning people in the general community, who display strongly narcissistic traits while wreaking havoc in the workplace or at home. They make clear that 'being highly narcissistic or a narcissist is not the same as having a diagnosed psychiatric disorder, or a pathological level of narcissism'. They do not concern themselves with people who have narcissistic personality disorder, a term used to describe pathological narcissism.

Twenge and Campbell do, however, acknowledge there are two types of narcissism: one covert, hypersensitive or vulnerable; the other overt, oblivious and grandiose. They focus on narcissists who are confident, exhibitionist and outgoing, 'the savvy narcissists who have the most influence on the culture', and not on the more vulnerable ones who might end up on the shrink's couch. The measure they use, the NPI, has been found to be skewed towards identifying the more overt narcissist, but has other imperfections; it can confound more confident individuals with genuinely narcissistic ones—more on the implications of that later.

How Does a Narcissistic Mind Work?

'I have done that,' says my memory. 'I cannot have done that'— says my pride, and remains adamant. At last—memory yields.

Friedrich Nietzsche

Nietzsche's savage aphorism calls us to attend to the self-deceptive capacity of the human mind—an assessment borne out by recent psychological research. Most people tend to have what psychologists call a 'self-serving bias', a tendency to see the self in a more favourable light than is strictly true. Once it was widely thought that human beings were rational animals who tested their hypotheses against reality. By the 1990s, however, research on people's perceptions of themselves showed a marked disparity between the way people assess information about the environment and the way they assess it about themselves. When it comes to the environment, they seek accuracy and revise understanding in the light of new evidence. Their behaviour is usually rational. Yet when it comes to assessments of themselves, the tendency is

THE LIFE OF I

turned on its head. Most people, when asked how good-looking or nice or intelligent they are, rate themselves more highly than observers. They are less concerned with accuracy than with protecting and keeping a positive image of themselves. What is at stake is not truth, but a sense of self one can live with. Academic psychologist Cordelia Fine calls it *A Mind of Its Own* in her witty and elegant account of the mind's weird manoeuvring in favour of maintaining a flattering self-image.

Yet while there is something universal here—indeed many people present to others a more attractive version of themselves, an ego ideal rather than a realistic sense of self—it is also true that people's claims become more modest in the presence of people who know them well. There is some kind of reality principle working, however imperfectly. In a narcissistic person, in contrast, these twists and swerves become somersaults on the high wire, a psychological acrobatic exercise in holding reality at bay. Narcissists temper their claims for no one, even when among people close to them who know their claims to be false. They rate highly on self-deception and denial. Their self-serving orientation takes an almost universal human characteristic to an extreme.

Narcissists' continual self-enhancement and bragging is specific, usually to gain a sense of agency or achieve social dominance. A narcissist will brag about being smarter, richer, more successful and better looking, but not about being more caring or compassionate. More important even than this is that a narcissist is prepared to pay a much higher price than a non-narcissist for self-enhancement and bragging. If necessary they are willing to alienate others and even to lose friends by impressing them with their superiority. Most people know that boasting puts other people on edge, or alienates them; the narcissist doesn't care. That is because they have been found to value communal traits much less than dominance and success in competition. Their strategy in life is to outdo others: a getting-ahead strategy, not getting along. Other people bring out not the best in them, but the worst. Other people are not treated as subjects in their own right, but as sources of narcissistic supply.

Narcissists may at first appear charming, attractive and socially dominant. They like to be the centre of attention. After longer contact, however, their self-centredness, sense of entitlement and selfish exploitation become plain. They hog the conversational limelight, making little or no room for others and their concerns. They interrupt and move the conversation back to themselves—called the shift response. Person A tells the narcissist of some difficulty they have just experienced. 'Tell me about it!' says the narcissist, who is about to prevent their friend from doing just that, seeming to tune in momentarily but actually making sure the conversation shifts them back to centre stage: 'Listen to what happened to me!' Alternatively, the narcissist might not make the normal supportive noises or expressions of the true listener; they give either minimal or no response ('Hmm … uh huh'), remaining disengaged or silent, perhaps looking bored, and paying little real attention. The speaker, lacking any encouragement, falls silent, at which point the narcissist dives in, recommencing their monologue about themselves. A popular joke captures it: 'Enough about Me!' says someone to their lunch companion, 'Tell me what *you* think about me!'

Baumeister thinks there is an element of addiction in the narcissist's desire for attention, praise and admiration. Others bring out the worst in them but also energise narcissists, drawing out the need to compete and offering the 'hit' produced by feelings of superiority. Because they treat others as objects rather than people worthy of respect, contact with narcissists over time becomes aversive. They are poor bosses and work colleagues; since they are hyper-competitive in interpersonal situations, they quickly take advantage of others, even close others. Non-narcissists are more likely to give credit to the team. In contrast, narcissists are likely to claim sole credit for work done in a group.

Twenge and Campbell take aim at a series of myths about narcissism, which have, they feel, blunted social concern:

1. **Myth: Narcissism is actually high self-esteem.** Narcissism is not just high self-esteem in the sense of a quiet and sturdy confidence in oneself, sturdy enough to accept criticism and take it on board. Rather narcissists feel superior; they are not just confident but overconfident and arrogant; they have an inflated view of their abilities, and are self-centred. They don't brag about how kind or compassionate they are, but about the Mercedes in the drive.

2. **Myth: Narcissists are insecure and have low self-esteem.** Narcissism is not, as the psychodynamic view suggests, just a defence against an empty or enraged self, a hidden sense of shame or low self-esteem. Narcissists do not big-note themselves because inside they feel weak or puny. They brag because they want to rub their listeners' noses in how successful they are. Here Twenge and Campbell draw on new ways of measuring hidden or implicit feelings about the self and explicit or conscious views of the self. Work on implicit versus explicit views has found that some views, like acceptance of racial equality, can be skin deep. Tests in which positive words like 'good' are paired, at speed, with black or white faces often show that people are unconsciously biased against other racial groups, even when they wish to be otherwise. If the psychodynamic view is right, then the narcissist will score high on explicit self-esteem but low on implicit self-esteem.

    The findings are mixed. Some research *has* shown just this pattern. But other studies have shown that the people who score high on the NPI do *not* seem to have low self-esteem when also measured for implicit feelings about the self: 'Narcissistic people found it just as easy—or even easier— than non-narcissistic people to hit keys for "me" when they saw words like great, good, wonderful and right and found it equally or more difficult to press the "me" key for words like bad, awful, terrible, and wrong.' They also showed higher unconscious self-esteem on items measuring a sense of agency such as 'assertive, active, energetic, dominant, outspoken, and enthusiastic', versus 'quiet, reserved, submissive, and inhibited'. They scored average on communal words like 'kind, friendly, generous, cooperative, pleasant and affectionate'. Narcissists also paired the letters associated with their name with flattering, achievement-orientated words but not with those associated with nurturing or caring. Twenge and Campbell claim, then, that 'narcissists have similar positive and inflated views of themselves on the inside and outside ... but believe that caring about others isn't all that important'.

3. **Myth: Narcissists really are superior people.** In fact, while narcissists judge themselves to be superior to others, no evidence exists that they outperform anyone or are especially talented or better looking. Winston Churchill joked of his political rival, Clement Attlee, 'He is a modest man with a lot to be modest about.' The narcissist, it turns out, is a braggart with a lot to be modest about. This is no accurate vanity.

4. **Myth: Some narcissism is healthy.** Here Twenge and Campbell take issue with the many psychologists who assert the need for some 'healthy' narcissism, pointing out that narcissistic faults of personality prove problematic for others over time: 'Hurting others is wrong and that informs our stance on whether self-admiration is healthy.' In a sideways move, they argue 'that it would be better for everyone not to concentrate on self feelings—positive or negative—so much'. Happiness comes from focus not on the self but on relationships, connecting to the world, spending time with children and family, or becoming lost in the 'flow' experience of art, sport and work.

5. **Myth: Narcissism is just vanity about physical appearance.**
   Narcissists are more likely to show bodily narcissism, look in
   the mirror more, wear revealing clothing or show cleavage,
   and post more flattering photos on Facebook. But they are
   also 'materialistic, entitled, and aggressive when insulted, and
   uninterested in emotional closeness'.

The Narcissist in Love

At the core of narcissism, according to both psychotherapists and
academic researchers, is an inability to love. Keith Campbell, one
of the authors of *The Narcissism Epidemic*, also wrote the self-help
book *When You Love a Man Who Loves Himself*. He wrote the popular book for general readers because, as a narcissism researcher,
he kept being inundated with poignant letters from traumatised
women trying to figure out what had gone wrong in a relationship. Just because someone leaves you doesn't mean they are a
narcissist. But these were no ordinary break-ups, where pain and
hurt and a profound sense of loss also occur but respect and care
for the former partner can remain. These were endings with a
bruising, destructive force in a category all of their own. (Think
strong winds versus Hurricane Katrina.) They had a common
pattern. They left the ex-lover confused over their grasp on reality,
gasping in disbelief.

Once someone forms an attachment, it is, for most, not
easily fungible with another. People become precious to us, even
irreplaceable. We are vulnerable to the temptation to stay in a
destructive relationship because of that attachment, even when
the behaviour of the loved one suggests we would be better off
ending it. Once attached to a *narcissist*, however, this risk becomes
exponential. Narcissists in romantic relationships deserve special
attention because in romance there are no precise rules. Once
someone is committed and in love, all kinds of outrageous behaviour are possible without being deal-breakers. These relationships

often sweep someone off their feet initially, before revealing the darker side: 'others exist for me.' There is only one point of view for the narcissist: theirs. If their will is ever thwarted or their grandiose illusions punctured, they can subject their partner to savage, rage-filled verbal—or worse, physical—attacks that leave the partner reeling. These are not people for whom the vows of 'in sickness and in health or for richer or poorer' have meaning. Narcissists are drawn to partners who make them look good— trophy wives or handbag husbands. They are there only in the good times, while their partner serves their needs, admires them unconditionally and reflects well on them.

Campbell cites some breathtaking ruthlessness when a partner was sick or vulnerable. One man bailed on his wife when she needed cancer treatment and lost her hair, because she 'spoiled his image'. In Australia, I heard of a man who filed for divorce, citing his wife's recent double mastectomy from breast cancer. 'Such a turn-off to be breastless,' he told her. A news item caught my eye, about a woman who threatened to end her marriage because her husband had not, for some months, been able to have an erection. Other examples from Campbell concern monstrous vanity: the character who compared himself to Jesus, or the boyfriend who took photos of *himself* to bed each night!

Studies show that people in committed relationships usually become 'unavailable' to others—tending to concentrate on the loved one's cherished attributes and be less responsive to alternative partners. Narcissists, in contrast, have been found to keep their eyes wide open, even while in a committed relationship, searching for other, better possibilities. They are more likely to be chronically unfaithful even when married. They're the ones with a wife *and* a girlfriend. Or two. Campbell says:

> To understand narcissists' approach to relationships, take
> every one of these ideas [of love, commitment, caring,

loyalty, responsibility and trust] and throw them away. In place of love, put love of the self; in place of caring, put exploitation; and to commitment, add 'as long as it benefits me'. Narcissists' approach to relationships is simple: it's all about them.

Narcissists keep a relationship while it feeds the ego and discard it if it doesn't. Most centrally, the other person is treated like a tradeable, replaceable commodity—with a use-by date. Narcissists are game players, Machiavellian in relationships, signalling commitment then pulling away, keeping the upper hand by following the principle that the one with 'the least interest in the relationship has the most power'. The partner is considered fuel, or what writer Sam Vaknin described as narcissistic supply, providing power, status and esteem. And woe betides the partner or lover who ceases to give narcissistic supply.

If partners of non-narcissists often experience a small decline in relationship satisfaction over time, for partners of narcissists it starts off higher but drops dramatically—almost to zero. Ex-partners of narcissists report feeling 'sucked dry', 'used up' or 'burned', or as if they have just navigated a minefield. They feel shattered and brood over what happened for a long time afterwards. They feel damaged and lose trust in other relationships. To love someone and realise they never cared for you is extremely destabilising.

Narcissism is also implicated in domestic violence. Narcissists' partners cannot express what they feel since it is met with 'denial, abuse and even violence'. If the narcissistic response to criticism or rejection is aggression and rage, then a partner leaving can result in violence. It gets worse. Male narcissism and a sense of sexual entitlement are factors in rape. Studies showed 'narcissistic men felt less empathy for rape victims, reported more enjoyment when watching a rape scene in a movie, and were more punitive toward a woman who refused to read a sexually arousing passage out loud to them'.

Interestingly, the culture has moved towards a wider embrace of narcissistic values in relationships. Contemporary advice from pop psychologists now often cautions against 'settling' for some-one imperfect, and recommends taking yourself as a love object! The title of one book—by one of these 'experts' on relationships, a star of the reality TV program *The Bachelorette*—says it all: *Better Single than Sorry: A No Regrets Guide to Loving Yourself and Never Settling*. Twenge and Campbell relay a conversation overheard between two college students, about one girl's longest relation-ship ever, of some six months. 'It feels really weird,' she said. 'I'm used to having time to myself, I'm used to being able to work on myself, instead of taking care of somebody else.' The idea that you can only have relationships if you love yourself is rife. (I have had more than one mother solemnly tell me that, with children, 'You have to put yourself first'!) Maybe, Twenge and Campbell suggest, we need a new cultural belief: 'If you love yourself too much, you won't have enough for anyone else.' (For all their decrying of psychodynamic theories, this notion takes them back to Freud's idea that an excess of libido invested in the self, self-love, withdraws it from the possibility of investing in others.)

Popular culture abounds with examples of shifts in sexual behaviour of a narcissistic kind. Consider. In 1957, Buddy Holly sang the hit single 'Peggy Sue'. Its lyrics express a kind of innocence about love, describing desire of a surprisingly (to modern ears) chaste kind. Then, in 1958, he wrote 'Peggy Sue Got Married', and the lyrics express anguish over 'the one' getting married to another. Holly's yearning songs now look seriously quaint. A study has shown that, by 2005, two-thirds of popular songs displayed aggression towards women or described sex in degrad-ing ways, used words like 'bitch', 'dick' and even made threats that the singer would 'beat' that 'pussy up'. Teenagers spend, on average, half an hour a day listening to such descriptions.

Perhaps it is unsurprising, then, that the world of quick sexual hook-ups and uncommitted relationships might become more common. People are used for short-term gain, and then discarded. Sometimes, very short-term. In an episode of *Sex and the City*, for example, the character Carrie picks up a man at a bar for sex but jumps out of bed and returns to work just after he has brought her to orgasm by oral sex. She checks out of the apartment and leaves him unsatisfied, in a swapping of gender roles in her opposite but more familiar scenario. In journalist Laura Sessions Stepp's book *Unhooked: How Women Pursue Sex, Delay Love and Lose at Both*, a young woman says she leaps out of bed straight away as it 'makes men feel feeble'. Her friend says, 'Sometimes you just want to screw them before they screw you.' Then there is the new cultural trend towards 'friends with benefits', where the key is to have sex without attachment, to remain uninvolved. Sociologist Zygmunt Bauman has a wonderful term for this; he calls it the 'permanent temporariness of relationships'. On an MTV documentary on the phenomenon, one girl confesses her feelings for a guy. He replies casually, 'I don't think I am attached at all.' She has violated, he asserts piously, the 'real friends with benefits' ethos, where 'none of this conversation would even come up'. He says to the interviewer that she 'isn't everything I'm looking for in a girl. This is something to keep me occupied for the time being; I'd rather be kind of with her than just be alone.'

The Narcissism Epidemic is, most importantly, an argument about rising narcissism in the younger generations. 'Overall, we've seen a massive increase in narcissism among college students,' Twenge says. Between 1979 and 2006, data on students who took the NPI showed that there was a 30 per cent increase in narcissism. One out of four college students answered the majority of questions in the narcissistic direction. The trend has accelerated, especially since the year 2000. This aspect of their argument—that each generation is getting more narcissistic—has been hotly debated; not all US scholars agree that it is higher among younger generations. Professor Johanna Wyn, director of the Australian Youth Research Centre at the University of Melbourne, is sceptical. 'Jean Twenge can't speak for Australians,' she says, maintaining that her research into gen X, born from 1973, and gen Y, born from 1989, shows strong orientation to family, friends and volunteering.

What is absolutely clear, however, from a wide consensus of the social psychology research is that overall narcissism is growing. As societies become more individualistic, Twenge and Campbell argue, the evidence is that they become more narcissistic: 'Orange polyester pants came and went, but narcissism has persisted, growing more widespread every year.' Even collectivist China, as it becomes a consumer capitalist society, has begun reporting trends towards higher scores of narcissism. While men still score slightly higher on narcissism, it is rising especially sharply among women, the traditional carers. Psychotherapists have also seen a jump in the number of people they treat with narcissistic disorders. By 2004–05, a national US survey showed that while only 3 per cent of those over sixty-five experienced narcissistic personality disorder symptoms, just under 10 per cent of those aged 20–29 did. Articles and books on self-esteem skyrocketed in the 1970s. A surge of interest in narcissism followed shortly thereafter. There are thousands of mentions of narcissism in the press each year, and six times as many articles on it in psychology journals as in the 1970s.

As to the real cause of the 'epidemic', however, Twenge and Campbell remain vague: 'No single event initiated the narcissism epidemic; instead Americans' core cultural ideas slowly became more focused on self-admiration and self-expression.' Why? From the self-absorbed and self-indulgent 1970s, the new values were 'replaced by a more extroverted, shallow and materialistic form of narcissism'. As part of a grab bag of causes, they mention celebrity worship and reality TV during the 1990s, the internet and the new social media, which have further entrenched the self-focus and self-admiration that have become the 'new cultural ideal'. Most centrally, though, they lay the blame at the feet of baby boomer parents: 'our parents treated us as royalty since before we were born.'

They point to baby bibs with self-aggrandising titles like 'Supermodel', 'Little Princess' and 'Magnet', and T-shirts emblazoned with 'Spoiled Rotten' or 'I'm in Charge', as evidence for the era of 'Your Majesty the Baby'. (In reality, this is much truer of later generations; these T-shirts weren't around for boomer parents.) Children's names also reflect the trend towards an assertive individuality and uniqueness, the desire to stand out from the crowd, signalling 'specialness'. No longer do parents choose common, plain names, as they did in the 1940s and 1950s, designed to be pretty much like other children's names, to help children fit in, be one of the crowd, like Anne or Karen, or Robert and John. Now they choose unusual names, like Paris and Mulligatawny, often with highly individualised spelling.

There has been a decline in traditional parenting values, Twenge and Campbell claim, and parents are now slaves to the child: 'More than any time in history, the child's needs come first.' Parents want to be friends, not the boss. They value obedience less than in the past, according to surveys; once the second most important aim of parenting, it has dropped to second last. Most importantly, they assert, 'we have become too indulgent ... we praise children too much ... we treat children like royalty'. They cite psychologists who claim that parents 'idealise children' rather than 'truly loving them'. Or, as psychologist Dan Kindlon says, cutting to the chase in *Too Much of a Good Thing*, 'we give our kids too much and demand too little of them. Schools, too, are part of the problem. Preschoolers in the United States, as a result of the wrong-headed self-esteem movement, sing songs like "I am Special, I am Special, Look at Me!"'

We must acknowledge the progress—we no longer accept the once common practice of beating children, and we take greater care with child health and welfare—but parental involvement has nevertheless become 'helicopter parenting' and over-involvement. Teachers have begun awarding prizes for participation. We have seen these trends in Australia. In 2014, the Australian Football League created controversy by banishing the scoreboard from the under tens; from then on junior games would have no winners or losers. Teachers here and in the United States complain that parents storm into classrooms, protesting about Peachblossom's low grades, instead of reading their child the riot act about making a greater effort. The tough lessons of life are avoided. Parents raise children to be 'winners not lovers'. Twenge and Campbell assert that 'a focus on individual achievement that leaves out feelings, love and caring is a recipe for narcissism'. About 80 per cent of Americans believe, according to a 2001 *Time*/CNN poll, that children are more indulged than in the 1980s. There can be no doubt about it, conclude Twenge and Campbell: children, nowadays, are spoiled.

Twenge and Campbell argue that with the core narcissistic personality installed by new parenting practices that concentrate on raising self-esteem, the media then operate as a 'superspreader' (using the term from epidemiology and disease control), whereby an infected individual then infects others. Movies, celebrity worship through tabloid magazines, and the transformation of ordinary people into celebrities via reality TV are superspreaders of narcissism. The desire for fame among children and adolescents has sharply increased. In one 1997 survey, given a choice between fame and contentment, only 17 per cent of baby boomers wanted to be famous, but just under one-third of young adults did. By 2006, 51 per cent of 18–25-year-olds listed it as an 'important

41

goal'. Dressing like and imitating celebrities has increased too. High school dances have suddenly come back with a vengeance, with skyrocketing expenditure on outfits, makeup and small details of appearance like manicured nails, fake suntans and elaborate hairdos. All this baffles many of the boomer parents, who thought they had thrown out quaint ideas like debutante balls along with girdles, unequal pay and the rest of the feminine mystique. Now wedding extravagance has begun again to be the norm, rivalling the French aristocracy before the revolution. Gwyneth Paltrow remarked that for modern women 'the whole wedding fantasy [is] their day at the Oscars'. A new term has been coined for the bride who develops a maniacal obsession with everything being perfect: Bridezilla. People begin married life heavily in debt, with the cost of a wedding equalling a deposit for a house, or their parents spend part of their retirement fund.

Then there are the 'Mega-Birthday Parties', occasions so elaborate you need an event manager to host them. One article about planning teenage parties was called 'Don't You Wish Your Party Was Hot Like Mine'. 'That said it all,' said Susan Reardon, a Litchfield County mother who was planning on spending US$12 000 on a sixteenth birthday party for her daughter, including 'specially designed invitations, a tented backyard with linen-covered round tables, a dance floor, a band, an ice-cream sundae bar and DVDs of the celebration for all the guests'. Litchfield, however, was not in the same league of hyper-parent as the New York CEO who spent US$10 million to stage a coming-of-age celebration for his daughter and friends in the Rainbow Room, atop the Rockefeller Center. The youngsters all returned home with a party bag that included a $300 video iPod.

Much of this expenditure, of course, like so much else, comes on credit. Such easy credit fuels 'grandiose, materialistic fantasies'. The financial meltdown, too, Twenge and Campbell assert, occurred because of changes in character: as credit got easy, insanely free lending principles for mortgages meant new expectations and a sense of entitlement to 'live like royalty' without the means to pay for it.

If psychotherapists identify the core problem leading to narcissism as emotional deprivation, which creates a character that aggressively defends against excess shame, for Twenge and Campbell it's excess gratification leading to hubris. Sounding at times like Old Testament prophets, *The Narcissism Epidemic* authors thunder that we are guilty of giving way to the seven deadly sins of pride, wrath, gluttony, envy, sloth, lust and greed. The way we live now is 'as eternal children, having our every need met and wish fulfilled'. Against this infantile paradise, Twenge and Campbell reiterate Freud's idea that civilisation depends on the renunciation of the 'pleasure principle' in favour of the adult world limited by the 'reality principle'.

There is, they claim, no evidence for the psychodynamic theories of cold and unempathic parents. They cite one study that found that children whose mothers are both warm and psychologically controlling—like a helicopter mother—are more likely to be narcissistic. Narcissists are more likely to agree with the statement: 'Looking back I feel that my parents sometimes put me on a pedestal.' Or 'When I was a child my parents praised me for everything I did.' However, as Twenge and Campbell admit, these studies were of adults recalling childhood, and were methodologically far from perfect. And in other studies, they concede, it seems it is less the helicopter parent—blades of over-concern whirring above the Spoiled One's head—and more like indulgence combined with neglect (for example, those adolescents whose parents do not know where they are at night) that are likely to create narcissistic children. In a British study, it is cold and unempathic parenting combined with over-praising. Yet still, Twenge and Campbell insist, the problem lies in spoiling, in a 'role reversal' between parent and child as to who is in charge, 'the era of the weak parent'.

* * *

The author of the 2007 book *Generation Me: Why Today's Young Americans Are More Confident, Assertive, Entitled—And More Miserable Than Ever Before* manages to capture both sides of the narcissistic coin. As well as tracking all the brash, self-centred and overconfident elements of *The Narcissism Epidemic*, she explores how rates of depression and anxiety have risen dramatically: the 'average college student in the 1990s was more anxious than 85 per cent of students in the 1950s and 71 per cent of them in the 1970s'. Children, too, are suffering. Schoolchildren who were not psychiatric patients in the 1980s reported levels of anxiety higher than those who were patients in the 1950s. As well as higher expectations, these youngsters have to cope with increased competition and insecurity over everything: college places, housing and partners. Their world is simply less secure. The author writes movingly of the number of young people she knew who committed suicide at college, while other friends suffered panic attacks and depression. She highlights the many social and economic changes that have resulted in less secure conditions of childhood. One of them is parental divorce:

> For many in GenMe, the instability began at an early age with their parents' divorce ... almost half of GenMe has seen their parents divorce, or have never known their father at all. This has a clear link to depression as children of divorce are more likely to be anxious and depressed ... the personal stories of children of divorce ... vividly illustrate the lifetime of pain, cynicism and uncertainty divorce can create among young people.

None of this adds up in any simple way to the 'spoiled rotten' thesis. This more sensitive and nuanced account shows the shadow side of our narcissistic society, which is incompatible with the Pollyanna version of modern parenting as too child-centred and with the child in charge. So who is the author? It is none other than Jean Twenge. Somehow in her later, jointly authored book with Keith Campbell, the flipside of narcissism—vulnerability and anxiety—has dropped out of the picture. *The Narcissism Epidemic* sounds altogether more Republican in spirit, sheeting home all blame onto the individual.

Surely we have a problem. The kind of omnipresence that helicopter parenting implies—all that excess attention, mollycoddling and overprotection—would require stable relationships and very different work patterns. Yet that is precisely our weakest point, where our hopes are most distant from our desires. There are longer working hours per family to make ends meet. Both parents are in the workforce at ever-younger ages of a child's life. Both the women's movement and the stagnation of middle-class incomes have contributed to this. One consequence has been books like *The Time Bind, The Second Shift, Nobody Home* and *The Commercialisation of Intimate Life*; portraits of overstretched families and the outsourcing of many previous functions of the family. None of that is consistent with the helicopter parent.

Among the consequences of this new individualism are family breakdown, commitment phobia, and the rise of loneliness and its dark companions: depression, anxiety and even suicide. There is a tendency for the deepest human relationships to be commoditised and to have meaning emptied from them, a world in which people seek fleeting connections in a society of strangers. In the wake of these changes, there has been for too many a collapse of meaning, with all the anxiety and anguish that comes with postmodernity's unbearable lightness of being.

In 1985—the time period that Twenge and Campbell argue is when parenting took a fatal turn towards spoiling and child-centredness—one of the most important books of American

sociology was written. *Habits of the Heart*, by sociologist Robert
Bellah, is based on extensive interviews. It is a troubling portrait
of the consequences of the new emphasis on the self. He notices
the difficulty adults have in articulating ideas of sacrifice and
obligation in relationships, and how easily others are discarded if
they no longer fulfil the needs of the self. He describes a 'sombre
utilitarianism' of 'self-preservation', where other people are treated
as 'instruments' for one's own self-fulfilment, often resulting in a
world of short-term relationships with other self-seeking people,
where 'the only measure of the good is what is good for the self'.

If the era since the 1970s has held self-indulgence, self-
fulfilment and self-actualisation as ideals, how exactly has that
era also managed to spawn parents who are supposedly so
self-sacrificing and self-abasing as to be ever-present, giving in
to their children's every whim? Just how do parents who are
in the workforce and working longer hours get the time to be
helicopters? Po Bronson, in the *New York Times*, agrees with the
idea that parents praise children too much, but he links it to
our high achievement culture and our greater absence from
children's lives:

> Offering praise has become a sort of panacea for the
> anxieties of modern parenting. Out of our children's lives
> from breakfast to dinner, we turn it up a notch when we
> get home. In those few hours together, we want them to
> hear the things we can't say during the day.

Let us take the argument that parenting is now ludicrously
child-centred. It is certainly true that children often govern not
just their own but also family choices about consumption in ways
undreamt of in earlier eras. But in other ways we have changed fundamentally to place parents' rights to freedom and self-fulfilment
ahead of children. We no longer stay together for the sake of the

children if we find ourselves in an unhappy marriage. So the very same children contributing to a decision on what brands to buy have little or no influence on the much more central question affecting their wellbeing of whether their parents stay together. How do these parents, some of whom live on opposite sides of the country to their children, or who lose touch with them altogether, get to hover? Do the children also dictate how much time they can spend with their mother or father? When parents return home from work? How much after-care, before-care or day care they have? Or are these choices more likely determined by parental finances—by interest rates on mortgages, rising house prices and indeed a desire for a certain material standard of living?

Could it not be that we are really looking at one kind of indulgence—for example, of material desire—combined with another kind of inattention? Could the 'spoiling' be the compensatory behaviour of overstressed and overstretched parents assuaging guilt? Is this simple spoiling or is it much closer to Freud's initial insightful guess; a mixture of emotional coolness combined with excessive overpraise, focusing on the child's achievements and indulgence of consumption patterns that rival those of royalty? Maybe there *is* more to this than meets the eye.

Chapter 3

Inside the Mask

These children get what they do not need and do not get
what they do need.

John Fiscalini, psychoanalyst

A DAM GOPNIK HAS written in the *New Yorker* about a new trend
to neuroscepticism: a push back against the way neuroscience is often treated as the gold standard of proof. Gopnik
likens our swings of fashion in explanations of human conduct
to the battle between the characters in the old TV program *Star
Trek*. Mr Spock assumed everything was rational, analytic and
able to be explained logically. Captain Kirk, meanwhile, believed
'what governs our life is not only irrational, but inexplicable
and the better for being so'. In the Age of the Brain, we are all
Mr Spocks now.

New brain-imaging techniques have given neuroscience a new
scientific authority. Cambridge University psychologist Simon
Baron-Cohen in *Zero Degrees of Empathy: A New Theory of Human
Cruelty*, explains that neuroimaging 'reveals abnormalities' in the
narcissistic person's 'empathy circuit'—those parts of the brain
known to be involved in compassionate understanding and iden-
tification with others. The narcissist lacks the 'double-minded'

ability to see someone else's perspective as well as their own, because 'a chip in their neural computer is missing'. The result is people 'imprisoned in their own self-focus'. German psychiatrists have similar findings. Using magnetic resonance imaging (MRI) techniques, they studied thirty-four people, half of whom had a diagnosis of narcissistic personality disorder. They found that narcissists have 'less gray matter in a part of the cerebral cortex called the left anterior insula'. We have known for a long time that narcissists lack empathy, Professor Stefan Ropke explained, but 'for the first time, we were able to show that it is structurally correlated in the brain'. In a striking result, after examining the region of the brain that 'has been tied to the regulation of emotion' and 'generation of compassion and empathy', they discovered that 'the patients with narcissism exhibit a structural deficit in exactly this area.' US neuroscientists from the University of Southern California found a strong correlation between people who scored highly on a measure of narcissism—the Machiavellian Egocentricity subscale—and much higher activity in the part of the brain concerned with the self, even while at rest. So even while snoozing, the narcissist's mind stays busy—thinking about themselves! They also found these same subjects were impulsive and struggled to control their impulses, leading to poorer decision-making.

As interesting as these findings from neuroscience are, none of those grainy images of the narcissist's brain get us close to a cause. Is their neural capacity for empathy impaired from birth? Or is it that they use their empathy circuit in relation to others so little that it begins to resemble a rusty old railway track smothered with weeds? Meanwhile the region of the brain concerned with themselves is so well cultivated that any thought concerning the self runs unimpeded along well-honed neural pathways.

Empirical studies by social psychologists like Twenge and Campbell also have their limits. We need ways of verifying insights, so empirical studies are always important. Yet there can be hubris in vulgar empiricism, if we believe only what is measurable, even if what we measure is sometimes banal, trivial or misleading. So how good are the tools of the social psychologists, like the Narcissistic Personality Inventory? Pretty good, but not infallible. While the NPI is undoubtedly a very useful measure, scholars admit it is best at identifying the grandiose, functioning narcissist. Some scholars have concerns that some of the items on it simply measure confidence, assertiveness and high self-esteem. That means high scores on the NPI may be conflating healthy, adaptive traits with narcissism. It also misses the vulnerable narcissist, who might be wrecking their own life and the lives of those around them.

A broader limit is that empirical studies where college students self-report and tick boxes, or react to ego threats in the lab, are only one sort of knowledge. Another kind comes from skilled clinicians, who spend hundreds or even thousands of hours, over decades, getting up close and personal with the narcissist on their couch. They are in a good position to observe the characteristic emotional patterns of narcissists. Their illuminating portraits are similar to what the anthropologist Clifford Geertz called 'thick description', only not of societies but of individuals: rich, evocative and detailed descriptions deriving from the process whereby, over a long period, a therapist gets to know the grooves and contours of the narcissist's soul. If the NPI is the measure used by the academic psychologists, outstanding therapists have contributed to the development of another widely used means of diagnosing narcissism for the US-based *Diagnostic and Statistical Manual* (DSM).

What one writer wittily describes as the psychologists' version of an auto repair manual, the DSM currently guides mental health professionals worldwide. It identifies serious 'biological' disorders such as depression, schizophrenia and bipolar, as well as various personality disorders. Roughly, a personality disorder describes someone who does not experience hallucinations or psychosis, but has serious and lasting impairment in intimate and social relationships and at work.

A narcissistic personality disorder according to the latest *Diagnostic and Statistical Manual of Mental Disorders* (DSM-5), published in 2013, is indicated by the presence of five or more of the following:

1. A grandiose sense of self-importance without commensurate achievement.
2. A preoccupation with fantasies of unlimited success, power, brilliance, beauty or ideal love.
3. A belief that he or she is 'special' and unique and can only be understood by, or should be associated with, other special or high-status people (or institutions).
4. A requirement of excessive admiration.
5. A sense of entitlement, that is, unreasonable expectations of especially favourable treatment or automatic compliance with his or her expectations.
6. Interpersonally exploitative, that is, takes advantage of others to achieve his or her own ends.
7. A lack of empathy, that is, an unwillingness to recognise or identify with the feelings or needs of others.
8. Envy of others or belief that others are envious of him or her.
9. A demonstration of arrogant, haughty behaviour or attitudes.

This new, updated volume has been under the cloud of a huge controversy. The press went crazy with excitement when it was announced that the category of narcissistic personality disorder was being abolished—at the very moment a narcissism epidemic was being declared! There were all kinds of witty riffs that the main people who would be displeased were narcissists themselves. With their disorder abolished they were no longer centre stage!

However, no abolition of narcissism was ever intended. Rather, the working group responsible for the new version of the DSM wanted to move away from describing a discrete syndrome, which delineates it from other personality disorders. They wanted instead to use a trait approach: narcissism is on a continuum—all of us have some—so how and why does it become problematic? Which kinds of psychological traits make for problematic, maladaptive narcissism? In the end, on strong advice from therapists, who have found the NPD checklist an extremely useful guide to diagnosis, they retained the category. In the new edition of the DSM, though, there is more emphasis on narcissism as a faulty system of self-regulation: the emotional roller-coaster of the narcissist's life; the way they are vulnerable to inflating with pride one moment and deflating the next. In those revisions, we can see the influence of gifted therapists like Elsa Ronningstam, a Boston specialist in narcissism.

So enough of Mr Spock's methods; time for the spirit of Captain Kirk. Let's look at the insights emerging from the craft of psychotherapy. Is a narcissist born a narcissist? Or are they made that way by experience? That is the central question that psychotherapists have been grappling with since Freud.

Freud: Love Turned Inward

It was Sigmund Freud who laid down the first outline. Like all of Freud's work, 'On Narcissism' is beautifully written and easy to read, although that ease can disguise the sophistication of his theoretical understanding. A tantalising sketch, it contains both insights and errors. It took the founder of psychoanalysis some time to come to think about narcissism. Freud thought that there exists an emotional unconscious that influences our behaviour: we are not who we consciously believe ourselves to be. He also stressed the common humanity between the mad person and the sane. In similar spirit, as an important antidote to dehumanising descriptions as monsters and 'emotional vampires', he believed that narcissism exists in all of us, on a continuum of those who do not have enough, through those who have 'healthy' narcissism, to those who suffer from its pathological variety. One can see what he means: the depressed and withdrawn self-mutilator at one end of the human spectrum, a mass killer like Breivik at the other.

Freud felt we all begin in a 'primary' state of narcissism, which is natural but which needs to be overcome as a child develops. Yet in some people this universal process is derailed, resulting in pathological narcissism. Love turned inward. The self was taken as the love object. For Freud, the great antidotes to neurosis were love and work: 'We must love in order not to fall ill, and we are bound to fall ill, if, in consequence of frustration, we are unable to love.'

Loving another is the opposite of a narcissistic state. Yet Freud could not stop imbuing this lovely insight with his somewhat misanthropic cast, that someone in love displays a marked 'sexual overvaluation' of their beloved. Here, in the state of romantic love, a person is invested in the loved one and therefore vulnerable to loss. This is the opposite of a narcissistic state; in an arresting phrase, Freud felt that 'Whoever loves becomes humble. Those who love have, so to speak, pawned a part of their narcissism.' More generally he thought of love as a finite resource: 'If there is too much self-love, there is not a lot left for loving others. And if there is too much altruism, there is not much love left for self.'

As children develop, the primary narcissism and euphoria of the period of infancy—being worshipped as 'Your Majesty the Baby'—gives way to a pained realisation of imperfections as they grow older and more is expected of them, as they are disciplined and criticised by parents and caregivers. Yet their old sense of self-perfection lives on, but becomes transformed into an ego ideal or ideal self they strive to live up to. Freud also thought that the renunciation of narcissism in the process of growing up makes people susceptible to being attracted to, fascinated by and envious of those whose narcissism seems intact. Children charm us with their self-contentment and inaccessibility. So too do those animals 'which seem not to concern themselves about us, such as cats and large beast of prey'. Likewise criminals and comics fascinate us by holding away 'from their ego anything which would diminish it. It is as if we envied them for maintaining a blissful state of mind—an unassailable libidinal position which we ourselves have abandoned'.

His view of narcissism in women reflected the patriarchal culture of his time. He felt women, as part of their general inferiority, are more narcissistic than men. Freud claimed that the onset of puberty in women 'seems to bring about an intensification of the original narcissism'. Instead of overvaluing her lover, a woman instead admires and loves herself. Yet this narcissism in women can drive men mad with desire:

> Women, especially if they grow up with good looks, develop a certain self-contentment which compensates them for the social restrictions that are imposed on them ... Strictly speaking, it is only themselves that such women love with an intensity comparable to a man's love for them. Nor does their need lie in the direction of loving but being loved; and the man who fulfils this condition is the one who finds favour with them. The importance of this type of woman for the erotic life of mankind is to be rated very high.

Freud simply got this wrong. All modern research shows that both genders can be narcissistic, but more men score highly on the NPI, and there are somewhat higher numbers of men with pathological narcissism. Nor do women find it difficult to love; consider all those plaintive self-help titles, like *Women Who Love Too Much*, written for women entangled with narcissistic and withholding males, or, for that matter, Keith Campbell's *When You Love a Man Who Loves Himself.*

Freud also tied female narcissism to what he saw as their biologically ordained dependency on men. Again, this will never survive the consciousness raising of feminism. Elizabeth Lunbeck, in *The Americanization of Narcissism*, points out that Freud was highly dependent, in ways that few males of that era acknowledged, on the care work done by a large number of the allegedly inferior gender. There was a small army of family women, in fact, who acted as 'ministering angels to the needs and comforts of men'. From his wife Martha and her unmarried sister Minna Bernays, to daughters Sophie and Anna, all these women worked incredibly hard on typing his manuscripts, distributing analytic manuscripts throughout Europe, arranging Freud's travel, or hotels for visiting analysts, managing his household, raising the children, laying his clothing out each day, preparing food and flapping around him, assuaging life's harsher vibrations. No one interrupted the Great Man's Muse at lunch, as he sat preoccupied and silent in their convivial midst, leaned back, lit a cigar and let his thoughts roam, perhaps to their greater 'narcissism', 'dependency' and alleged penis envy. On the other hand, they may not have been so much envying his penis as his ability and power to have a profession for which he was admired, to saunter into lunch prepared by others, and to eat undisturbed.

Freud did graciously concede that in motherhood women might overcome their narcissism: 'in the child they bear, a part of their own body confronts them like an extraneous object, to which, starting out from their own narcissism, they can then give complete object love'. Sons especially benefit from this; Freud acknowledged the importance of being loved, although only, it seems, for the boy child: 'a man who has been the undisputed favourite of his mother keeps for life the feeling of a conqueror; that confidence of success often induces real success'. One can see his point; think of someone like former prime minister Paul Keating, for example, whose mother could not remember him ever doing a single thing wrong as a child, beyond throwing someone's hat into a tree!

Then again, Freud was quite grim about parental love:

> Parental love, which is so moving and at bottom so childish, is nothing but the parent's narcissism born again, which, transformed, unmistakably reveals its former nature … a revival of and reproduction of their own narcissism, which they have long since abandoned … At the most touchy point in the narcissistic system, the immortality of the ego, which is so hard pressed by reality, security is achieved by taking refuge in the child.

We all know parents or grandparents who bask in the reflected glory of their wunderkinder, veering past pride into a grotesque hubris. They seem to be establishing the child as an extension of *their* superiority and specialness rather than recognising any real qualities of the child. Yet, putting such examples aside, this view is extremely cynical. As Australian psychoanalyst, Neville Symington points out, it overlooks the selflessness in parenting, the moral achievement in setting aside one's own narcissism to answer a child's needs, helping them develop strong relationships with others, and the huge sacrifices made in raising a child as one contribution to the wider world. Narcissism is usually transformed, not revisited. Symington is right. We should not confuse ordinary, good-enough parenting with the narcissistic variety.

In later works, Freud spoke of the devastating nature of narcissistic mortification—the emotional shock when a person's ideal sense of themselves collides with an uncompromising reality that forces a drastic, downward revision of their self-concept. The more grandiose the sense of self, the more likely such collisions are.

It is this central relationship of narcissism and shame that has preoccupied psychoanalysts ever since.

Heinz Kohut: Inside the Mask

It was not until a new character type began to frequent psychoanalysts' couches in the United States—displacing the older sexual neuroses common in Freud's time and instead struggling with issues of self and identity, including narcissism—that Freud's perceptive but incomplete early sketch gave way to more systematic contributions on the subject. One of the most famous and influential is from Heinz Kohut, a Jewish refugee who fled the Nazi regime to America and practised from the 1940s onwards, culminating in works like *The Analysis of the Self.* He treated not extremes like Breivik but affluent Americans with a much milder variant of the disorder, who were functioning but deeply troubled.

Listening to his patients, Kohut thought that inside the outer mask of a braggart, there was a hypersensitive, vulnerable core. He heard a 'never listened to story', begun long ago in childhood, of a failure of empathy, of a child's needs being painfully overlooked as narcissistic parents centred their attentions on their own needs. Kohut was an exceptionally empathetic therapist, tuning in and listening as attentively to the cadences of *how* patients said things as to *what* they said. He argued it is essential that the 'vulnerable' part of the narcissistic patient be accepted and treated empathetically. The patient is never wrong, only the therapist. He was concerned not to rush to interpretation or note slips of the tongue, which makes the narcissistic patient feel self-conscious, criticised and shamed. The parent's face is like a mirror. A child looks at that mirror and sees themselves there, as the parent sees them. The expression on the parent's face may show not interest but disinterest, dislike instead of love and acceptance, and disappointment, even disgust and rejection, triggering shame instead of pride. Kohut felt these failures lay in the early environment, with unempathic parents failing to mirror and support with acceptance the natural grandiosity in a small child, puncturing it too harshly, leaving a lasting disposition of shame before the eyes of others.

Kohut naturalised narcissism. He was the great exponent of 'healthy narcissism', which he said is present in everybody, and is a natural part of the psyche. There is too much moralising in responses to the narcissist, Kohut felt, a 'negatively toned evaluation' overlooking 'the contribution of narcissism to health, adaptation and achievement'. This moral disapproval came in part from Freud's idea that you start life as a little narcissist, and that overcoming narcissism and becoming able to love other people is part of maturing. In this vision, it is a moral as well as developmental achievement, then, to be able to love. Often, Kohut felt, therapists impose 'the altruistic value system of Western civilisation', trying to replace the patient's narcissism, their self-love, with the love of others. This misses the zest for life, the confidence, creativity and exuberance that comes from 'healthy narcissism'. Lunbeck, very Kohutian in spirit, shares this view. She criticises what she sees as the dour moralising tradition of Lasch and his modern counterparts, the social psychologists Twenge and Campbell, for losing sight of the essential nature of healthy narcissism. Many psychotherapists confronted by the self-hatred and malignant sadness of intractable depression might agree with her.

The emphasis on independence and separation, obscured, Kohut felt, how embedded in relationships we are, including in adulthood. Everybody needs affirmation from other people; it is essential to maintaining psychic balance, self-esteem, keeping afloat in the world and helping to regulate emotions. A child is pushed out of a friendship group and rushes home to tell their mum, who empathises and then dusts them off and helps them figure out ways of linking up with other kids in the grade. You are passed over for a promotion at work and you immediately ring your spouse or best friend, who commiserates. After being dumped by a self-centred boyfriend or girlfriend, you feel like an unattractive worm so you have dinner with a close friend, who shores up your battered sense of self. And so on. No one can go through life, Kohut felt, without such people. But if things go well in development, any one of those distressed people could reverse the roles; *they* could become the person turned to, depended upon, giving comfort, succour, empathy. Kohut thought that our 'self' does not come into being in isolation but is embedded in relationships with others. Of course he was right. All of my examples are of what psychologists call 'emotional regulation'. In good relationships, close others do this for us all the time. We never lose this need.

Yet there can be desperation over *not* being looked at. A child who feels invisible experiences an anguish that speaks to something primal in the human condition. The problem for the narcissist, Kohut thought, is that their self is so fragile that this need becomes extreme. Other people are treated greedily, exploitatively, not like other human beings, but like objects in the service of bolstering their self-esteem. Grandiosity in narcissism takes a pathological, defensive cast. Through the special relationship with a therapist, called transference, where the therapist allows themselves for a time to be used ruthlessly by the patient, Kohut saw the possibility of repair over time. Permitting regression and dependency in an atmosphere of empathy enable the narcissistic person to become less so. In Kohut's view, it is imperative that the therapist move gently around such sensitivities rather than challenge them too early. Instead of drawing attention to how demanding someone was, Kohut might simply have said, 'It hurts when you are not treated the way you feel you deserve to be treated.'

Take the case of one of his patients, Miss F. She felt isolated from others and unable to achieve a satisfying intimacy with anyone. On an emotional roller coaster, she was subject to abrupt shifts in mood; oscillating from excitement and elation while in a grandiose state, cherishing her 'secret preciousness which made her vastly better than anyone else', only to collide with reality and plummet downward into a deflated, bland state of frozen immobility. She did not establish relationships with people on the basis of real attraction, but because they would soothe her 'painful narcissistic tensions'. Simply put, she sought out people who might puff her up, give narcissistic supply, rather than establish real friendships and love relationships.

Her family was not untypical in mid–twentieth century America. Her mother, a depressed homemaker mother receiving very little help from the withdrawn father, was often emotionally unavailable. As she turned to her father, after disappointing rebuffs from her mother, he 'further traumatised her by vacillating between … fantastic love and emotional disinterest and withdrawal'. Her brother was cruel, and perhaps a grandiose narcissist, grabbing all the family limelight. Miss F, in contrast, as the overlooked child, was a vulnerable narcissist. What struck Kohut was not so much the *content* of what she said, as its emotional texture, her 'high pitched' needy tone, the voice of a small, fragile and vulnerable child.

Sessions would begin with Kohut feeling bored. He would struggle to concentrate, so flat and calm were her comments, without any emotion. Yet, halfway through, something would trigger her narcissistic rage at his remaining silent, or not giving her any support. Kohut was able to calm her by 'mirroring' her comments thus far and summarising them, but without any interpretation. In contrast, Miss F found any offered insights deeply threatening. She would fly into a rage, her voice rising high and shrieking with anger, if he tried to offer any. She would accuse Kohut of 'undermining her'. She was extremely demanding but taught him, he felt, the need for complete empathy. Miss F's behaviour represented the adult version of the insistent need for attention of the young child who had never been listened to. If Kohut gave his own interpretation, she experienced his intervention as a verbal assault; he 'instantly became her depressed mother, deflecting all of Miss F's needs onto herself'.

Miss F's real story, as it unfolded, was this. Often she would skip home from school, bursting with pride, 'joyfully anticipating' telling her mother about some success. But instead of her mother's face 'lighting up', meeting and sharing her joy, her mother's 'expression would remain blank', she would appear to listen, then invariably deflate her, 'imperceptibly the topic of conversation shifted and the mother began to talk about herself, her headache and her tiredness and her other physical, self-preoccupations'. In short, here was a role reversal: the mother turned to the child for attention and comfort, to look after her. This scenario is not uncommon when an emotionally remote or absent father offers little succour, support or nurturance to the caregiving parent. Miss F's mother was unable to remain in the position of the nurturing adult. Our joy in life is amplified by being shared, being mirrored by others, and joyfully accepted and celebrated. Exuberance, when shared, rises to a crescendo before subsiding. Puncturing a child's excitement and joy can lead to the potent and toxic emotion of shame. As a child Miss F was robbed of maternal acceptance, affirmation and enjoyment. Devastatingly: 'Nothing she did as a girl evoked pleasure or approval.' Miss F ended up feeling empty and depleted and unable to have loving relationships.

Kohut understood that his role was to become the inexhaustibly patient listener, the very first person to properly hear this woman's 'never listened to story'. This empathetic stance, this being there, fully attentive and responsive to her, was more important, he argued, than actually interpreting her plight in the light of the then standard Freudian Oedipal dramas. As the woman navigated her way through her rage at Kohut, she was gradually able to locate it in the past, where it ought to be—at those memories of feeling unheard and unresponded to.

Some of Kohut's patients latched onto the therapist like limpets, attempting a merger, as if the analyst was a 'mere extension of the patient'. Their domination of the therapist could be intense; getting them to behave *exactly* as they wanted was very difficult to deal with. Again, Kohut argued for an empathetic approach, suggesting the incorporation of another person gave the narcissist's fragile self a balustrade, the scaffolding of security to help hold their disintegrating psyche together. Over time in therapy, these functions could be increasingly integrated into the psyche. Such patients, however, could be tyrannical and dominant, exacting a brutal toll on the therapist. Many found them exhausting to deal with, as difficult as those who were psychotic.

Kohut noticed that as his relationship with his patients developed, they often reverted to a stage where they placed the therapist in the place of the parent, experiencing for the first time the blissful state of basking as 'the gleam in their mother's eye', an experience they had missed out on. Kohut was 'invited to participate in the child's narcissistic pleasure and thus to confirm it'. He thought this gleam in the parent's eye is central to psychic health; in this he was much more lenient on the question of narcissistic needs being gratified than many. To want to exhibit ourselves as children before our parents, our adoring audience, Kohut considered normal and desirable. He drew attention to a passage from Anthony Trollope's novel *Barchester Towers*, of a mother crooning to her baby:

> 'Diddle diddle ... dum ... hasn't he got lovely legs?' said the rapturous mother, '... He's a ... little ... darling, so he is; and he has the nicest little pink legs in all the world, so he has ... Well ... did you ever see? ... My naughty ... Johnny. He's pulled down all Mama's hair ... the naughtiest little man ...' The child screamed with delight ...

Kohut thought that this *being enjoyed* is the basis of healthy narcissism. Visit any doctor's surgery and watch babies and toddlers cruising around, looking back at their mother or father and basking in their doting smiles, and you can see immediately what Kohut meant. It *is* commonplace. He also allowed for some continuation of this into adulthood. It is hardly surprising that after experiencing such joy, some people grow up wanting to bask in the admiration of others, to exhibit themselves to recreate this pleasure, or to recreate it by having 'fantasies of grandeur'. Kohut agreed with Freud's view of the internal pot of gold bestowed by being a mother's favourite. He pointed to the ways grandiosity is linked to creativity, and pushes people towards outstanding performances and achievements, like those of Goethe, Freud and Winston Churchill.

In the TV show *Mad Men*, the character Megan is an aspiring actress. Her acid-tongued mother says of her: 'It is hard to have the temperament of the artist without the talent.' For the person with mediocre endowments in the talent department, Kohut thought that wild grandiosity would be disruptive in many life situations. Therapy has to do for the patient what the parents have not: tame their pretensions to grandeur.

In a healthy family, the child who is supported but not indulged gradually relinquishes this self-centredness and becomes orientated towards realistic goals. Their early grandiosity is integrated into a secure sense of self-esteem and willingness to embrace and move towards worthwhile ideals in life. If there is 'trauma', however—by which Kohut meant the absence of empathetic parenting—the grandiosity is split off, becoming part of a protective fantasy about the self, no longer subject to the reality principle.

Before leaving Kohut, I want to state clearly my approach in this book to ideas of 'healthy narcissism'. There are undoubtedly hugely positive qualities in people to which it would be terrible to give the pejorative label narcissism. But 'healthy narcissism', I think, is a fundamental category mistake. The word 'narcissism' has *always* carried an ambiguously negative inflection since ancient times, when the Greek myth first depicted the youth Narcissus pining away as he gazed into the lily pond.

Now think of all those self-help books—*Children of the Self-Absorbed: A Grown-up's Guide to Getting over Narcissistic Parents*, or *Emotional Vampires: Dealing with People Who Drain You Dry*. Our natural language embeds a harsh judgement in the word 'narcissism'. How, then, can we attach something desirable and admirable to it, as in the adjective 'healthy'? Surely here the emotional weight of each word—'healthy' and 'narcissism'—cancel each other out. It is easy to understand what this clumsy phrase is aiming for: it is trying to capture all the modes of self that are positive but not excessively so, neither prideful nor shame-ridden, like self-confidence, zest, joie de vivre, exuberance, self-enjoyment, self-belief, pride, self-esteem, ambition, drive, an unwillingness to be put down, self-efficacy ... But why on earth do we need one vague, misleading and pejorative term to cover all of these distinctive states and feelings when we have our wonderful natural language?

Consider, for example, 'pride', 'prideful' and 'hubris', three excellent words that convey precise meanings about the feelings experienced. There is quite a lot of research now showing that in narcissism the pride felt is hubris, inflated and phony, rather than authentic or just pride, where the feeling is earned through real-life achievements. A visiting US academic psychologist listened to my account of this distinction and immediately offered a good example. He told me about one of his students who was a gifted marathon runner. She was so modest he only found out by accident; she hadn't told anyone about it. Her reason for running was intrinsic, the challenge of endurance itself, not because it enabled her to be seen as superior in the eyes of others. But she also took a natural, unalloyed pleasure in the recognition given to her by her teacher and classmates when they found out. Kohut would approve! But why call this by the ugly name 'healthy narcissism'? Why not call it just or authentic pride, based on real hard work and achievement? And to distinguish it from that lovely, natural pleasure, let us use a precise word, 'hubris', to describe the egoistic, excessive pride shown by celebrity rapper Kanye West, when he boldly declared:

> People get mad at me saying that I am a creative genius, but it's just obvious. It's, like, factual. I would write creative genius when I go through the airport … I would put that on customs [forms], where you put what your title is, except for two reasons: it takes too long to write and sometimes I spell the word genius wrong.

That's narcissism! I agree with those psychoanalysts and psychologists who argue 'healthy narcissism' is a misnaming that has sent us chasing after psychological red herrings ever after. Let us keep the word 'narcissism' for negative qualities all the way through to the pathological and malignant.

My last doubts concern the *results* of Kohut's therapy, tenderly tiptoeing around his narcissist. Surely one test of therapy for narcissists is whether they get along better afterward with others, rather than emerging—their insecurity and low self-esteem shored up—a more confident narcissist? One woman told me that her husband was made worse by therapy. He remained in therapy for years, at taxpayers' expense, after being diagnosed with an NDP. The diagnosis and therapy, which acted as a kind of alibi, had absolutely no effect on his self-centred behaviour. In fact, she felt he quite liked his regular audience, and became more entitled and arrogant; the therapeutic alliance worked to entrench all his complaints about her, and, of course, he was always the victim. She was never able to talk to his therapist and explain what she lived with: the rages, the infidelities, the denigration, the continual self-focus. In one empirical study, more narcissistic people actually did okay; hardly surprising since they tend to feel good about themselves. It is *the people around them* who suffer from their inflated sense of self.

The Blood of Others: Otto Kernberg

To get the narcissist to consider the effect of their behaviour on *others* was the central concern of Kohut's contemporary and equally influential rival Otto Kernberg. Another Jewish refugee fleeing the Holocaust, Kernberg was struck by the kind of patient who kept turning up on his couch, for whom there was as yet not even a name. His approach to narcissism was tougher with the patient than Kohut's. Kohut looked at things from the narcissistic person's point of view. For Kernberg, the ultimate goal of therapy was to move towards a relationship of enough trust so that it was possible to gently confront the narcissistic person, gradually bringing to them an awareness of the impact of their narcissism on others. He explained: 'You have these patients with severe distortions that ruin their lives. No doubt about it, these people have not been able to maintain work, a profession, a love relation. And with ... psychotherapy ... you are able to change their personality, improve their lives.'

Kernberg's patients were more often hospitalised, and their pathology was more severe than in Kohut's patients, who were closer, perhaps, to the 'worried well'. Kernberg's patients were also more aggressive. They contributed to his work on malignant narcissism, where the condition shades into psychopathy. Although his writing is complex and esoteric, he explained the syndrome lucidly and deftly when interviewed, highlighting that narcissists can be both grandiose and vulnerable at the same time. Pathological narcissism is an 'ego trip' where an 'exaggerated love of self' is combined with a 'devaluation of others'. Narcissists are 'very full of themselves' but this grandiosity exists paradoxically alongside vulnerability; they are prone to feeling rejected and are easily hurt. Sadly, all the self-love means an impoverishment of their interior world, 'because the richness of life comes from our gratifying intimate relations with significant others, as well as ideals outside of ourselves'.

Kernberg also thought cold, unempathic parenting was to blame. But he added something else. There is unhealthy grandiosity in the way narcissists are raised; they are overvalued in some way. Many of his patients had some sense of 'specialness' thrust upon them as children. Two of his patients were dressed up as a kind of 'object of art' and offered for public admiration in a grotesque way. Fantasies of power and greatness linked with exhibitionist trends became central: 'The child growing up took refuge in this exhibitionism to cover for the emptiness inside coming from lack of affection.' Perhaps the child was regarded as brilliant or was the one supposed to fulfil family aspirations: 'A good number of them have a history of having played the role of "genius" in their family during childhood.'

Kernberg also thought parenting cannot account for everything: there is at least some element of being 'born that way'. He felt the narcissist has very high innate levels of aggression, which could be constitutional or environmental. This is linked to their competing against and intense envy of others. They are always comparing themselves with others, and greedily wanting what others have. Listening to narcissistic people on his couch, Kernberg noticed how they split the world into all good and all bad. In the therapy room, there was always a bad guy and a good guy: one person who was devalued and another person who was idealised. Instead of aspiring to acquire the qualities of admired others, however everyone except the self was devalued, and thought of with contempt. Love relationships were usually fleeting, superficial, with little capacity for empathy, as in the Don Juan syndrome, where people are used as sexual objects without attachment. One of Kernberg's patients commented after many failed love relationships that 'her boyfriend had finally exploded, saying, "No man will ever be able to give you the kind of attention you want. The only place you'll ever see that kind of attention is what a mother gives to a baby!'"

Kernberg disagreed fundamentally with Freud's ideas about the 'primary' state of narcissism, from which a child matures. Instead, he said, pathological narcissism could not be more different from a small child's charming, even endearing self-centredness, which coexists with 'genuine love and gratitude', and whose demands are related to real needs that can be satisfied. Children, Kernberg argued, have nothing like the ruthless, greedy demands, the insatiable desire to be superior or the insistence on being the centre of attention of the adult narcissist, nor the cold haughtiness typical of pathological narcissism. A well-tended child is loving and contented. In contrast, an adult narcissist's thirst for attention can never be slaked, the insatiability of their desire is hidden behind feelings of disappointment, passive-aggressive resentment or even rage directed towards others failing to fulfil their (unreasonable) needs. They are always aggrieved.

Most children are also curious and interested in others, have a trusting and profound love for their parents, and experience real grief when separated from them. Beneath the surface charm, in contrast, the narcissist has little real interest in others, disregarding them, and only idealising them when they are a source of narcissistic supply. Their interest is really in what the other person can do for them. Unlike children, the narcissists Kernberg treated were unable to depend trustingly on other people. There was contempt and devaluation in the narcissist's relationship to others, 'in striking contrast to the warm quality of the small child's self-centeredness'. A non-narcissistic child does not need everybody to admire them, nor do they need to be the exclusive owner of all that is good and valuable in life. Kernberg found that by two or three years old, the narcissistic child lacks 'normal warmth and engagement with others, and [has] an easily activated, abnormal destructiveness and ruthlessness'. Hence, 'pathological narcissism is strikingly different' from normal development.

Perhaps because of his much darker view of the narcissistic character, and the implications for others in their life, Kernberg's approach in therapy was more confrontational than Kohut's. Convinced that greed and demandingness are not simply aspects of normal development, Kernberg believed these traits must be confronted and examined from the standpoint of their impact on others. At the extremes, the most dangerous variant, which he called malignant narcissism, involves the fusion of the super ego or conscience with unmodulated aggression from the id—resulting in someone who feels that their destruction of others is actually a moral act. Someone like Breivik. Hardly surprising then that he focused on the importance of 'developing guilt and concern for others'. But Kernberg also thought they were incredibly difficult patients to treat. Their brittle grandiosity cannot tolerate insightful interpretations as they feel them to be injuriously critical rather than admiring. As a consequence, narcissists might storm off before any real change is achieved.

One of the difficulties is that the narcissists—who feel themselves to be so admirable, even perfect—naturally find it hard to sit at the feet of an expert. Psychiatrist Glen Gabbard cites just such a patient, who complained long and loud of how '"doctor what's his name" had interrupted him a lot and was not a good listener... [He] talked at great length about his need for a really "special" therapist. He even speculated that there might not be anyone in the city gifted enough to really understand him ...' If the therapist made an interpretation he would say: '"You have the same problem as my other therapist. You're always inserting yourself into this. I'm not paying you to talk about you or your feelings. I'm here to talk about myself."'

On the other hand, sometimes narcissists can idealise people around them. If Groucho Marx joked that he didn't care to belong to a club that would have him as a member, the narcissist is more likely to think such a club is obviously full of equally superior people. Declared closeness to these idealised figures in the narcissist's life is fake: 'It regularly emerges that the admired individual is merely an extension of themselves. If the person rejects them, they experience immediate hatred and fear, and react by devaluing the former idol.' After dethroning their former idol, the narcissist immediately drops them. In short, there is no real involvement with the admired person; a simple narcissistic use is made of them. The narcissist, Kernberg believed, is the quintessential expert at 'moving on'. They lack the ability to experience mourning after a loss. Another simple way of putting this is that they lack the capacity for a real and healthy attachment to another human being.

Relationships for a narcissist are 'like squeezing a lemon and then dropping the remains'. But the narcissist is also terrified of other people, who seem more sinister and nasty than they really are, since they project their own rage-filled and aggressive impulses onto them. The further Kernberg got in analysis, the closer he came to

> the image of a hungry, enraged, empty self, full of impotent anger at being frustrated, and fearful of a world which seems as hateful and revengeful as the patient himself … the available remnants of such self-images reveal a picture of a worthless, poverty-stricken, empty person who feels always left on the 'outside' devoured by envy of those who have food, happiness, fame.

Such patients are afraid of belonging to the ranks of the 'mediocre' rather than the rich and powerful. Anything 'average' seems to them worthless and despicable. Sometimes treatment can free them from the obligation to be exceptional. One of Kernberg's patients progressed enough in therapy that they actually yearned to be average!

Kernberg thought that unless treated, narcissists age badly. Rather than take pleasure in encouraging the achievements of younger people, they can end up bitter and alone, having alienated so many people.

Mr Spock and Captain Kirk

'No one,' said Charles Darwin, 'can think clearly in a moment of shame.'

It is the psychoanalyst Helen Block Lewis who has been the most powerful influence in orienting contemporary therapists towards understanding narcissism as a defensive manoeuvre against bypassed shame. She noticed that her therapy sessions were full of unacknowledged shame, experienced by her clients as a jolt, a shock, but then quickly hidden. Her influence threads through many of the more recent contributions on narcissism by psychoanalysts like Francis Broucek, Michael Lewis and Elsa Ronningstam. When people feel the unbearable scorch of shame, the emotion is so painful, it must be escaped. One common response is the desire to hide, to wish the world could swallow you, that you could disappear, that the ground would open up and you could vanish, and so on. Shame ranges from milder feelings of embarrassment all the way to mortification, a word that has *mort*—dead—as its root. What is so devastating is suddenly being seen, exposed to the eyes of others, before we are ready for it, with our flaws showing, being seen in ways we desperately don't want. Jean-Paul Sartre captured this beautifully when he wrote, 'shame comes upon me like an internal haemorrhage for which I always felt unprepared'.

Anyone with an inflated sense of self is likely to have many more unpleasant encounters with reality—and hence experience more shame—than a person without that grandiosity. All the boasting, self-display, self-promotion and swaggering can be a monumental defence, warding off this excruciatingly painful emotion. Most of us can acknowledge, at least to ourselves, that we feel ashamed of some aspect of ourselves or something we have done. Shame is an almost unbearable feeling but we can admit it into our consciousness and look at it. We can, through experiencing and acknowledging it, also modulate and defuse it.

Shame is also a very different self-conscious moral emotion from guilt. Careful empirical work by psychologists like June Tangney support what psychotherapists like Kohut said about narcissism creating a shame or rage spiral. Her work reveals that guilt is a much more pro-social emotion than shame. When someone feels guilty, they are much more likely to apologise to the person they feel they have wronged, and to try to make reparation. The focus is where it should be: on the wrongful action and the wronged person, rather than on the offending self. Guilt says, 'I did *that to you.*' This means when people feel guilty they are more likely to take responsibility, are less likely to resort to denial, or an aggressively defensive stance, with hugely important relationship and social benefits. With shame, because the focus is on the whole self—'If *I* did that I must be worthless'—the person feels their very identity is on the line. They are much more likely to resort to denial, or enter the shame or rage spiral that Kohut and others have described.

Doris McIlwain, a perceptive Australian psychologist from Macquarie University, with an interest in narcissism, pointed out to me an apparent paradox at the heart of narcissism: if a narcissist is so confident, why the *rage* when threatened? Criticise a narcissist, she said, and watch out! Outside the specialists, few people understand this shame or rage spiral. Both psychotherapists and empirical psychology on moral emotions reveal that the essence of narcissistic rage is *bypassed* shame, the attempt to ward it off by expressing not ordinary anger, but a wild out of control rage, as if the person is fighting for their very life. And in a strange way they are.

Let us focus on McIllwain's point for a moment, about why such an apparently confident person might react like that. Baumeister originally linked high but *unstable* self-esteem to narcissistic aggression. What later scholars have shown is that a stable sense of authentic self-esteem does not result in these toxic and damaging responses to criticism or failure: 'When we deal with self-esteem, we are asking whether the person considers himself adequate—not whether he considers himself superior to others.' This is authentic self-esteem. Far more problematic is self-esteem that is contingent on success, or on the admiration of others.

US psychiatrist Donald Nathanson draws attention to what he calls the four points of the Compass of Shame: Withdraw, Attack Self, Avoidance Behaviour and Attack Other. Withdrawal is easy to understand. Someone feeling shamed disconnects from others and reels back inside themselves—the only 'safe haven'. This is demonstrated in shame's characteristic posture, of slumped shoulders, a submissive expression, and eyes cast down. This is a non-verbal form of supplication, a plea to be forgiven and reintegrated into the human herd. Attack Self is seen in creative forms as self-deprecating humour—lowering ourselves in an amusing way before anyone else does. But Attack Self can be pathological too—as in the withdrawal into a shame-ridden, 'morbid depression', where people may berate themselves endlessly as failures. Then there is Avoidance, often achieved by alcohol and drug abuse. Shame, says Nathanson, is 'soluble in alcohol' and 'boiled away by cocaine and amphetamines'. All these drugs can create grandiose states, and interestingly narcissism has a strong correlation with alcoholism.

Most problematic of all the responses, however, is when shame is dealt with by entering an 'Attack Other' state. By attacking and lowering others, a shamed person can feel better about themselves, laughing at someone, expressing contempt, like all the internet trolls. Mass killers like Breivik, and school shooters like Eric Klebold and Dylan Harris, often experience a series of humiliations prior to the deadly acts; a shame or rage state has spiralled out of control and become an Attack Other script with deadly assault weapons.

Nathanson makes the extremely interesting observation that in Western culture over the last half-century, the dominant response to shame has shifted from Withdrawal and Attack Self to Avoidance and Attack Other, 'from a culture of politeness and deference to a culture of narcissism and violence'.

'Facing reality should be an aim in life,' says Clive James, but 'it hardly ever is.' For the narcissist, the stink of shame has to be held away at all costs. The psychoanalyst Annie Reich describes how the narcissist suffers 'repetitive and violent oscillations of self-esteem,' and retreats in the face of narcissistic injury into a grandiose fantasy world where the self is superior, strong and omnipotent rather than weak, puny and defenceless. Broucek adds to this by suggesting the narcissist's behaviour is not always defensive. They can also be activists, engaging in a 'seize the day' pursuit of the pleasurable, including even addictive feelings of elation and pride. Rather than wait for others to bestow praise, they praise themselves. Jessica Tracy from the University of British Columbia, along with her colleagues, caught this in the apposite title of an important article entitled 'The Emotional Dynamics of Narcissism: Inflated by Pride, Deflated by Shame'. A great deal of social psychologists' careful empirical work is not at all antithetical to a nuanced account of the 'mask theory' of narcissism by psychoanalysts. And influential contemporary analysts like Elsa Ronningstam use the findings from neuroscience to better understand and treat the narcissistic patient. So it seems that Mr Spock and Captain Kirk were on the same spaceship, after all.

Chapter 4

The Roots of Empathy

What we are in search of is a picture of the patient's forgotten years that shall be alike trustworthy and in all essential respects complete.

Sigmund Freud

Zero Empathy

WHEN RYAN WAS admitted to an American Ivy League university, he threw a party. Admission to a good university was just one more felicitous event in a life of privilege. Ryan's parents were wealthy, so he was given all that a teenager might desire, like a brand new Lexus SUV. Attractive and popular, he seemed assured of a bright future.

For the boy who had everything, this was to be quite some party. As well as the usual truckload of alcohol and the loud music, Ryan had planned another treat for his friends' entertainment. It was to invite Amy, an intellectually disabled girl from his neighbourhood. And to rape her in front of the others.

When interviewed by Bruce Perry, the brilliant US psychiatrist who specialises in disturbed children, Ryan said, in a polite, well-modulated voice: 'We did her a favour. I don't know what the problem is, really. She never would have gotten laid by anyone as good as us.'

Perry found Ryan 'perhaps even colder' than any sociopath he had interviewed. Until the police arrived, he thought it was a big joke, boasting about it. It was clear that here was a boy who, on the surface, lacked nothing in the way of material goods. He came from a stable two-parent home, with two apparently together and successful parents. No poverty, alcohol or drug abuse, no personality disorders, no domestic chaos, nothing obvious that might account for his behaviour. Yet in his callous treatment of the girl, his calculated enjoyment of her public humiliation, his sense of superiority ('anyone as good as us'), his entitlement ('we did her a favour') and his willingness to exploit and treat her like an object, in his absolute lack of empathy, the sheer narcissism is palpable.

Surely here, then, is an example par excellence of Twenge and Campbell's spoiled narcissist—indulged by parents and given no sense of limits. Indeed there was evidence of the parents covering up all kinds of misdemeanours, which should have signalled alarm bells to any parent, just prior to the crime. Even after the arrest, when Perry was interviewing Ryan, the parents' 'main goal was to protect him from further consequences'. They were prepared to pay anything to get him off the hook. There must be a psychiatric diagnosis—depression, perhaps—to help him exit the charges? Ryan sounds very much like a spoiled child, to a grotesque degree.

Yet what Perry found was that this indulgence existed alongside something very different. Ryan's father worked long hours and left the child-rearing to Ryan's mother. Although Ryan's mother stayed at home, she had actually delegated most of Ryan's upbringing to nannies, right from the start. Before giving birth, she had decided that having a child should not interfere with her social life and charity work. She believed that 'quality time' was all that children needed. The nanny could do the rest of the parenting.

Attentive and sensitive caregiving can be given by people other than a child's parents, so that did not at first concern Perry.

But when Perry inquired about the nanny's view of Ryan, he got a shock. 'Which one?' Ryan's mother, Amanda, asked. There had been eighteen. The reason for the high turnover was that Amanda kept noticing that Ryan was more attached to the nannies than he was to her. Even at eight weeks of age, he was brighter and more affectionate with his primary caregiver, the nanny. Amanda fired her. When she hired another, going back to her busy schedule, the same thing happened. The baby bonded to the nanny. He 'almost seemed frightened of his own mother when she interacted with him in the brief "quality time" moments'.

By the time Ryan was nine months old, he screamed and struggled until his nanny returned, whenever his mother tried to hold him. So she fired the next one, and the next. 'Over-involved' she called them. When asked by Perry what an average day in infancy had been like, it was clear that Amanda had no idea. She simply hadn't been present. Neither, due to his work patterns, had Ryan's father.

By the time Ryan was three, he no longer cried when nannies came and went. He rarely cried or seemed to feel anything much at all. Perry pointed out that in this affluent American family, who gave so much to him materially, the 'boy who had everything' was actually emotionally deprived; Ryan had more changes in caregivers in his early childhood than many do in a Romanian orphanage.

Ryan would be one of those terrifying human beings that Baron-Cohen describes as having 'zero degree of empathy'. Without empathy, as Baron-Cohen observes, all kinds of narcissistic behaviours become possible and others become impossible. Without full attentiveness to the Other, all manner of insensitivity, self-centeredness and even human cruelty in relationships and politics become possible. What we call *evil* becomes possible.

Yet the counterpoint is true too. With empathy, cruelty is impossible. Simone Weil thought that if one had empathy, or the 'ability to see another person's perspective on the world, one could not act unjustly'. In contrast, empathy in narcissism is crucially attenuated or missing altogether. It is not only at an individual level; group narcissism underpins racism, sexism and homophobia—refusing to extend empathy and a common humanity to those who are different from oneself, seeing them instead as inferiors one is entitled to exploit. Empathy is deeply involved in overturning longstanding injustices caused by hierarchical notions of people, replacing such group narcissism with another of Weil's profound insights: 'Respect is due to the human person as such and is not a matter of degree.' It is such an essential ingredient in moral conduct, friendship, love, getting along with others, philanthropy, considerate behaviour, generosity, altruism and what the Greeks call *caritas*, or loving kindness, that we need to take seriously the kinds of upbringing that allow it to flourish and those that leave it to wither early on the vine.

Baron-Cohen rightly points to the exceptionally well-developed research showing that at the centre of the development of empathy is the process known as attachment, the deep and profound bonds formed between infant and parents. Without attachment, there is no empathy for those one hurts. As Perry observes grimly, 'If a child feels no emotional attachment to any human being, then we cannot expect any more remorse from him after killing a human than from someone who ran over a squirrel.'

So what is the kind of upbringing that promotes the development of emotional and moral qualities that are *not* narcissistic? What creates empathy? What creates the basis for strong and sensitive relationships with peers and parents? What makes for a child who has a capacity for emotional self-control, who doesn't become all puffed up with hubris when things go well, or melt down in shame-filled rage when things don't go their way? Or an adult, who does not cheat on their lover or exploit their spouse, but is capable of the give and take necessary in a long-term loving relationship?

As it happens, we have an extraordinarily solid body of research and evidence answering all these questions. On both sides of the Atlantic, contemporary psychotherapists like Britain's Sue Gerhardt and US-based psychiatrist Dan Siegel, are paying tribute to the important new findings of attachment scholarship. To understand its development, however we need to leave the experts in North America for a moment and cross the Atlantic to the United Kingdom.

The Roots of Empathy

During the cataclysm of World War II, many infants and children were separated from their parents. Anna Freud and Dorothy Burlingham, who worked in a British wartime nursery for such children, were among the first to notice the profound effects of separation. They were troubled by the behaviour of children raised in institutions, or shifted around from placement to placement. As with the Romanian orphans of our era, the plight of these institutionalised children galvanised humane imaginations. Separation could have dramatic physical consequences in babies, who could fail to thrive or grow. In extreme cases, children disintegrated to skin and bone, even dying. This institutional 'failure to thrive' was widespread enough to be given a name: 'hospitalism'.

Emotionally, the pattern was more complex. After going through an initial period of intense and angry 'Protest', searching and crying for the lost mother and father, children might then go through a period of intense sadness that one researcher called 'Despair'. After that period of intense misery and mourning, the children who 'recovered' seemed strangely transformed. This phase was termed 'Detachment'. On the surface the children were charming and pleasant, even indiscriminately affectionate. One psychologist remarked, 'They were affectionate to everybody. The foster parents would find that they would call someone Daddy who they saw for the first time in the street.' Love has a particularity to it, a preference for the loved one. Yet for these children, attachments were replaceable; one man, any man, was as good a Daddy as another. Underneath surface cheer, they seemed indifferent, lost to any deep emotion, and incapable of any deep attachment or relationship. They seemed, in fact, 'to lack any feeling for others at all', displaying 'incorrigible behaviour problems that often included sexual aggressiveness, fantastic lying, stealing, temper tantrums, immature or infantile demands, and failure to make meaningful friendships'. These children were good at getting attention and getting what they wanted out of people. They were cold and exploitative, and lacked empathy for others. Their behaviour was clearly the result of disrupted stable attachments—the absence of ordinary continuity of good-enough parental love.

A young psychiatrist named John Bowlby became interested in disruptions to bonds with parents when he conducted a research study on young delinquents found guilty of theft. Many of the thieves demonstrated a curious detached quality that Bowlby christened 'affectionless psychopathy'. Bowlby was struck by the fact that all but two of them had been subjected to prolonged early separations. One child, Derek, came from an ordinary, good-enough family without any neglect or abuse. At eighteen months, however, he had been hospitalised for nine months. It was standard procedure at this time for hospitalised children not to see parents, and he remained in hospital without seeing his mother or father the entire time. Coming home, he 'seemed a stranger', even calling his mother 'nurse'. His mother commented, 'It seemed like looking after someone else's baby.' He remained always 'strangely detached, unmoved by either affection or punishment. His mother described him as 'hard boiled'. Just as later researchers would show the importance of attachment in the emergence of empathy—so crucial for the moral development of children—these young children had little empathy or feeling for others: 'None of them seemed to have any sense of the meaning of what they had done. They could not say why they stole, and they seemed impervious to the wrong they had done others.'

Behind the hostility and detachment, however, Bowlby felt there was a tragedy, a child so traumatised by loving and then losing their parents that their emotional life dried up; love was never to be risked again. Instead, love was turned inward, and was invested in the self. The child became its own love object. Underneath, Bowlby felt, was a deep and unreachable depression: 'Behind the mask of indifference is bottomless misery and behind the apparent callousness despair.'

Institutionalisation could transform a vivacious and affectionate toddler into a different child. They exhibited indiscriminate friendliness to strangers. During parental visits to children undergoing prolonged separations researchers found they now seemed indifferent, as if denying the need for any relationships. Neither crying nor clinging, they seemed only interested in the presents parents brought, not the parents themselves: 'They searched bags and stuffed chocolate into their mouths. "Don't be greedy," perplexed parents would say.' One observer wrote, 'Feeling for their parents had died because of the passage of time and had been replaced by hunger for sweet things which did not disappoint.'

Children destroyed toys brought by parents, as if in anger at their deserting parents. When her mother bought her a doll, Mary, 'using hands and teeth', silently 'rent it apart'. Going home at three and a half, Mary 'squirmed out of her mother's embrace, then stood as if not knowing what affection was about'. No longer fitting into the 'reciprocity of family life', Mary was 'self-centred' and 'intent on looking after herself; for more than a year her needs had not been met by others'; she defeated family members and teachers with her ruthlessness.

Another way of rendering this behaviour in children, however, is that self-focus, self-love—narcissism—is their defence against being or feeling abandoned. Too painful to invest love in other human beings who will only disappear, the only person they can rely on is themselves. And along with attachment—those profound loving ties that bind—most tellingly, the capacity for moral action, empathy, disappears too.

Insecure Attachments

Separation of this kind, however, is an extreme situation, and not all that common. It was not long before an American colleague of Bowlby's, Mary Ainsworth, became interested in another, but related, question. Her focus was not what happens under extraordinary circumstances—when a child *loses* an attachment—but how, in ordinary everyday homes, strong and healthy attachments are formed. Ainsworth had a stable but unhappy background in which her mother was physically present but felt emotionally unavailable to the young Mary. She just wasn't 'there' for Mary when she needed her. From the outside her home looked secure. From the inside, though, Mary felt it was anything but.

Ainsworth set up a research project first in Uganda, then in Baltimore, spending many hours observing mothers and babies interacting. Despite vast cultural differences, Ainsworth found similar attachment behaviour in both countries, 'suggesting that babies everywhere spoke the same attachment language'. Motherhood had long been sentimentalised but it was perhaps the first time anyone bothered to actually observe and record in great detail how real-life mothers behaved with babies.

While this early work in attachment centred on mothers, it is now recognised that it is equally applicable to fathers or other caregivers. Ainsworth observed that mothers who were most attentive, sensitive and promptly responsive to their children's signals in the first year of life had babies who, at twelve months, cried less and seemed more secure and cooperative. This was the opposite of what behaviourists like John Watson advocated: to leave the baby

alone lest they be spoiled. In contrast, babies who had been left
to cry for long periods without comfort became more demanding,
difficult and anxious by twelve months. Often the mothers of such
babies found themselves 'suffering from anxiety and depression'
and 'really incapable of attending to anything else'.

Ainsworth noticed that the secure children were more likely
to be exploratory in their mother's presence, rather than clinging or demanding attention. She dubbed this phenomenon the
'Secure Base'. She felt it was an internal thing—the more a child
feels someone is ready and able to be attentive, the more they feel
'held' in someone's mind, the more they feel free to go. Watch
children at a park and you can see what she means; when parents are attentive, they will explore happily, but when the parents
are distracted or inattentive, they will immediately cease playing
and try to re-engage the parent. Ainsworth designed a test in the
laboratory to assess how these babies responded to a mild stress:
being separated briefly from their mother in what came to be
called the 'Strange Situation'.

Securely attached babies cried on separation but on their
mother's return immediately sought them out, were easily
comforted by them, and returned to playing. There were other
attachment patterns. One was termed 'ambivalent': the baby
expressed both distress and great anger—like crying and hitting their mother at the same time—and an inability to draw
comfort from the mother's return. Another was the 'avoidant'
pattern: where the baby turned away, or seemed indifferent to
their mother's return, despite sharp rises in stress levels measured
by increases in heart rate. Later research added a 'disorganised
and disorientated' pattern, found in high proportions of abused
and neglected children, where the response is one of confusion or
contradiction—like freezing, or circling.

'The thing that blew my mind was the avoidant response,'
Ainsworth says. These babies were the group that appeared the

most insecure at home but were blasé, almost indifferent, in the Strange Situation—in short, they looked precociously independent. At home these babies cried and showed more, not less, separation distress, were clingier, whinier and so on. Most importantly, their caregivers had been rated by observers as 'interfering, rejecting or neglectful'. Ainsworth made a lateral leap. She noticed these avoidant babies behaved in a fashion similar to the older child who Bowlby described as being detached, coming home from hospital and ignoring the mother or pretending she wasn't there. This suggested that these children were using the same coping mechanism, of shutting down attachment needs. Later tests showed that the avoidant babies were just as stressed as the other babies: their heart rates and cortisol levels rose in the Strange Situation, yet they displayed a curious shutdown, displaying no emotional needs: 'Already by the age of twelve months ... [they] no longer express ... their deepest emotions or the equally deep seated desire for comfort and reassurance that accompanies it.'

It is now clear that it is *behaviour on reunion*—whether and how the baby asks for comfort and reassurance—that is the most important indicator of inner emotional security, not the inevitable separation protest itself. When Bowlby viewed the videotapes of the Strange Situation, he was amazed at how much was revealed of a one-year-old's internal emotional world and their capacity or incapacity to communicate their emotional needs freely to others. As we have learned, many psychoanalysts have found that shame about being dependent on others is at the centre of their adult patients' narcissism. Given that, consider these gestures from children who have been physically abused. On being reunited with their mother in the Strange Situation, one child went and lay down with their face pressed up against the wall, as if hiding in shame from their desire for comfort. In another, a child covered their face with their hands in an apparent gesture of shame, rather than move towards their mother. The Strange Situation reunion actually assesses, by interpreting the language of gesture, how a child feels they will be treated when they need comfort and show vulnerability, and whether those feelings are acceptable or unacceptable.

The Moral Consequences of Secure Attachment

Alan Sroufe, a psychologist in Minnesota, took up the question of what happens to children with different attachment patterns as they grow older. What he found shows very clear social and emotional advantages for securely attached babies, but especially that these benefits contribute hugely to *moral* development. The psychoanalyst Alice Miller maintains that the true opposite of depression is not gaiety or absence of pain but vitality. Kohut emphasised the importance of early relationships in cultivating lifelong zest, or 'healthy narcissism'. In Sroufe's study the two-year-olds assessed earlier as secure had such vitality they sparkled, were enthusiastic and were persistent in problem-solving. Secure children were more responsive to instructions, were more co-operative with their mothers and showed less frustration. They expressed more positive emotions and delight, and they laughed, smiled and shared more pleasurable feelings with their mother. Confronted with the same task, in contrast, their anxiously attached counterparts became worried and whiny, collapsing under pressure.

Sroufe and his colleagues felt they were onto some central issue in early development. While their early research had been with a low-risk middle-class sample, they now moved to study a group of mothers in a higher risk group, disadvantaged by sole parenthood, poverty and low education. The children were assessed at birth on temperament, but the caregiver's qualities were more important. The study showed that the security of attachment could be largely predicted at birth: mothers who showed little interest in the baby at birth were more likely to have an insecurely attached child.

When the children in the poverty sample reached preschool age, Sroufe enrolled them in a specially created preschool on the Minnesota campus. None of the teachers knew the children's previously assessed attachment classification. Sroufe and his colleagues found that preschoolers who had been judged securely attached as infants were significantly more flexible, curious and socially competent. Securely attached children were more sympathetic to the distress of their peers, more assertive about what they wanted, and more likely to be leaders. They had higher levels of self-esteem, and ego resilience. While secure attachment by no means made children bulletproof, similarly positive findings persisted throughout their schooling.

They were also more independent. The preschoolers who had avoidant attachment relationships as infants—those forced to self-reliance too early, whose dependency needs were rebuffed —were more dependent, and made more bids for attention, seeking out the teacher at a greater rate than securely attached children. They were least likely to directly seek attention or ask for help when they had been hurt or disappointed. Some 'expressed their needs for adult attention in bizarre ways'. One approached his teacher 'through a series of oblique angles', was 'frequently sullen or oppositional and not inclined to seek help when injured or disappointed, however, spoke poignantly of [his] avoidant patterns'.

Children with an avoidant attachment pattern tended to be far less able to engage in fantasy play than securely attached children. Where they did engage in such play, it was often 'characterised by irresolvable conflict'. Avoidant children tended to victimise others, engaging in repeated acts of cruelty. Ambivalent children, with their desperate clinging and need for reassurance, kept coming back for more, almost as if they had no experience of not being treated badly. They were prepared to seek contact at any price: one approached his tormentor and begged, 'Why don't you tease me? I won't get mad.'

Sroufe's study found that in every pair where there was victimisation, there was an avoidant and ambivalent child, with the avoidant child doing the bullying, the ambivalent child submitting. None of the securely attached kids showed any victimisation, nor did they let themselves be pulled into relationships with hurtful dynamics. They 'either found a way to make the relationship positive, withdrew, or met the aggression with just enough force to discourage it. It was as if such behaviour was foreign to them and they would have nothing to do with it.'

Teachers reacted very differently to each attachment style. They tended to treat secure children in a warm, matter-of-fact, age-appropriate way. They excused, indulged and infantilised the scattered and clingy ambivalently attached children. They were controlling, cold and angry with the avoidant attached children, and described them as 'mean, lying, everything is hers'. Watching all this, Sroufe and his colleagues, who knew the children's backgrounds, winced, feeling a great sense of loss and frustration. These children began life by being rejected, and now had those harsh lessons reinforced by the teachers' behaviour. 'Whenever I see a teacher who looks as if she wants to pick a kid up by the shoulders and stuff him in the trash,' Sroufe says, 'I know that kid has an avoidant attachment history.'

Sroufe linked these behaviours to Ainsworth's extensive observations of children in the home. He felt strongly that the avoidant children's 'piteous behaviour pattern had their origin in the rebuffs the children had suffered'. Their experience of emotional unavailability, rejection or physical abuse at home made it natural to inflict it on others. So too did the empathy and sensitivity shown by secure children come from their family: 'How do you get an empathetic child?' asks Sroufe. 'You get an empathetic child not by trying to teach the child and admonish the child to be empathetic, you get an empathetic child by being empathetic with the child. The child's understanding of

relationships can only be from the relationships he's experienced.'
By contrast, ambivalent children:

> seemed too preoccupied with their own needs to have any
> feelings left over with others, and avoidant children some-
> times seemed to take pleasure in another child's misery ... In
> the same situation a secure kid would get a teacher and bring
> the teacher to the child or stand by and look concerned.

Avoidant attached boys were 'off the charts in every measure
of aggression, assertion and control seeking'. They appeared
hungry for attention and approval (their dependency scores were
also highest) but sought attention in ways that were often disruptive and aggressive. Avoidant boys in whom aggression was
'particularly marked' were more likely to 'bully, lie, cheat, destroy
things, brag, act cruelly, disrupt the class, swear, threaten, argue,
throw temper tantrums, become defiant'.

Following the sample through to adulthood, Sroufe found
that security of attachment in infancy—despite coming from a
sample marked by poverty, single parenthood and disadvantage—continued to show strong benefits. By middle childhood,
secure attachments create a capacity for what the philosopher
Martin Buber called the intimate 'I and Thou' of friendship. At
preadolescence, children make friends more easily, spend less time
with adults and more with their peers. Interpersonal sensitivity
and empathy continue to develop. Insecure children's friendships
are more marked by jealousy and possessiveness. They display
more behaviour problems, and are more 'hostile, non compliant,
hyperactive' or whiny, anxious and needy.

The Internal Working Model

Why are there so often such lasting, though not inevitable, consequences of these attachment patterns? As child developmentalist

Ron Lally says, we need to realise how much is at stake: in the early years 'children are putting on spectacles with which to view the world'. What is developing is an internal working model of self and others. The model develops through what Daniel Stern describes as 'representations of interactions that have been generalised (RIGs)'. If every day, every week, month after month—as opposed to the occasional lapse in otherwise good-enough but imperfect parents—in a consistent pattern, a parent rebuffs a child's need for comfort, the very plasticity of the brain at this age means that it becomes a deeply entrenched kind of learning. A small child experiences the world *tout court*: as if all the experience they have is what the world is like. Their brains are still developing, so an insecure or disorganised attachment ends up being generalised; as a way of starting life, it is a little like setting out on a hike with a damaged compass. What begins in a pattern of interaction in relationships becomes generalised into wider expectations of the world, coded unconsciously, as part of the structure of the mind. It becomes a kind of internal emotional map of the world.

The internal working model, deriving from interactions that are repeated and then generalised by the infant, 'reflects the child's relationship history, codifying the behaviours that belong to an intimate relationship, and defining how he will feel about himself when he is closely involved with another person'. Yet for the child with an insecure attachment, the internal working model actually is a poor, even distorted guide to reality. For example, the child who feels unloved may come to generalise and believe themselves to be unlovable, and will expect rejection, threat or hostility. As with the adult narcissist, who is full of mistrust, anger and envy, who sees other people as objects to be dominated and exploited, these children's internal world can be an 'eat or be eaten' affair.

In contrast, secure attachment helps develop what Daniel Goleman calls emotional intelligence. It builds the capacity for meta-cognition, or the capacity for self-reflection, for knowing the complexity of feelings, like having more than one feeling at a time, or that someone can feel one thing but say another—the capacity, as Peter Fonagy puts it, of 'mentalising', *thinking about thinking*. It is this capacity that is so strikingly missing in narcissism. A secure child also develops a sense of what is inside another person's mind, that they might have the same capacity for hurt as they themselves do. This is central to developing empathy, the ability to put yourself in someone else's shoes, thinking with care and attention about what they might be feeling, or how they might react, and respecting their right to a different point of view. Anxiously attached children are less likely to develop such capacities, as if the painfulness of emotions forces them to simply cut off thinking about feelings. As one child put it, 'If I started crying I would never stop.'

Fonagy suggests that, in extreme cases, abused children can develop *no* 'theory of mind', because it is so unbearably painful to acknowledge the hostility or even hate that is in their parents' feelings towards them. One possible consequence is the incapacity to empathise or recognise that one's actions might bring hurt, pain and distress to another person. At the extreme, they could become a person like Breivik.

Narcissism's True and False Self

Just how children develop such powerful ways of seeing the world—for good or ill—is demonstrated in some stunning work by infant specialist Daniel Stern. He was a really unusual combination, both very empathetic and perceptive about what he was observing but also very analytical, a real systemiser. When he videotaped mothers and babies interacting, he decided to slow the tapes down to try to understand how they were relating to each other. He discovered a world of 'intimate communication ... what was once dismissed as rather charming but meaningless babble turned out to be as rich and unexpected as the universe of "cavort-ing beasties" that Anton van Leeuwenhoek observed when he put an ordinary drop of water under his newly invented microscope'.

The new research showed that there is an intimate, intricate mother and baby 'dance' going on. Stern turned to musical metaphors when he found infants responded with extraordi-nary precision to 'matching' by the mother of rhythm, contours of emotion, intensity, timing and imitation; there was even a kind of beat to these exchanges. Disruptions of these 'astonish-ing attunements', as he called them, resulted in a puzzled and perturbed reaction from the infant. Like later conversations, these exchanges involved taking turns in making contributions. Babies, it was found—contra Freud—do *not* begin life in a state of solipsism or primary narcissism. Pathological narcissism hap-pens when things go wrong. Babies seek and respond to social exchanges from their earliest moments after birth. They can discriminate between their own mother's breastmilk pads and other mothers', turning their little heads towards them. They mirror and imitate their father's expressions and show both joy and excitement whenever they have an effect on the world. They switch off and withdraw if they feel helpless. Far from meaning-less baby talk, parents and infants are engaging, from the very beginning, in lengthy and complex reciprocal exchanges. Even in the earliest months, when there is little control over movement, there is nonetheless a prolonged 'conversation', where infants respond, attune, and take turns or bring an exchange to a close just by looking away:

> Gazing is a potent form of social communication. When watching the gazing patterns of mother and infant during this life period, one is watching two people with almost equal facility and control over the same social behaviour … infants exert major control over … contact … they

91

can avert their gaze, shut their eyes, stare past, become glassy eyed ... reject, distance themselves from, or defend themselves against mother ... reinitiate engagement and contact when they desire.

Stern's work elaborates on the ways in which babies might come to be secure or insecure in Ainsworth's Strange Situation. Babies were found to be exquisitely sensitive to misattunement as well as attunements, whether the rhythm of spoken words, touch, gesture or expression. Stern asked mothers to purposely misattune—to first match a baby's excitement over the discovery of a toy with their own gesture, say, jiggling their bottom, then to deliberately do the same thing more slowly. Undershooting the baby's response drew a bewildered, almost hurt reaction. On the other hand, no parent ever attunes perfectly all the time, and fortunately it does not appear that infants need them to do so. More worrying are longer-term or more fundamental disruptions to this process. An experiment by Edward Tronick showed the potentially catastrophic effect of maternal depression. Tronick asked mothers to create a 'still face', mimicking the expressionless face often shown by depressed mothers who, as a consequence of their illness, emotionally withdraw from their children and present a face that is lifeless, without animation, drawn in upon her own pain. The babies in Tronick's experiment reacted to a still face with profound distress, alternating with attempts to reanimate their mothers' faces.

Stern concludes:

It is clear that interpersonal communion, as created by attunement, will play an important role in the infant's coming to recognise their feeling states are forms of human experience that are shareable with other humans. The converse is also true: feeling states that are never attuned to will be experienced only alone, isolated from the interpersonal context of shareable experience. What is at stake here is nothing less than the shape of and extent of the shareable inner universe.

Taking this last point, Stern's work also shows how patterns of interaction enable parts of the self to come alive and be acknowledged and accepted—whether in word or gesture—or be unattended, go underground, be disconfirmed or banished. At worst, such misattunement opens the possibility for the development of what psychoanalysts like Donald Winnicott, John Bowlby and Alice Miller have long been interested in: a 'false self', one externally compliant with the world but whose authentic responses are lost and substituted with 'acceptable' responses.

* * *

At a children's birthday party I attended, there were parents with a toddler aged about eighteen months and his older sisters. There were a number of other families with young children present, displaying the usual warm and affectionate chaos. Yet the interactions between members of this family were strikingly different. The father, a successful businessman, seemed depressed, withdrawn, and was known to be a workaholic. Perhaps because she received so little help, relations with his wife were tense and angry. More recent research into why attachment patterns can go wrong, highlight the importance of the relationships and support networks that mothers are embedded in. Sadly, some mothers have little help from extended family, while the father's lack of participation in childrearing makes them more like single mothers within marriages. In an entire day, there were few positive interactions between any of them. The boy was retrieved and roughly dumped in new spots to prevent him from doing something that, from a toddler's point of view, is incorrigibly interesting. There was no physical affection from either parent, and not much psychological or emotional contact either. No one looked at each other. There was no secure-base behaviour so evident with the other parents and their children—venturing off and checking back to see if his parents were keeping an eye out for him—he was precociously independent. When he evinced a need, the resentment was palpable. His mother was contemptuous when he became needy or whiny. When he cried and an older sister went to help, she stopped her: 'He's just having a sook.' The word 'sook' was spat out with disgust. When naptime came, there was a furore. The parents emerged from his bedroom, anger rising like smoke, as his cries continued and then finally subsided.

Later, when he woke up, everybody else heard his increasingly hysterical cries but neither parent appeared to, and neither moved. Everybody was distressed. It was as if he just wasn't in their minds. Finally another guest went up to get him.

There *were*, however, some positive moments in the day, and they link to Stern's interesting discussion of the idea of the false self. The little boy was clearly also very intelligent, and the parents were both clearly very proud of this fact. At one point they both boasted about how independent he was. When he solved a difficult jigsaw puzzle all by himself, he was admired as being not just 'very clever' but also 'very advanced', ahead of his peers, cleverer and better than other children, and he turned around to look at his mother and father. There was grandiosity here; they described his academic ability in inflated terms: 'gifted', with the keynote being his *superiority* to other children his age. The atmosphere was suddenly less chilly. Their heads swung back in an unmistakable gesture of pride. At this the little boy turned around, and for the first time that day, there was eye contact.

So what might a theoretically informed observation tell us about this mind-in-the-making, and how does it relate to narcissism?

I am not arguing that an avoidant attachment is the same as having a narcissistic personality disorder. Many avoidant attached people lack the extroversion and other orientated behaviours of narcissism. They are more withdrawn. So the two categories do not map over each other entirely. There is a much higher percentage of children with avoidant attachments than there are adult narcissists. Kernberg adds something important: that a child is partly born that way with certain traits that predispose them to narcissism. There is modest confirmation in the literature for this: some temperamental traits like impulsiveness, aggression, disagreeableness, and negative emotionality may be part of a child's disposition right from the start, making a parent's job harder. With respect to nurture, Freud observed that, as well as rejecting or cold parents, narcissism needs grandiosity and an overvaluation of the child too. We know that an avoidant attachment can result in aggression, braggardly behaviour, wanting and seeking attention in unpleasant ways, an inability to control hostile emotions like rage and anger, and impaired relations with peers. We know that these, too, are aspects of adult narcissists. But what about the sense of superiority and the sense of entitlement, to be treated better and to have the right to exploit others?

Suppose we add another element to a child born with a difficult temperament who develops an avoidant attachment. So far I have only discussed how the negative—soft, vulnerable—parts of this toddler's spirit have been rebuffed, often with anger, dislike and even contempt. Yet the attunement and positive moments, which every child hungers after and needs in order to feel connected to these two most powerful and adored beings in his life, *only occurs in relation to his achievements*. Such joy and pride in him as there is—in scant supply—centres on his being independent, intelligent, reflecting well on them as parents, performing his 'cleverness' and—crucially—being superior to and outperforming other children. *Then he is valued*. And suppose this goes on day in, day out, in a pattern since infancy. It is as if they are tuning into one part of the child, bringing it alive, but disavowing the rest of him. Both parents are in the powerful position of interpreting the world to a child. For this little boy, his parents have had a very particular bias, and part of him has been lost in translation.

On the one hand, such a child might well develop a bias against 'communal' orientation, since the relational world, already by the age of one, has turned out to be something of a disappointment. This may well affect his trust and belief in relationships too: it might be better to keep the upper hand and snatch what you can get from short-term relationships than to invest and risk vulnerability and rejection.

On the other hand, it is in the competitive domain, in the achievement stakes, that the child *does* receive the positive, warm responses he craves. And these are warm moments that are so few and far between that to animate the normally hostile parent with approval and gain praise might well be addictive. The child becomes the adult who is addicted to pride in achievement, deflated by shame in being all too human, terrified, as Kernberg and others have discovered, of depending on and being vulnerable to others. Kernberg also found that in the patients who had been feted throughout childhood as a 'genius' or as 'special', there were often not only feelings of loneliness and emptiness underneath the grandiosity, but also a longing to be 'average'.

It gets even more interesting. In the first few years of childhood, by the time these persistent attachment patterns are entrenched, language is either non-existent or rudimentary. Here the work of Allan Schore, a psychologist and neuroscientist, is particularly illuminating. One of the many startling findings from recent neuroscience is that in one fundamental Freud was right. There *is* an unconscious. As the brain continues forming in the first two years after birth, it is very experience-dependent. It is in the context of relationships with parents that our sense of self and expectations of others are formed. This all occurs well before language is sophisticated enough to capture emotional experiences, before the brain can store and recall explicit verbal memories, before such capacities can help us remember what we felt or how we were treated. Our *emotional* history of the early years is stored unconsciously, giving it an unacknowledged capacity to shape our perceptions and actions. The child treated thus does not have the language to put into words their feelings of shame around dependency. It remains bypassed shame, unacknowledged, and therefore toxic.

When children start to understand language, however, words become a core part of the translation of experience into cognitions and memories. Yet, as Stern says, insecure attachment can actually help develop not an authentic but a false self. Language can both 'greatly extend our grasp of reality' and 'provide for the distortion of reality as experienced'. It can force apart experience as it is lived and as it is verbally represented. What is not recognised verbally by the parents—what is never put into words—may be disavowed by the child as 'not me'.

In order to maintain his all-important connection with the parent, the child continually reshapes himself in relation to what he feels his parents want—his acceptable and not acceptable identity. He keeps private or represses qualities that are true, and offers up the qualities—a version of himself—that the parent seems to want, attributes that make up a false self. Much of what is true and important about the child is left silent and invisible. The 'never saids' of childhood involve choices about what is desirable and what is unacceptable. The deepest message is that it is not okay to be who you really are.

In an insecure avoidant attachment, the child actually behaves by disavowing the dependency needs that have so aroused the anger of his carers. The little boy whose cortisol levels shoot up in the Strange Situation behaves instead not like the needy little toddler he actually is, but *as if* he is someone else, a more grown-up, precociously independent child. These are the terms and conditions of his parents' love. His parents' love is not unconditional at all.

Stern says that in the creation of a false self and a true self, experiences become split: some are selected and enhanced because they meet the needs and wishes of someone else, even if radically different from the experiences determined by the true self. As language develops, *the false self becomes the child's avowed and acknowledged reality*. It becomes the spoken words of 'who he is'. The false self is privileged and becomes his acknowledged identity, while his true, actual self is disavowed and unacknowledged. Because his true self, or aspects of him, has aroused disgust in his carers, shame makes it likely that part of him will be banished to his unconscious. Only one aspect of the child is affirmed, recognised and expressed verbally as true, as what is reality. Why does a child comply with this rather than defy the parent and assert his true self? Primarily, Stern says, it is the primal, profound need for experiences of being with another person, the longing for intimate communion. 'Only connect', as E.M. Forster said. As we know in cases of child abuse and neglect, a child will go to inordinate lengths to protect their parent in their mind, feeling shame rather than rage after sexual abuse, for example. They will blame themselves rather than blame the adored parent. In our much less extreme example, it is mainly or entirely in the domain of the false self that the infant is able to experience a sense of closeness, communion and sense of validation.

Adult Narcissists

What about such a child grown up? In one of his last books, *A Secure Base*, Bowlby made an important link between the tapes he had watched of children displaying avoidant attachment in the Strange Situation study and the patients who were turning up increasingly on the therapist's couch—described in the United Kingdom as having a false self, and in the United States as suffering from narcissism.

> The picture such a person presents is one of assertive independence and emotional self-sufficiency. On no account is he going to be beholden to anyone and, in so far as he enters into relationships at all, he makes sure he retains control. For much of the time he may appear to manage wonderfully well, but there may be times when he becomes depressed or develops psychosomatic symptoms, often for no reason he knows of.

Alice Miller also writes insightfully about the false self and narcissism. For Miller, 'healthy narcissism' can be characterised as the full access to the true self; the narcissistic disturbance can be understood as a fixation on a false or incomplete self. The key for Miller is narcissism in the mother (I would argue *both* parents): 'What happens if the mother [father] ... is herself in need of narcissistic supplies? ... If the mother [father] tries to assuage her own narcissistic needs through the child?' None of this, Miller says, cancels out strong affection for the child. Indeed the parent may love the child passionately as her 'self-object' but not in the way they need. The child develops in relation to the parents needs, not their own. They do not exist as a separate being, with legitimate feelings of their own that are recognised and validated by the parent.

Miller found that all but two of her narcissistic patients had insecure, depressed mothers. She outlines a role reversal—where the child ends up satisfying unmet needs in the mother rather than the mother meeting the child's needs:

> the child, an only one or often the first-born, was the narcissistically cathected object. What these mothers had once

failed to find in their own mothers, they were able to find in their children: someone at their disposal who can be used as an echo, who can be controlled, is completely centred on them, will never desert them, and offers full attention and admiration. If the child's demands become too great (as once did those of her own mother) she is no longer so defenceless, does not allow herself to be tyrannised: she can *bring the child up* in such a way that it neither cries nor disturbs her.

In order to maintain their parents' love, the children 'only developed those capacities which they felt their parents needed and admired'. Other qualities went unrecognised or were hidden from their parents and themselves 'in order to avoid rejection or shame'. If a person realises that 'he was never loved as a child for what he was but for his achievements, success and good qualities', and that he sacrificed his childhood for this 'love', this will shake him very deeply, but one day he will feel the desire to end this courtship. The 'love' 'leaves him empty handed' as it is given to the false self, not to him.

While I have concentrated here on links between narcissism and avoidant attachment, anxious ambivalent attachment has also been implicated in more vulnerable forms of narcissism. This is the baby who reacts with anger and by clinging in the Strange Situation, whose strategy of getting needs met is to have their emotional reactivity switch flicked permanently on high. As pre-schoolers they are prone to histrionic and needy behaviour—the 'cry baby'—exaggerating vulnerability in order to gain attention. As adults, this behaviour pattern may become entrenched in highly conflicted love relationships marked by anger and anxiety, constantly 'leaning out for love', expressing misplaced anger, unreasonable demands and an aggrieved neediness that their partner is meant to assuage, sadly alienating the very person they are so dependent on.

The Paradox of Affluence?

Clearly narcissism is unlikely to emerge from a secure attachment and responsive, sensitive parenting, which have been shown over and over again to result in empathy and an enhanced capacity for the communal and relational world. It is more likely to come from the combination of inattention and indulgence, with grandiosity thrown into the mix. The idea of spoiling, helicopter parents only captures one aspect of the story. It is clear from the evidence that narcissism does not map over debates between conservatives and liberals about the best family type, or over the 'Motherwars' over working and staying at home. It can develop in very varied family forms: intact and separated, when fathers are present and when they are absent, with stay-at-home mothers and working mothers. However, let's take one aspect of contemporary childrearing: the fact that more families have both parents working. These profound changes have occurred in the United States with a minimum of government investment in high-quality childcare; rather the provision is mainly private and for profit. In that country there is no paid parental leave, so more infants than ever before, at ever younger ages, go into early day care. In and of itself, high-quality childcare ought not have a negative outcome. Yet according to the most sophisticated longitudinal study ever done on the subject, only 9 per cent of US childcare was of high quality. The study also pinpointed children who were placed in care for longer hours. By kindergarten age, the study found children in longer hours of childcare were three times as likely to

> receive high ratings on items that could be considered to reflect assertiveness, such as bragging/boasting, demanding of lots of attention, and arguing a lot, and disobedience/defiance, such as talking out of turn, being disobedient at school, and being defiant, talking back to staff, but aggression as well, including getting into many fights, showing cruelty, bullying

or meanness to others, physically attacking other people, and being explosive, showing unpredictable behaviour.

Changes in society don't only affect working parents badly. There would be plenty of at-home parents among those whom Dwight Vidale, one of the teachers at an affluent high school interviewed in Paul Tough's *How Children Succeed*, speaks about when he says that he sees a lot of helicopter parents, 'always hovering around, ready to swoop in for the rescue'. Yet he also says, crucially, that the hovering is about achievement: 'that doesn't mean they are making emotional connections with their kids, or even spending time with their kids'. Perhaps that is why, as Tough notes, the documentary *Race to Nowhere*, which paints a grim and depressing portrait of contemporary adolescence, became something of an underground hit in privileged schools. It depicts an 'overachieving girl who committed suicide, apparently because of ever increasing pressure to succeed that she felt at school and at home'.

These affluent, privileged kids, riveted to the screen of *Race to Nowhere*, will be among those who go on to college and, perhaps, those who complete Twenge and Campbell's Narcissistic Personality Inventory. The film shows an interview with psychologist Madeline Devine, who wrote a bestselling book, *The Price of Privilege: How Parental Pressure and Material Advantage Are Creating a Generation of Disconnected and Unhappy Kids*. In it she presents an array of evidence to show that today wealthy parents, whether at home or working, 'are more likely than others to be emotionally distant from their children while at the same time insisting on high levels of achievement, a potentially toxic blend of influences that can create "intense feelings of shame and hopelessness" in affluent children'.

Low levels of maternal attachment, high levels of parental criticism, and minimal after-school supervision were linked to problems. Dan Kindlon from Harvard also found similar evidence of worse emotional wellbeing due to the wrong kind of pressures on affluent children:

> The emotional disconnection that existed between many affluent parents and their children often meant that parents were unusually indulgent of their children's bad behaviour. Parents making more than one million dollars a year, by a wide margin, were the group most likely to say they were less strict than their parents.

The pressures are all in the wrong direction. 'While pushing children to excel,' Tough says, parents 'inadvertently shield them from exactly the kind of experience that can lead to character growth.' Or as psychoanalyst John Fiscalini observes so insightfully: 'These children get what they do not need and do not get what they do need.'

One of the most important studies of parenting and narcissism was done by Otway and Vignoles. They put recollections of young adults to the test with different psychodynamic models: Freud, Kohut, Kernberg and Theodore Millon, who thought parents spoiled children (it is his theory that Twenge and Campbell's explanation is closest to). What Otway and Vignoles found was confirmation of Freud's view: 'Seemingly the future narcissist receives constant praise from his or her caregiver, but this is accompanied by implicit messages of coldness and rejection rather than warmth and acceptance, and thus, we speculate, the praise—which is also indiscriminate—may come to seem unreal.'

This leads to the distinctive combination of grandiosity and fragility noted in narcissists. They also found that covert, or vulnerable, narcissism, in particular, is associated with anxious ambivalent attachments.

The assertion that narcissists are not vulnerable or shame-prone is not as secure as it might look. Erin Myer and Virgil

Zeigler Hill cleverly used a bogus lie detector test while assessing narcissism and self-esteem. In this way they were able to get past the possible inaccuracies of tests based on self-reports—given that narcissists do not like to admit failure, weakness or vulnerability in any shape or form, their responses on NPI-type tests could well be prone to self-enhancing. What they found was stunning confirmation of the psychodynamic view. Women with higher levels of narcissism reported higher levels of self-esteem when there was no threat of a lie detector. When confronted with one, however, they changed their story. These narcissistic individuals reported *lower* self-esteem than people who were low in narcissism. They actually didn't feel as positively about themselves as they pretended. The researchers said they were 'briefly able to peel back the grandiose façade that are worn by narcissist and catch a glimpse of how these individuals actually feel about themselves'. The results

> provide compelling evidence for the idea that the grandiose feelings of self-worth reported by narcissists may not be the entire story concerning how they feel about themselves … provide support for the psychodynamic mask model of narcissism … [and] for the idea that narcissists inflate their feelings of self-worth on self-report measures and that these overly positive self-evaluations may disguise underlying feelings of self-loathing and inferiority as suggested by Kohut and Kernberg.

At least some other empirical studies support this. Carefully honing in on the nature of shame and pride in narcissistic individuals, there is also evidence that once primed with words like 'failure' and 'humiliation', narcissists are more likely to react defensively or with aggression. Many of these studies, however, are limited by the fact that they are dealing with college students' self-reports and recollections of their childhood.

What we need are longitudinal studies from early child-hood to adulthood observing parent–child attachment and child characteristics at the preschool age and followed right through to adulthood. Then we might have a really solid foundation to understand the causes of narcissism in so far as they are environmental. Phebe Cramer from Williams College in Massachusetts set out to do just such a study. She found that it was neither 'permissive' parents—both warm and affectionate but failing to set appropriate limits—nor 'authoritative' ones—who have a felicitous balance between warm affection and sensible limit setting—who correlate with the development of narcissism. Rather she found evidence that supports Kernberg's view: 'authoritarian' or cold, harsh, insensitive parenting has the strongest relationship to precursors of narcissism like wanting to be the centre of attention, or lacking empathy for, or being aggressive to, age mates in the preschool years, and to signs of pathological narcissism at age twenty-three.

Who Cares For the Caregivers?

Across history many child-rearing environments—what is called the Environment of evolutionary adaptiveness, or EEA—were extremely harsh. Although 'secure' attachments have desirable consequences for children, and when they are adults are conducive to forming strong stable bonds with others, attachment scholars now think that in harsher circumstances insecure attachment might be more adaptive. According to child developmentalist Jay Belsky, 'patterns of rearing that are negative, inconsiderate and coercive lead children to behave in ways that are self-centred', or more suited to a dog eat dog world. Feminist and anthropologist Sarah Hrdy concurs:

> ... it might be highly adaptive for an avoidantly attached
> individual to learn to downplay love, to dismiss the

importance of close human relationships ... Rather
than rely on those around him, the most advantageous
course open might be for the child to become self reliant and avoid developing empathetic feelings for others
around him...

Or more narcissistic. A new study published in April 2014
combines British and US data to show a troublingly high rate—
forty per cent— of children with insecure attachments. Given the
importance of secure attachment to the development of empathy,
it is a worrying finding. Two other important studies by Sara
Konrath and her colleagues from the University of Michigan
complete this picture. In 2011, using a wide ranging meta-analysis
of seventy-two studies, Konrath compared empathy among college students from the 1970s and early 1980s with students from
the later generations of the 1990s and 2000s. The later cohorts
displayed a significant decline especially in empathy but also in
the ability to take another person's perspective. As narcissism
rises, empathy goes down. The reduction in empathy was particularly pronounced after the year 2000. As Konrath suggests,
those students showing the strongest declines are the children of
the parents of the 1980s who first showed up in Jean Twenge's
research as being part of a more narcissistic generation.

In April 2014, Konrath published another landmark study.
Because insecure attachments are associated both with increases
in narcissism and with waning empathy, she looked at whether
there was a rise in such attachments among young adults attending college during the period 1988 to 2011. She assessed the adult
versions of insecure attachment by using the specially designed
Relationship Questionnaire. The categories are Secure (the sequel
to the secure child), Dismissing (the sequel to the avoidant child)
Preoccupied (the sequel to the ambivalently attached child), and
Fearful (the adult sequel to the disorganised and disoriented

attachment child). The percentage of secure adults declined from 48 per cent in 1988 to 41 per cent in 2011. Meanwhile the number of adults with all forms of insecure attachments increased—from 51 to 58 per cent. The number of students showing up an Avoidant or Dismissing adult attachment especially increased, from just under 12 per cent in 1988 to almost 19 per cent in 2011. Dismissing attachments are associated with a positive view of the self, and a negative view of others; consistent with this, Konrath found declines in trust in perceptions about others. She also found a decline in trust among Americans in data gathered in 2013—two thirds of Americans in 2012 thought other people couldn't be trusted compared with 58 per cent in 1988. (Still a very high number.) This mistrust, however, was much more pronounced among younger people.

Could it be that we are developing a new EEA? Are we developing, by one social-policy plank after another, a new social ecology inhospitable to childrearing—an 'Avoidant Society'? Konrath clearly thinks so. Like the avoidant, narcissistic adult, this society is less empathetic, more ruthless, colder, less kind, more competitive; it sees people as winners or losers, is impatient if not hostile to the display of dependency needs not just in children but in anyone vulnerable, is attracted to economic and personal ideas of self-sufficiency and independence, and is dismissive of attachment needs.

Decades ago, John Bowlby warned that if you want parenting to go well, you must care for the caregivers. The huge empirical research on attachment since then has produced powerful confirmation of this argument. In the radically changed circumstances of the new century, what practical alternatives are we offering to nourish connection and the kind of embeddedness in the social networks which help parents and children flourish? So much of the writing on narcissism reads as if individual parents en masse took a wrong turn after 1970. Parenting comes not from thin air but from a social and economic context; they were simply responding to the seismic shift in values and increased competition in the new capitalism. It is not parents, but policy-makers and employers in the United States who have responded to women's increased workforce participation by reluctantly agreeing to a mere three months of unpaid leave on the birth of a child. In Australia we have done better, but the period that is currently funded is only eighteen weeks, with the proposal under the Liberal government to extend and make a more generous payment for the first six months of a child's life. There is still a long way to go to reach the more generous periods of time offered in Scandinavian nations of up to three years.

This brave new world is a whole lot larger than its symptoms— the self-esteem movement or the college kids with unrealistic ambitions or the helicopter parents rushing in to rescue a child whose grades are poor. Another way of looking at narcissism is that it is a quality required for survival in the hyper-competitive paradise of the new capitalism. Many CEOs have been found to be more narcissistic, for example, than other folk, while people who are especially materialistic and susceptible to buying luxury brands have been found to be raised in emotionally cold homes. Narcissism in this light is not maladaptive at all. It is a new character type, just as Lasch said, not just thrown up by the inexorable cultural logic of the new economy, but positively required by it.

Chapter 5

Others Exist for Me

I'm such a magnificent guy ... yet every single day I have
to be insulted by beautiful blond girls walking with stupid
obnoxious douchebags ... I deserve them more.

Elliot Rodger

'I AM NOT a monster ... I am not a violent guy ... I am a happy
person inside.' The speaker went on, telling the packed
courthouse that he was just a normal guy, a good person and
father: 'If you asked my daughter she would say, my dad is the
best dad in the world.' He believed in God. 'I am not a murderer.'
Speaking of the house in Cleveland where he had lived with three
women, he said, 'There was a lot of harmony'. The women often
asked *him* for sex. 'All the sex was consensual. The girls were not
virgins. They had multiple sex partners before me.' He gently
remonstrated with one of them over her risky behaviour: 'She got
into my car without even knowing who I was.' About this error of
judgement, he was magnanimous: 'I don't blame you.'

The speaker was Ariel Castro, a former bus driver facing 977
counts of rape and two counts of aggravated murder. He had
abducted three teenagers, Amanda Berry, Michelle Knight and
Gina DeJesus, and held them captive for eleven years. In a moving

address to the court, Knight spoke of their horror: 'Days never got shorter. Days turning into night turned into years. Years turned into eternity.' Knight knew she might never again see her son Joey, who was two and a half years old when she was abducted. Castro kept them chained up, tortured them and brutally raped them repeatedly. They were in constant fear for their lives, as he told them of other women he had killed. They were forced to play Russian roulette with a gun. They were fed once a day and lived in a freezing, boarded-up basement blocked off from the world. Or were sent to a boiling attic for punishment. When he raped them, he put them in the basement on a chain with motorcycle helmets over their faces to muffle any screams of pain. He made them watch their grief-stricken families' responses to their disappearances on television. When Knight became pregnant on five occasions, he starved her, jumped on her stomach and punched her repeatedly until she miscarried.

Castro's remarks, 'I'm not a monster, I'm sick', were part of a bizarre, rambling, self-justifying monologue when he was being sentenced. He pleaded guilty—to avoid the death penalty—but spent the time in court not apologising for the harm he had done but denying any personal responsibility. Everything was someone else's fault. He distanced himself from his crimes by calling them not 'my victims' but '*the* victims'. And as he saw it, *he* was the real victim. Psychologising his own crime and appealing for sympathy, he claimed he had been abused as a child himself. Then it was pornography's fault; his addiction to porn made him do it. Then it was his first wife's fault. She had, as the court heard, suffered broken noses, several dislocated shoulders, broken ribs, knocked-out teeth, and a blood clot in the brain causing an inoperable tumour after Castro's savage beatings. After receiving numerous threats to kill her and the children, she took out a restraining order. But he wasn't guilty of domestic violence: 'She wouldn't quiet down … The situation would escalate until the point where she would put her hands on me and that's how I reacted, by putting my hands on her.' Indeed, without his first wife's cruelty to him, he would not have committed the sexual crimes for which he was being wrongfully tried. He felt victimised by prison authorities; he demanded his entitlements as a father, wanting rights to see his daughter. Eventually, Castro burst into tears of self-pity.

Against all this stood the brute facts. He had abducted three terrified women, viciously raped them again and again for a period of eleven years, deprived them of liberty and held them captive as sex slaves. He had murdered Knight's babies in utero. The judge rounded on him in moral fury. 'No single prison term adequately reflects the enormity of your conduct,' he said. He sentenced Castro to life imprisonment plus 1000 years. He was an 'extreme narcissist' and a sexual predator.

Indeed.

The Castro case is so extreme that in his life as a sexual predator we can see every aspect of malignant narcissism—the total focus of the needs of the self, the complete lack of empathy to the point of absolute cruelty, the astonishing sense of entitlement, the vicious exploitation, the grandiose, self-enhancing delusions, and all the breathtakingly weird distortions of thought denying the stark reality of what he had done. Ideas of stranger rape, abduction and serial rapists haunt our imaginations. Yet cases of stranger rape are much rarer than the most common form of sexual coercion: acquaintance or date rape. This is the terrain of the university party that turns nasty, or the post-victory football party that becomes a gangbang, where our frail ideas of 'consent' occur in highly charged, often ambiguous sexual situations, where heavy alcohol and perhaps drug use create a twilight zone of what sociologist Michael Kimmel calls 'plausible deniability'. Could narcissism, albeit of a less extreme kind than Castro's, also be in play on such occasions?

Night Games

In Melbourne in 2010, after the Grand Final in which the Colling-wood football team emerged victorious, celebrations continued into the wee hours at an address in South Melbourne. On the same night, three young university friends from the same residential college were at a nightclub in South Melbourne. 'Sarah Wesley' (not her real name) was hoping to meet up with a VFL player, Nate Cooper, whom she had met some weeks earlier. At about 4 a.m. Sarah went to the house in South Melbourne and consented to have sex with him. They walked past several Collingwood players, including Dayne Beams and John McCarthy, who were sitting in the living room on the way to Nate's bedroom. Then, all of a sudden, she was surrounded by several other naked footballers in the room demanding she have sex with them too. Later, she was followed into the alleyway outside by another player, 'Justin', who also tried to have sex with her. By the next morning she had filed rape charges.

In court, a policewoman was asked to confirm notes from her interview with Sarah:

> '"Had consented sex with Nate" … then goes on to say: "Nate introduces victim to Dayne Beams"?'

> The policewoman, her finger tracing the words in her notebook in front of her, nodded. 'Correct.'

> '"Then Collingwood player, felt compelled to have sex but … not forced." Not forced?'

> 'Correct.'

> '"Two to four other naked males in the room?"'

> 'Correct.'

> '"Then they grab her and force her to perform oral sex on male and vaginal rape?"'

'Correct.'

'"Remember saying 'No'"?'

'Correct.'

'"Felt trapped."'

[The policewoman] nodded again and repeated after him,
'Felt Trapped.'

Anna Krien's riveting book *Night Games: Sex, Power and Sport*
describes this event along with its aftermath, the charges of
rape laid against 'Justin', and the trial. The police, for reasons
not really explained in Krien's account, did not proceed to lay
charges against the other Collingwood footballers. Justin was
later acquitted. Krien evokes very well the ambiguous circumstances that Sarah found herself in, the grey zone of alcohol and
'Testosterone Flats' where a young woman, having consented to
sex with one man, suddenly finds herself in a situation seemingly
drawn from a gangbang porn script.

A number of infamous cases like this have recently come
to light, like the one concerning the Cronulla Sharks, from the
National Rugby League, on a pre-season tour of New Zealand.
Nineteen-year-old Clare, a waitress at the hotel where the team
stayed, began by kissing two players in their room. Suddenly
the room was full of players. Over 'the next two hours, at least
twelve players and staff came into the room. Six of them had sex
with Clare, the others watched'. Some masturbated while they
watched, others flipped her over and rubbed their penises in her
face. To the *Four Corners* journalist investigating, Sarah Ferguson,
Clare said: 'Every time I looked up, there would be more and
more people in the room, and, um, there's lots of guys in the room
watching, ah, maybe two or three that were on the bed doing
stuff to me.' Matthew Johns, a famous, senior rugby star and TV
personality, was thirty years old at the time, and one of the first

players to have sex with Clare. She said he 'found it hilarious', 'laughed and joked throughout' and 'kept it going'. Five days after the event, Clare made a complaint to police. The players were interviewed but all steadfastly maintained she consented to each and every act. No charges were laid. Clare was devastated, and her life derailed; she began drinking heavily, withdrawing from social contact, before attempting suicide.

In the cases of Clare and Sarah, precisely what kind of active 'consent' are we talking about? Rabbits freezing in the spotlight 'consenting' to the gun trained on them? Frightened people often have this reaction, feeling powerless to do anything to resist. In Sarah's case, exactly how much freedom did she have to resist? Krien writes of Sarah's friend saying to her:

> How could she even begin to consent to that? How'd she even have time to consider what she wanted? ... it sounds shithouse. Those men had all the power ... She was in a strange house, in a bedroom with most of her clothes off, and a bunch of guys she does not know come in expecting to fuck her, I mean, did they even prepare themselves for the possibility of her saying no?

Krien is haunted by the comments of the accused, Justin, who claimed that when Sarah said she had had enough, he asked her to first 'Finish me off'. The expression keeps returning to her. Outside the court Krien chats with another journalist who agrees that she's also heard that one many times before. What irks Krien, I think, is the sense of entitlement displayed in the comment, to women 'finishing off' a man: a special, quite particular female obligation to bring a man to orgasm. But more on that theme of entitlement later.

'Night games' and the scandals that follow don't only concern football players. Our defence forces have been rocked by one scandal after another. In 2011 'Kate', an eighteen-year-old cadet from the Royal Air Force Academy, went public after she discovered that while she was having sex with another recruit, she had been filmed and Skyped into a different room, where four other cadets watched. According to fellow recruit, Naomi Brookes, Kate was jeered at in the academy and on social media sites: 'They would say things like, "Oh, she's such a slut, she deserved it, she was asking for it," that sort of mentality where the blame is really placed on the woman, and in no capacity did the comments engage with her not consenting to it.' Luckily Kate found a staunch ally in Stephen Smith, then Defence Minister, and an investigation was launched into this and a number of other disturbing incidents concerning the defence forces over subsequent years. When a Facebook site for former and serving defence force members turned up, displaying troubling racist and sexist attitudes, Australia's Sex Discrimination Commissioner, Elizabeth Broderick, investigated these incidents and made stern recommendations to end the culture of sexism in the Australian Defence Force. However, less than a year later, the so-called 'Jedi Council' scandal surfaced, in which ninety people were implicated over emails containing explicit and offensive images and text of women in the defence forces. Broderick said she was 'appalled at the range of people implicated' in this latest scandal, not only junior ranks but senior army personnel, including a lieutenant colonel, majors, warrant officers, sergeants and corporals. But the Australian Defence Force and various football leagues were not alone.

* * *

'Fucking Sluts! No Means Yes! Yes Means Anal!' came the jeering chants from dozens of young men, members of the Delta Kappa Epsilon fraternity—which George W. Bush belonged to—at one of the United States' most prestigious schools, Yale University. The men were chanting on Old Campus, where most of the

new female students lived. The incident—not an isolated one—
occurred in 2010. It became a cause célèbre, and the US Office
of Civil Rights opened an investigation into allegations by sixteen
students that Yale University had failed 'to eliminate a hostile
sexual environment' and thus violated the federal law concerned
with gender discrimination in education, Title IX, the 1972 amendment to the 1964 Civil Rights Act. Initially the amendment had
had a huge and positive impact on women participating in high
school and college athletics, although it did not refer specifically
to sport but was directed against all forms of discrimination in
education. Part of it states, 'No person in the United States shall,
on the basis of sex, be excluded from participation in, be denied
the benefits of, or be subjected to discrimination under any education program or activity receiving federal financial assistance.'

The stakes were high: if Yale was found guilty of violating
Title IX, its federal funding—amounting to some US$500 mil-
lion—could be removed. It was not the first time Yale had been
sued by female students under Title IX for a hostile sexual
climate; that was in 1977, some twelve years after the first women
were admitted to the previously all-male university.

Fast forward to the contemporary scandals and, despite
women now being a majority at Yale, the problem has, if anything,
intensified. The Pre-season Scouting Report—an email ranking
new female students for sexual desirability and stating 'how many
beers it would take to have sex with them'—pretty much sums it
up. Yale student Alexandra Brodsky, who was sexually assaulted
in her freshman year, said grimly:

> In my immediate circle of friends, I know six or seven
> women who've been raped. I think it is hard to go through
> Yale and not have a roommate, a friend, a girlfriend expe-
> rience some sort of harassment ... We'd come to Yale
> for this incredible, life-changing experience and found

gender-based barriers standing in our way … you got in
because of your 4.0 GPA and 1600 SAT [perfect scores],
and suddenly you're worth three beers.

Instances of sexual misconduct, and the furore that invariably
follows, whether in the Australian Defence Force, the Australian
Football League, the Australian Rugby League, Yale University or
Australian universities, are individual flashpoints in a wider cultural collision. These seemingly disparate events have an internally
consistent logic. Looking at individual incidents is concentrating
on spot fires without recognising the bushfire that is burning.
Often the new social media—posting photos or Skyping sexual
acts and coercion, or trolling someone—act as a megaphone and
intensify the problem, but are not in themselves a cause. Rather,
all the events above are dispatches from the front line of a much
larger, deeper and ongoing cultural clash, between the new regime
of sexual liberalism and the great movement in the late twentieth
century towards women's equality. The whole society, as writer
Helen Garner once put it, is seething with issues of sex and power.

To borrow the term coined by Canadian philosopher Charles
Taylor, the *Sixties* were the period of the 'Great Disembedding' of
Western culture from its religious heritage. Among those elements
of the old regime overturned were our longstanding assumptions
about human hierarchy, white over black, men over women. One
of the transcendent political movements to emerge from that
period was the women's movement; the other was anti-racism.
As philosopher and writer Raimond Gaita has suggested, those
liberation movements expressed a desire for justice far deeper
than mere equal opportunities: 'Treat me as a person; see me fully
as a human being, as fully your equal, without condescension …
These are calls to justice conceived as an equality of respect …'

However, a sexual revolution was occurring at the same time.
Alongside patriarchal control of female sexuality, the longstanding

117

oppression of homosexuals was being challenged. The contraceptive revolution, and widely available abortion, saw control over fertility pass, for the first time in human history, from men, church and state to women. A new culture of sexual liberalism was born. It concerned not only how we behaved but also what we viewed. Censorship laws were relaxed; the pornography market exploded; the raunch culture emerged.

The women's movement was both a participant in, and the beneficiary of, the sexual revolution. The greater openness and less shame-ridden culture around sexuality helped destigmatise contraception and enabled women to step down from the pedestal of the asexual Madonna to become, if not like the pop star Madonna, at least sexual beings with desires and needs of their own. All of these vital aspects of women's emancipation drew impetus from, and were strengthened by, the sexual revolution.

Yet the relationship between women's liberation and the new sexual freedom has never been uncomplicated. The two movements have often been in tension. This was caught by a chance remark of Stokely Carmichael, which instantly entered the lexicon. When female activists in the anti-Vietnam protest movement got fed up with brewing the tea and demanded their own political positions, Carmichael made the jibe, 'The only good position for women is prone'.

Over time, another reason for the ongoing tension has become clear. As the above incidents illustrate, any assumption that we have arrived at our post-feminist equal opportunities destination is false. Rather the sexual liberation revolution is actually much more complete, more successful, more far reaching than the feminist revolution. The uneven nature of social change changes everything

Jostling alongside welcome signs of women's newfound status, and a more relaxed, tolerant, open and liberal society on sexual matters, many of the contours of the new sexual liberalism remain shaped by male dominance. Often these truly ugly incidents flash out into the public realm, bearing the indelible signature of misogyny.

I will come to how research is showing the effects of narcissism on some men's propensity to engage in sexual coercion shortly. For the moment, I want to build up my case of how, in a culture of narcissism, 'prevailing conditions'—an endorsing and affirming host culture—can bring out narcissism in susceptible people. This precursor 'culture' is the necessary precondition of sexual narcissism, coercion and assault. It is an incubator of sexual narcissism. Sociologist Michael Kimmel gives it a name: 'Guyland'.

Guyland: Narcissism and Sexual Aggression

Guyland, Kimmel says, is 'a culture of "entitlement, silence and protection" based on a shockingly strong sense of male superiority and a diminished capacity for empathy'. His focus is on the coming-of-age period between sixteen and twenty-six, when boys become men. His assertions are based on the evidence compiled from his interviews with more than four hundred US college students, from whom he quotes copiously. As an example of the culture of entitlement, he cites being a guest on an episode of a TV talk show called 'A Black Woman Took My Job'. 'Why "*my*" job"?' Kimmel asked the panel pointedly, zeroing in on their unexamined prejudices, the sense of entitlement that assumes jobs should rightfully be reserved for white males. While women often struggle with the legitimacy of Sheryl Sandberg's idea of 'leaning in'—feeling entitled enough and assertive enough to pursue careers without being seen as ball-breaking bitches—Kimmel points out that in contrast men are more likely to feel an entitlement to power.

From one perspective, *all* patriarchal cultures may be considered institutionalised forms of narcissism. Patriarchy is a system that inscribes and legitimates male superiority, dominance and privilege, in which women, in Søren Kierkegaard's words, 'exist for someone else'. Women bear the brunt of care and low-status work, while high-status and well-rewarded public and business endeavours are reserved for men. Men having always had a quota system is a feminist joke about affirmative action, referring to the centuries-old ban on women from education, the priesthood, professions and government. Since the sixties, we have been attempting to turn all this around. What is clear from Kimmel's work, however, is that despite feminism, despite the high number of women attending tertiary colleges, a sense of entitlement has by no means disappeared among these young men. The sense of entitlement is particularly high among athletics and football college stars, who are treated like celebrities. It goes beyond the young men themselves, to the way university administrations, coaches, parents, the media and the wider world treat them. The sense of entitlement surfaces especially in relation to sex.

Consider this example. On 7 December 2001, a group of high school football recruits came to the campus of the University of Colorado for a weekend. Colorado had just hit the big time, becoming one of the top teams in the inter-collegiate competition. 'The university,' reports Kimmel, 'had also become a hot bed of sexual assault by high-profile athletes.' Several recruits and some existing team members had sex with women at an off-campus residence. On 8 December, three of the women filed charges for rape and sexual assault. They also sued the university 'for facilitating the gang rape and failing to prevent it'.

What had happened was this. The new recruits were taken around by team members, who were meant to show them a good time. 'Sometimes, at other schools, recruits are also met by pretty co-eds who are paid by the alumni association to "escort" the recruits. Everyone knows these escorts will have sex with them.' One of the recruits told police that the football players had been promised sex: 'They told me that ... we gonna all get laid and you know ... see how we do it ... They told us, you know, this is what you get when you come to Colorado.' The young men became angry when this promise was not fulfilled. One said 'he didn't have fun because he didn't hook up with any women'; another said, 'What's up on the girls? You didn't give me no girls.' Note the sense of entitlement. A party was hastily arranged by some groupies and players, and several other non-groupie women got caught up in it. They were in their pyjamas and fast asleep when they were rudely awakened by young men demanding sex.

One of the young women, Lisa Simpson, woke up to find a hulking recruit standing by her bed. 'I'm a recruit,' he said. 'Show me a good time. Suck my dick.'

Kimmel acknowledges that celebrity college athletes do have groupies, for whom 'their wealth and notoriety for partying, is a sexual turn on'. But these women were not groupies. They were no part of any agreement to 'show the players a good time'; they just happened to be in the wrong place at the wrong time: the same location that the men chose for sex. Simpson and the others were just tucked up in bed, lights out, fast asleep; the recruits and team members had gatecrashed their world, expecting entitlements and sexual favours from whoever was female and in the vicinity.

The culture of protection at the centre of Guyland worked here too. The university administration, coaches and team officials immediately and steadfastly sided with the men. (Boys will be boys, bros before hos.) Staggeringly, so did some women. Joyce Lawrence, a member of the commission investigating the scandal, said, 'The question I have for the ladies is this: why they are going to parties like this and drinking or taking drugs and putting themselves in a very threatening or serious position'. As we have seen, this is an egregiously false account of the events.

In the end, all the guilty men got was a gentle slap on the wrist, guaranteed not to injure the limbs of future stars who might bring glory to the university. Their community service consisted of working out in the weights room or giving people tours of the faculty. 'Even the athletic director called it a "sham"', says Kimmel. 'Attitudes like this are what sustain predatory sexual entitlement. That's how the culture of protection works.'

Eventually the university settled with Lisa Simpson. She was awarded US$1 million in damages. The university acknowledged no wrongdoing, but simply wanted to 'put the matter to rest'. A year later, the football program tried again to enlist one of the guilty recruits: 'He was a good player after all.'

Great Expectations: Male Sexual Entitlement and Slutbus.com

Where does such a sense of entitlement come from? Without being a direct cause, one part of the puzzle, according to Kimmel, may be that our porn-saturated culture gives men a misleading idea that women's sexuality is like that depicted in porn, where no guy ever has to take no for an answer. Young men, brought up on such images, feel angered by reality, women 'withholding what they, the guys, believe is their due: sex'. Then Porntopia becomes 'the place where [young men] can get even, where women get what they "deserve" and guys never have to be tested, or face rejection'. The realm of sexual fantasy can be an area of play-acting in which aspects of aggression and desire not acted on in everyday life can be expressed. That said, the rise of rougher and more violent 'gonzo' porn has led to concerns that it represents a backlash against women's advancement:

> The men who make pornography have a good idea what their male viewers want. Over and over again, they describe a male consumer who is angry, sexually frustrated, and eager to enact some sort of revenge on women. In interviews with pornography producers, journalist Robert

122

Jensen found this sort of motivation as a constant theme. 'I'd like to show what I believe men want to see: violence against women,' said one producer to Jensen, explaining why the 'money shot' (the man ejaculating on the woman, usually on or near her face) is the critical moment in the pornographic spectacle ... Men get off behind that, because they get even with the women they can't have.

Kimmel emphasises this theme of retribution against unavailable women. However, there may well be differences in the emotional texture of male responses according to age. Studies have shown older men are more likely to engage in solitary porn watching, as an escape from domestic obligations, with a 'deep kind of sadness born in intimations of inadequacy, a collapse of their unchallenged prerogatives in the boardroom as much as in the bedroom. This sadness turns out to be the dominant emotion among adult male consumers.' They prefer less extreme porn than young men, and for women to look as if they are experiencing desire and pleasure. One middle-aged man said, 'It gets me away from the ordinariness of life, makes me a hero of some sort ... So there is this big gap, between the way I'd like things to be and the way they are, and there's a certain amount of sadness that comes in realising that.' Performance artist Tim Cayler admitted feeling snowed under with work and childrearing responsibilities, and said of sex with his wife compared with porn, 'I would have to commit myself to an act that I may or may not be able to consummate, you think that is easy? The little black dots, they are easy.'

The young men interviewed, in contrast, not only spoke about women 'more with contempt than desire' but used porn as a part of 'bros before hos' male bonding rituals:

Each time I happened on a group of guys engaged in pornography consumption, they spent a good deal of time jiving with each other about what they'd like to do to the girl on the screen, yelling at her, calling her a whore and a bitch and cheering on the several men who will proceed to penetrate her simultaneously.

For these young men, the dominant emotion is *anger*—or, as I would put it, rage over a thwarted sense of entitlement. Younger men who come of age watching porn have a taste for more extreme acts like double penetrations and gang bangs. They have been set up for disappointment. In reality women are very different from those depicted in porn: in pornography no one ever says no; women are instantly available, instantly orgasmic, entirely orientated to penetration in every orifice, up for sex with a whole football team. Actual women have needs and desires of their own, may refuse sex, and, when they have it, expect respect and mutuality.

As young men collide with a reality very different from the porn fantasy world of panting, ever-available and willing women in pornography, resentment grows. Not yet secure in their identities, not yet fully formed, they 'daily confront the baffling combination of sexually active but seemingly unavailable young women'.

Consider the popularity of slutbus.com or bangbus.com. The standard plot line is that young men pick up a girl for a laugh in a minibus and offer her money for taking off her clothes. Then they up the ante until she agrees to have sex for money. The rest of the video shows her having sex with all of them, after which they tip her out of the car and hold out a wad of bills, driving off just before she gets a hold of it.

Matt, from the University of Georgia, says:

> I'll confess, although I know it's not very PC or any-thing, but ... I love where these stuck up college bitches are like drunk and finally just give head to like 20 guys

and get fucked by the whole football team and all. It's like they're always walking around campus in their little shorts and you can see their shaved pussies sometimes, but they think they are like, way too hot for me. But then these films, and, they're like these same bitches, and they finally get what's coming to them … [laughs] I mean get what's coming *on* them.

Disurbingly, these young men see it not as a scripted porn show with actors, but as a truthful documentary. They actually believe women, lots of women, behave like this. One of the men complained to Kimmel, 'Why aren't they like that here at Amherst?'

It is in this distorted mental universe that the date-rape zone exists. Casual sex, combined with alcohol or drug use and imaginations primed by porn, establishes multiple volatile situations where, pious instructions about 'appropriate behaviour' and consent fall by the wayside. Consent is assumed. A Yale undergraduate interviewed pointed out how confusing it was to be lectured every other week on 'appropriate behaviour' and sexual assault, then go to wild, drunken parties on the weekend where everything was 'completely illegal and off limits'.

It is hardly surprising, in such circumstances, that the grey area of 'where consent ends and sexual assault begins' can lead to rape. Consider these remarks by students: 'It's not "don't stop until she hits you". It's "don't stop until she *hurts* you".' And 'If she's drunk and semi-conscious, she's willing.' Another student, 'Bill', confessed:

Sometimes I can't believe what I've done to get laid. Like I've said I'll only put in a little—can you fucking believe that? Like—I won't come in your mouth … I know this isn't PC and all, but a couple of times I've pushed girls' heads down on me, and like one time this girl was so drunk she was near passed out, and I kind of dragged her into my room and had sex with her. When she came to, she was really upset and started crying and asked why I had done that. I think I said something like, 'because you were so pretty' or some bullshit, but really it was because, well, because I was drunk and wanted to get laid ... And she was like, there.

This has nothing to do with political correctness, and everything to do with the legal requirements for a charge of rape. With such attitudes, it is not surprising assault rates are so high that before each weekend, all the hospital emergency rooms near campus stock extra rape kits. As Kimmel says: 'Alcohol creates a zone of plausible deniability. Where no one is supposed to take responsibility ... for what he or she wanted to do.' Kimmel's aim, as a sober sociologist, is to get us to look past the reassuring concept of a 'few bad apples' or of individual deviance, to see how the culture of Guyland—with its sense of entitlement, protection of transgressors, and silence about crimes like date rape—is implicated as a kind of precursor culture to what can go wrong on party night.

Entitlement, along with something Kimmel doesn't name but portrays throughout his book, exploitation, is crucial to the more pathological aspects of narcissism. And narcissism, researchers have shown, plays a crucial role in sexual assault.

Narcissism and Sexual Coercion

Why do some men, but not all men, commit the acts of sexual aggression that exist along a continuum from manipulating and pressuring to resorting to more forceful physical coercion and ultimately rape? After all, both rapists and non-rapists inhabit Guyland and watch porn. *Most* men do not rape. So why is it that some do? One key individual variable, it turns out, is narcissism.

It shouldn't surprise us. Narcissism is all about denial of another's unique perspective on the world. It trashes it. It obliterates it. And that makes sexual predation much more likely.

In a seminal article in 2002, Roy Baumeister and his colleagues pulled together a lot of evidence in an overview of different studies finding connections between narcissism and sexual aggression. They do not suggest it explains all cases. By no means are all narcissists sexually aggressive. They may well find other fields in which to dominate, exploit and be treated in the manner they become accustomed to: as CEOs of business, in politics, as celebrities in the media and so on. Or they may simply engage in the game-playing that Keith Campbell outlines—being a serial philanderer while in committed relationships. But if how we as parents, football coaches, armies, schools and universities treat boys and young men creates a higher sense of entitlement, we need to start taking the research on the link between narcissism and sexual aggression very seriously.

Consider what we have identified so far as the darker core aspects of narcissism: private fantasies of, and a constant hunger for, being admired; a sense of entitlement; a sense of superiority; a willingness to exploit; impulsiveness and a lack of empathy; and, perhaps most importantly of all, a retaliatory aggression when the inflated ego is threatened. In the drug- and drink-filled haze of university and after-game parties and hook-ups, the narcissist might be a dangerous person to be around. Among the predators, sexual aggression is clearly associated with higher levels of narcissism. As Baumeister suggested, it may not even always be a *stable* trait, since success and being treated like a star—for example, in the case of Dominique Strauss-Kahn, former head of the IMF, who was accused of raping a maid—can sufficiently increase narcissistic traits in individuals to promote the possibility of sexual aggression. The same pattern is shown in studies of young men when they become celebrity athletes; both consensual and coercive sexuality rise sharply. Indeed 'defenders of star athletes accused of rape often invoke an inflated sense of entitlement as a defence: they propose that these young men become accustomed to having women cater to their demands, and so they have difficulty accepting or believing that a woman will say no to them.' Acquired situational narcissism is the technical name for it. Success can make someone feel unique, superior, special, privileged and with entitlements ordinary mortals don't have.

Narcissists have high self-esteem, but it is unstable. This is why they are more aggressive and vindictive after negative feedback or failure. They have revenge fantasies against people who, they feel, put them down. Their daydreams consist of grandiose fantasies of sexual exploits and heroic achievements, in which other people admire the narcissist's superiority. More of their significant social relationships are shallow. They can be charming but are, beneath the mask, contemptuous of others and indifferent to their feelings. 'Such a picture,' concluded Baumeister, 'seems well suited to a sexual predator: someone who is skilled at getting women to do what he wants, willing to use whatever method works, and unconcerned about anyone but himself.'

When a woman refuses sex, a man has a choice. He can either accept it or resort to increasing forms of manipulation and coercion. But why don't all men react aggressively when told no? One study shows that high empathy scores reduce a man's likelihood of acting in sexually aggressive ways. All the qualities of narcissism, in contrast, make sexual coercion more likely. Studies show that men scoring higher in narcissism are more likely to accept rape myths such as 'when a woman says no she means yes' and 'if a woman is raped she asked for it', and so on.

Narcissists are also more likely to make egotistical self-attributions, to take from any success a grandiose, global case about themselves—I am a brilliant person—with the counterpoint threat hovering in the ether upon failure—I am nothing. In sexual contexts this might run as 'I am an irresistible stud,' versus 'I'm not desirable'. With such a lot at stake, it is hardly surprising, then, that as a consequence they find failure intolerable, and can react to sexual rejection with rage. They have much more to lose than someone with a more modest self-concept who does not place their entire sense of self on the line at every turn. In the case of date rape, initial sexual activity inflates the narcissist's pride; a woman's subsequent refusal deflates it, causing anger.

Grandiosity would make a refusal especially galling to a rapist, especially if he knows the woman has had sex with other (in his eyes, lesser) men. Agreeing to sex is seen as an expression of admiration, while a woman's refusal seems like a judgement on his sexual worth. And then there is the sense of being special: respecting constraints like gaining consent—well, ordinary rules and laws do not apply to the likes of them.

In Baumeister's view, for the narcissistic rapist 'the paramount gratification is egoistical'. What infuriates is thwarted entitlement. The prevalence of acquaintance rape may mean that the victim has had sex previously with the offender—in one study 59 per cent of cases had this pattern—leading to an increased sense of entitlement in the male. Another study, on self-confessed perpetrators who had not been prosecuted, said the rapes involved consensual sexual activity such as heavy petting or oral sex just before, then refusal. The women's right to refuse further sexual activity encounters a mind that is distorted by the acceptance of rape myths, such as when a woman says no she means yes. Sexually coercive men are more likely to believe that aggression is sometimes justified, especially if she has 'led him on'.

It is a narcissist's propensity to resort to denial, too, that is implicated in the cognitive distortions sexual aggressors deploy. *Surely no woman can refuse someone as desirable as me*, goes the logic. In one survey, only 3 per cent of men admitted to having forced sex, yet between 15 and 22 per cent of women said they had been forced. A narcissistic man cannot bear to admit the woman did not want him, so 'blindly rationalise[s]' the fact that it was force rather than his being a wonderful lover that made the woman submit.

This kind of denial is even more extreme among convicted and incarcerated rapists, who exemplify this denial to an extreme degree. David Champion, in his *Narcissism and Entitlement: Sexual Aggression and the College Male*, cites examples where rapists have insisted that they buy the victim dinner after the rape, or ask to see them again: 'Sometimes after we'd had sex [i.e. after he'd raped the victim] I'd give the girl my phone number, but none ever called. I guess they figured I didn't give them the right number.' Others ask to kiss the victim before they release her, or ask her if she enjoyed the experience.

Diana Scully's study of imprisoned rapists shows an inflated sense of self; a number 'claimed to be multitalented superachievers, better at almost everything than anyone else'. One man claimed the rape he committed produced 'a glow, because she was really into oral stuff ... She felt satisfied, fulfilled, wanted me to stay, but I didn't want her'. Many refused to acknowledge, even where weapons, abduction or breaking and entering had occurred during the crime, that what they had done was rape. It was clear it was a matter of pride rather than cunning; those already in prison for rape and murder preferred to admit to the murder than to the rape. Scully reports that only 10 per cent of the rape deniers thought their victims would 'hold unfavourable opinions of them'. Instead, even when they had used a weapon, they thought of themselves as 'fabulously skilled lovers whose partners [often the ones who had testified to put them into prison] were invariably thrilled and grateful for sex, some specifically said that their victims had complimented them on being good lovers'. Forty-five per cent of the rapists thought the victims would describe them positively as 'friendly, gentle, good and desirable'. Even some of those rapists who admitted they had committed rape still claimed the woman enjoyed it. 'I don't think a woman has ever said no to me,' said one. As Baumeister comments, this is 'an especially shocking statement coming from a man serving a prison sentence for rape'.

The Quest for Admiration

Sex for the narcissist is an aspect of desiring admiration, of gaining narcissistic supply. Sexually aggressive men are more likely to discuss conquests with peers than are others. They are more likely to report coercive behaviour to their peers as consensual sex, to enhance their standing with others. Eighty-five per cent of date rapists in Eugene Kanin's study said they had a great deal of pressure exerted by best friends to seek sexual encounters. Only 35 per cent of the control participants said they did. Among younger respondents, the difference was even greater. A German sample shows similar findings: 'Sexually coercive men perceive themselves to be under peer pressure to make and report sexual conquests. Their prestige and esteem in the peer group depend on how well they succeed at bedding the various women.'

Narcissistic competitiveness is not the only story, though. Narcissists can also see themselves through another trope: the perpetual or heroic victim, always treated badly by others, the long-suffering one who is hard done by in life. While this may seem contradictory to the 'wonderful lover' fantasies, in another way it is not at all surprising. Grandiose expectations on the part of the narcissist of being treated in a manner that they deserve means they will be forever disappointed by other people, leading to feelings of being victimised. When you are a 'victim', aggression can be reinterpreted as self-defence.

With narcissists who are sexually coercive, this false sense of being victimised is important. Baumeister said, 'Many studies suggest that sexually coercive men consider themselves to have been mistreated by women and bear vague grudges against females and that the act of rape may seem to them a form of gaining revenge for this mistreatment.' (Think of Kimmel's resentful students cheering at slutbus.com.) Studies have shown rapists can even object to the way a woman carries herself if it conveys a sense of superiority—a personal putdown—so the rape is a way of putting her in her place.

In a laboratory study by Baumeister, Bushman and Van Dijk, male undergraduates completed the NPI and then watched an excerpt from an R-rated movie that depicted rape. They manipulated participants for entitlement by showing half the students a consensual sex scene before the rape, and the other half just the rape, without any lead-up. Narcissists, they reasoned, would feel greater entitlement following the consensual sex scene, and be more favourable to the subsequent rape. This was exactly what they found; participants higher in narcissism enjoyed the clip more than non-narcissistic men, and found the sexually coercive scenes less off-putting.

Lack of Empathy

In rapists, the attribute that might inhibit sexual coercion in less narcissistic men, empathy, is missing. In the examples of football teams, the defence force and universities, it is not hard to find lack of empathy for the women, not only from the acts themselves but also in the display of them via technology. Baumeister describes the lack of empathy as 'decisive' in rape. It seems to be more about being *unwilling* to use empathy than being *unable* to. Narcissists can understand others all right when they want to, possessing what is called cool empathy—they know how someone is reacting at a cognitive level but don't 'feel' it (what is called 'warm empathy'). They simply tune out from others when they want to. In the case of acquaintance or date rape, if the narcissist can turn empathy on and off, it may be that he deploys it to win a woman's love but then turns it off when he rapes her, 'undeterred by the distress of the victim'.

One study found sexually coercive men are only defective in deciphering women's *negative* signals. They see what they want to see: that which preserves their inflated self. Rapists scored high on reading facial signals, but this could imply the cold empathy of the Machiavellian: understanding someone's feelings for manipulative purposes, but not caring about them. Such insight may aid rapists in seducing and raping women. Another study shows rapists are aroused by narratives of both rape and consensual sex, while non-coercive men are aroused only by consensual sex. The latter also show empathy rather than sexual desire, when shown pictures of a woman when she is upset. In contrast, sexually coercive men rated a distressed female face as equally attractive as a non-distressed female face. These men are twice as likely to report engaging in sexual aggression against women on multiple occasions. Rapists then, are not turned off by a woman's distress. They are indifferent to it. Most importantly, they find humiliation is the most arousing stimulus of all:

> Rapists showed the highest levels of physical sexual arousal—higher than to consensual sex—in response to stimuli depicting humiliating rape ... what turns them on is not hurting the female victim but humiliating her. Humiliation is a matter of status and esteem rather than physical pain or injury, and the central importance of esteem lends further credence to our focus on narcissism as a decisive factor.

Narcissistic men also have greater trouble when asked to identify with the victim after watching a videotape of rape. They more easily identify with the perpetrator. When they identify with the victim, they show greater belief in rape myths.

Finally, there is alcohol, which not only lowers inhibitions but in susceptible people can create a disinhibited narcissistic state.

The likelihood of rape increases with alcohol, a pattern that is well established. In one survey, 40 per cent of rapists had histories of chronic alcohol abuse and 50 per cent reported being drunk prior to assault. While there are no studies directly showing the ego-boosting effects of alcohol and its effects on willingness to rape, we know it does increase other violent acts. Baumeister thought the key is in the narcissistic response: studies show alcohol, by creating 'feelings of personal superiority and egotism increase the likelihood of sexual coercion'.

Narcissistic Injury

Narcissistic injury can be a 'triggering factor'. When a narcissist's grandiosity—his fantasies of being irresistible—is punctured, he can react with self-righteous fury.

In the terrible rape and murder of Jill Meagher in 2012, a popular young woman was quietly walking home in Brunswick, Melbourne, after drinks with colleagues. Her killer was a serial rapist on parole after earlier multiple rapes. He had violent fantasies about exerting power over women and took particular pleasure in humiliating them. This highly unstable man had brutally raped a number of prostitutes by first soliciting their services and then parking his car with the passenger side next to a fence. He viciously assaulted them anally and vaginally, including with his fist, leaving shocking internal injuries, all the while threatening them with death: 'Did that fucking hurt? See, look who's got the power? See, I can do whatever I want.' On the night he encountered Meagher on Sydney Road, he had been humiliated by his girlfriend, who, fed up with his jealousy, had walked out on him while they were drinking earlier in the night, and once at home wouldn't pick up the phone. That was the first rejection. Then, walking along, he spotted Meagher and asked her a question. Then he touched her bottom. Note the sense of entitlement in touching the bottom of a stranger on the street. Meagher slapped his face—the second rejection and narcissistic injury. He then reacted violently, forcing Meagher into an alleyway, viciously raping and strangling her in a rage, before dumping her body near Gisborne.

While narcissism by no means accounts for all acts of sexual coercion, it is undoubtedly an important part of the deeply troubling puzzle.

In May 2014, another terrible crime of narcissistic vengeance transfixed the world. A young Californian student, Elliot Rodger, hacked to death three of his male housemates and then, in a drive by shooting, murdered two young women and another man. In several videos posted online, and in a 140-page manifesto called *My Twisted Life*, Rodger told his story—why his life had led to this point. The themes of murderous anger born of social isolation, narcissistic injury, envy and humiliation abounded. Seated in his BMW in one video post, a present given to him by his mother, he tells why, in his 'Day of Retribution', he will take revenge upon the women who have rejected him sexually, and men who he believes have all the sex he wants and can't get. With an aggrieved sense of entitlement, he ponders the slights and rejection he has suffered from women: 'I'm such a magnificent guy and I'm beautiful ... civilized, intelligent, sophisticated ... yet every single day I have to be insulted by hot beautiful blonde girls walking with stupid obnoxious douchebags ... I deserve them more.' In another clip he says he is 'perfect' and 'fabulous' and yet has been made to feel 'so invisible as none of the girls pay any attention to me ... such an injustice'. He complains 'unbelievable', pointing to his US$300 Giorgio Armani sunglasses and his BMW—a 'better car than 90 per cent' of the other boys at college have. Yet despite this felt perfection, no young woman has wanted him sexually. So they, and the men who are their lovers, must die.

Narcissism is undoubtedly an important part of the deeply troubling puzzle of sexual crime. As the brilliant cultural critic

Guy Rundle argues, writing about the Rodger case in the online magazine *Crikey*, our world of hyper-individualism increasingly produces winners and losers, those who feel passed over and excluded. 'Toxic narcissism is to our current social order what rickets was to 19th century capitalism—pervasive, so common as to be half hidden, a byproduct of the system itself.' Yet, as Rundle says compassionately, 'things could be otherwise'. Understanding narcissism and its familial and social causes takes us beyond mere description of a syndrome, to a haunting sense of loss, an intimation of a world that might be different.

Chapter 6

It's Not about the Bike

Whatever you're doing, those other fuckers are doing more.

Tyler Hamilton, describing teammate Lance Armstrong's philosophy

CHAMPION CYCLIST LANCE Armstrong's story seemed like a modern fairytale. It spoke deeply to the American Dream—the belief that anything is possible—to the idea of the self-made man and the power of one individual pulling himself up by the bootstraps. In this tale, an all-American boy grew up with a poor but saintly, hardworking single mum, Linda. Just seventeen when Lance was born, she refused all the advice to give him up. His biological father abandoned him when he was a toddler.

Linda stayed true, raising her boy against all the odds. 'Son, you never quit' was her favourite refrain. For his adoring mother, Lance became everything, the source of all love and meaning in her life. In Linda's eyes, he could do no wrong. Briefly, it seemed the perfect union. Then, when he was still very young, about three years old, she introduced a wicked stepfather. He was cruel and punitive, constantly finding fault with Lance's unruly behaviour,

137

and beating him with a large wooden bat. The boy hated his step-father and was only relieved when the marriage finally broke up. His mother was his 'best friend and most loyal ally'. She gave him everything he needed, even on her limited wages. It was just the two of them again, against the world.

Other than with his devoted mother, Armstrong didn't really have a place in the world. He was rejected not only by both his fathers, but also by his more affluent schoolmates for not being made of the right stuff or wearing the right clothes. 'I felt shunned at times,' he said. 'I was the guy who did weird sports and who didn't wear the right labels ... My mother and I couldn't keep up with the Joneses, so we didn't even try.'

Riding through the yellow cornfields under bright blue Texan skies, the hyperactive and fearless Armstrong discovered a talent for cycling and, in particular, a truly remarkable gift for endurance. Soon he was winning big competitions; he became state champion, and made money; he had an income, a car of his own. Already a self-made man, while 'other kids drove cars that their parents had given them, I drove the one I had bought with my own money'. Armstrong became a world champion while still very young. He arrived in Europe with his undoubted talent and plenty of chutzpah, handing out baseball caps with his name on them and newly printed business cards.

Then, quite suddenly, it all went wrong. Armstrong was diagnosed with testicular cancer. It had already spread into his lungs and brain. With only a 20 per cent chance of surviving, he now began the fight—and race—of his life. After the most brutal chemotherapy, and surgery on his brain, he beat all the odds and survived. At first just a skinny bald guy with scars all over his scalp, Armstrong made it back to his bike, gradually returning to full strength.

Don't be a quitter, his mother had said and, undaunted by the ravages his body had been through with cancer treatment,

Armstrong now set his sights on the legendary cycling marathon the Tour de France. The race is regarded as perhaps the greatest endurance test of humankind. It is not hard to see why it captures the imagination. Over three weeks, lithe, super-fit and wily cyclists ride through the French countryside, with its fields of soft purple lavender and contrasting yellow sunflowers, charming seaside towns and snow-capped peaks. With grit and courage they climb up savage mountains like the windswept, barren moonscape of Mont Ventoux, then take the winding, tree-lined descents at terrifying speed.

Of all the winners of the Tour de France, Armstrong seemed the greatest of them all. He dominated from 1999 to 2005, winning no fewer than seven consecutive Tours, making him the greatest cyclist, and perhaps the greatest sportsman, of all time. In his acceptance speech for his seventh victory, Armstrong said, 'For the people who don't believe in cycling, the cynics and the sceptics, I'm sorry for you, I'm sorry you can't dream big. And I'm sorry you don't believe in miracles.'

Miracles are also the rather immodest theme of his internationally bestselling memoir *It's Not about the Bike*. Everybody likes a winner, and by now the most famous cancer survivor in the world, worth more than US$100 million, was a philanthropist and head of the influential Livestrong charity. He commanded US$150 000 as a speaking fee, and was often asked on talk shows like *Oprah*. Now on the celebrity A list, he frequented the red carpet, became a friend of President George W. Bush and lover of actress Sandra Bullock, and was briefly engaged to musician Sheryl Crow. Lance Armstrong had it all. He was even, at one point, negotiating to buy the race that had made him famous, the Tour de France. He had become a 'Citizen Saint', inspiring cancer sufferers, many of whom sought an audience with him, hoping for a healing touch from the Great Man. The Citizen Saint image was more than saleable. Armstrong had also, according to his agent, become that highly desirable commodity: a brand. Bill Stapleton, his manager and friend, explained:

> In the beginning we had this brand of brash Texan, interesting European sports, a phenomenon ... Then you layered in cancer survivor, which broadened and deepened the brand. But even in 1998 there was very little corporate interest in Lance. And then he won the Tour de France in 1999 and the brand was complete. You layered in family man, hero, comeback of the century, all these things. Then everybody wanted him.

Lance had a message: dreams do come true, if only you work hard, and never, never give up. It was about finding—as Oprah liked to put it—'one's best self'. It *is* possible, said the Lance Armstrong story, for one individual to triumph over all the odds: 'This isn't Hollywood or Disneyland. My story is amazing, but true. I'm very lucky and I have a completely pure conscience.'

All, however, was not what it seemed.

From Hero to Villain

In early 2013, at around the same time Anders Breivik was complaining about the hardships of his life in prison, a flinty-eyed Lance Armstrong entered the studio of Oprah Winfrey—that modern confessional box—and admitted that it was all 'one big lie'. He confirmed he was a long-time doper, a fraud, a liar, a cheat and a bully. After decades of denial, protesting his innocence, spreading vicious smears and filing million-dollar lawsuits against anyone who alleged that he used performance-enhancing drugs, Armstrong—in front of millions worldwide, and to a wide-eyed Oprah—finally acknowledged the truth. He was stripped of all seven Tour victories, and lost millions of dollars of sponsorship overnight. It is possible, since he has lied under oath, that he will serve time in prison. As one commentator quipped, this was a fairytale in which the hero turned out to be the villain.

It should not be thought that Lance Armstrong's conscience had finally got the better of him. There had been a number of exposés by courageous journalists like *Irish Times* writer David Walsh, and in French papers like *L'Équipe*. Back in the United States, though, anyone challenging Armstrong's extraordinary results was treated as suspect, as if they were jealous, or were downright un-American. Lance's Tour victories were bookended by two major doping scandals. In the infamous Festina affair, in 1998, a Belgian masseur named Willy Voet was stopped and searched by French police while crossing the border. In Voet's boot were a staggering number of performance-enhancing drugs, 250 vials of erythropoietin (EPO) and 400 containers of other substances. Other teams frantically flushed thousands of dollars' worth of drugs down toilets. Then, after the 2004 Athens Olympics, teammate Tyler Hamilton was stripped of his gold medal, and given a two-year ban. After Armstrong retired, teammate Floyd Landis was busted for testosterone use only four days after his victory in the 2006 Tour.

Armstrong's confession was the long-term result of a dogged pursuit by the United States Anti-Doping Agency (USADA). The agency had already got some big scalps, like sprinter Marion Jones. In 2010 Landis finally confessed to doping and pointed the finger at Armstrong and the rest of the US Postal Service team. A Grand Jury investigation by USADA subpoenaed many former teammates and their partners. Some of those interviewed had already been willing to tell the truth to the few who wanted to listen. For others, however, it was only under threat of perjury charges that they broke with the 'omerta'—the code of silence among bike riders about doping, with the severe penalty of being shunned and driven from the sport if broken.

Under oath, former teammates like Hamilton, Landis and Frankie Andreu all gave evidence that Armstrong had not only doped but instigated a highly organised, systematic program of doping for other riders on the US Postal team. In fact, to those who followed pro cycling closely, Armstrong's confession was simply the final instalment in a long-running saga. The true story had few heroes but a couple of heroines. Betsy Andreu, Frankie's wife, was one of them.

Betsy was from the Midwest, a devout Roman Catholic who had old-fashioned values about absolute truth and honesty in all things. She saw things in black and white, with no shades of grey: you were a truth teller or a liar; you rode clean or used drugs and were a cheat. Integrity mattered to Betsy Andreu more than winning, money or fame. No matter what the consequences, win or lose, there was just one righteous path. While other cyclists' partners might have been collaborators in doping, like Haven Hamilton, or seen it as 'a necessary evil', as Armstrong's former wife Kristin was alleged to have called it, Betsy was adamantly opposed to doping. It was a sin.

When the Andreus visited Armstrong in hospital after he was first diagnosed with testicular cancer, an oncologist came into the room. Betsy asked if Lance wanted privacy. He said no. What she then heard changed their lives forever. Testicular cancer is rare, and can be associated with steroid use. The doctor asked if Armstrong had ever taken performance-enhancing drugs. He said yes, and casually listed them all: testosterone, steroids, human growth hormone, cortisone and EPO. Betsy was horrified. Dragging Frankie outside, she demanded to know if her new fiancé also took drugs: 'I'm not fucking marrying you if you are doing that shit,' she screamed at him. Betsy refused to congratulate Lance when he won his first Tour in 1999. She also went on record in David Walsh's book *L.A. Confidential* about Armstrong's hospital bed confessions, and again to USADA. Despite being labelled a crazy, jealous bitch by Armstrong, Betsy was a truth teller. And the truth was that, despite testicular cancer being linked to excessive steroid use, when Lance Armstrong returned to bike racing he also returned to doping—with a vengeance.

The Circus Strongmen

Old forms of doping, like testosterone and steroids, aid strength and recovery. But they are small beer compared with the new forms of blood manipulation available since the late 1990s. It was here that the genius of Armstrong's sports doctor Michele Ferrari—nicknamed Dr Evil—came in. Ferrari was a new breed of trainer, super-scientific in his approach. He removed the vagaries of racing, the romance of a rider's 'feel' for how to train, when he was on form and when to attack. Ferrari took to number crunching; it was not magic that created champions, but science. The essence of a cyclist's success lies in his VO_2 max—his maximal oxygen consumption rate, which equates to the power per kilogram he can generate. And that power is dependent not just on muscle power, fitness and weight (the leaner the better), but most crucially on his blood: specifically how many oxygen-carrying red blood cells he has. 'A cyclist is only as good as his blood' was Ferrari's motto.

A rider's haematocrit number measures how many red blood cells he has. It is usually around the low forties. Over a long Tour, it drops even lower. Enter the drug EPO. A naturally occurring hormone produced by the kidneys, EPO stimulates bone marrow to produce more red blood cells, which carry oxygen. By the mid-1990s, however, artificial EPO had become available. It was designed, ironically enough, to help cancer patients recover from anaemia induced by chemotherapy. It did not take long for the use of EPO to enter competitive sport generally, and especially long-distance cycling. Using EPO, haematocrit numbers can be boosted to more than fifty. Even for a recreational rider, that increases peak power output by 12–15 per cent. It also increases endurance, the length of time cyclists can ride at 80 per cent of their maximum performance. For a world-class athlete, this translates to about a 5 per cent increase—or, as sports scientist Ross Tucker explains, 'roughly the difference between first place in the Tour de France and the middle of the pack'.

It was not just Lance Armstrong who took it. In fact, after its discovery in the mid-1990s, it was very hard to be a successful pro racer unless you took EPO. All world-class cyclists in the EPO era were presented with a Faustian bargain: sell your soul, start doping, keep up, and become a player. The alternative was to muddle along in the middle of the pack, exhausted by the pace, or withdraw from the sport altogether, with your conscience and integrity intact, but at a high price—your talents wasted. Others rode clean, or *pan y agua*—Spanish for bread and water—but ran the risk of suffering long-term health damage from what came to be called passive doping. This was the propensity for a clean rider to suffer long-term muscle damage by pushing himself beyond endurance in trying to compete against the unnatural speeds produced by doped riders—like Greg LeMond, three-time Tour winner, who suffered from mitochondrial myopathy, a degenerative muscle disease, in the final year of his career when EPO took over. Doped riders simply had far more red blood cells to power up the mountain. Hamilton describes it:

> the race would start and the speed would crank up and up. Pretty soon we were hanging on for dear life … We had no chance to win … the reason was the other riders were unbelievably strong. They defied the rules of physics and racing. They did things I'd never seen, or even imagined. They could attack alone, and hold off a charging peloton for hours. They would climb at dazzling speed, even the bigger guys who didn't look like climbers. They could

perform at their absolute best day after day, avoiding the usual peaks and valleys. They were circus strong men.

Under such pressure, many became corrupted. There is very good evidence that in the Tour de France and many other races, large numbers in the field of bike riders—called the peloton—were using EPO. Consider: from 1980 to 1990, the average speed of the peloton was 37.5 kilometres per hour. That was the pre-EPO era. Yet between 1995 and 2005, when EPO use dominated before reliable detection, the average speed of the peloton rose to 41.6 kilometres per hour. One rider, the outspoken anti-doping advocate Christophe Bassons, estimated it averaged around 50 kilometres an hour, 'as if the roads of France were one gigantic descent'. That is an increase of about 22 per cent in speed. Once methods for EPO testing began claiming high-profile dopers, Armstrong and Ferrari turned to another form of cheating: blood transfusions.

Frankenstein and the Bags of Blood

When Tyler Hamilton was first told by US Postal's team manager, Johan Bruyneel, that he would be flying in Armstrong's private jet to Valencia in Spain, to have a blood transfusion, he was shocked. Previously he had thought of this practice as 'Frankenstein-ish, something for Iron Curtain Olympics Androids in the eighties'. But, disarmingly casual, Bruyneel shrugged and made the procedure sound boringly normal. 'Whenever I watch the likeable gangsters on *The Sopranos*,' said Hamilton, 'I think of Johan.'

Armstrong's scheme was to take out blood at manageable intervals before the race, then, with this self-created blood bank, reinfuse it at strategic points during the Tour. Once in Valencia they went to a deserted hotel. There, Dr Del Moral

set an empty transfusion bag on a white towel on the floor next to the bed ... Then the needle, I'd seen a lot of needles but this one was huge—about the size of a coffee stirrer. It was attached to a syringe that was in turn attached to a clear tubing that led to the waiting bag. I looked away; felt the needle go in. When I looked again, my blood was pumping steadily into the bag on the floor … watching a big clear plastic bag fill up with your warm dark blood. You never forget it.

The stored blood was reinfused three weeks later during the Tour. The bags of blood, 'shiny, swollen like berries', were taped to picture hooks in the hotel rooms with white athletic tape. Hamilton shivered and got goosebumps, his body taking a sudden chill as the blood, kept in refrigerators to avoid risk of infection, flowed into his veins. From where he was lying, he could see Armstrong's socked foot in the room next door as he was also infused. After an infusion during the 2000 Tour de France, Hamilton noticed a strange sensation:

I felt good. Normally at this point in the Tour, you feel a bit like a zombie—tired, shuffling, staring. Now, however, I felt springy, healthy. Euphoric even … I caught sight of myself in the mirror: I had some colour in my cheeks. Lance and Kevin seemed energised too.

Back on the bike the next day, it worked. Up the infamous 'alabaster death-head' of Mont Ventoux, the toughest climb of the Tour, Hamilton couldn't quite believe the speed Armstrong was travelling, whizzing up the mountain as if on a city training ride, on flat terrain.

But the decision as to who was transfused was controlled by Armstrong's caprice. So complete was his control over the US Postal team that if he resented a teammate doing well and threatening his dominance, he could withhold transfusions and make them race *pan y agua* or, better still, make them race just after a blood donation, while weak and depleted. Then they were sure to be humiliated. After Hamilton beat Armstrong and won a major race, the Criterium du Dauphine, this was exactly what happened to him. Forced to race the next day while Armstrong rested, he felt weak and tired after the blood extraction, and ended up having to abandon the race. It was Armstrong's way of keeping the others humble.

Is Lance Armstrong a Narcissist?

Interesting as the story of Lance Armstrong is in itself, what is striking for this book is the connection between his behaviour and narcissism. Let me offer some examples. He had a strong sense of entitlement. Narcissistic men are more likely to continue to play the field even when in a committed relationship. Armstrong's notorious appetite, even while married, for all-night sessions with strippers, female fans and the groupies who hang around cycling stars earned him the nickname FedEx, after the shipping company with the slogan 'When it absolutely, positively has to be there overnight'. That sense of entitlement extended to competition. Hamilton comments that one reason we love sports is all the unpredictable, fallible human elements. Yet 'Lance believed in his bones that, if he worked hard, he was *entitled* to win every single race … he couldn't withstand the idea of losing.' If Armstrong won, he considered it normal. Rather than give credit when other people beat him, he described their success angrily as 'not normal'—his code for a rider using drugs. Yet Armstrong's victories were far from 'normal'; experienced observers watched him surge up mountains with his mouth closed, not even puffing, sitting in the saddle, while other non-doped riders' heads lolled back, their mouths open, gasping for breath, bodies swaying from side to side as they stood on the pedals, showing all the normal signs of exhaustion.

Armstrong was exploitative. He ruthlessly used his teammates for his own self-interest, racing them when they were sick, injured and exhausted. He even manipulated access to team doping programs in order to keep them submissive. Narcissists refuse to acknowledge the role of others in their success, while less narcissistic people are happy to attribute their success to the team. Armstrong fits the pattern.

Psychoanalyst Kernberg wrote of how people on the receiving end of a narcissist often feel used and then discarded. They have an ability to just move on, with utter ruthlessness. Other people, even long-term friends, don't seem real to them. Because there is no real attachment to the other person, it is easy to let go. This was exactly Armstrong's pattern. He might begin by seeming charming and charismatic, but he was known for 'icy archipelagos filled with former friends who have been, as one puts it, excommunicated'. Once they stopped serving the interest of the self, they were discarded: 'Lance has a thing about friendships,' says Hamilton, 'they all follow the same pattern. He gets close to someone, then, click, something goes haywire, there's a conflict, and the friendship ends.' When long-time friend Kevin Livingston asked for a raise in salary after the first Tour de France win, Lance shook his head: 'I don't know who the fuck Kevin thinks he is.' Hamilton was shocked. Livingston was Armstrong's closest friend, who had always sacrificed his own interests to help him win the Tour, and had stood by him when he had cancer. But for Armstrong, this loyalty 'wasn't the question'. Kevin was replaceable. 'Kevin thinks he's gonna get paid,' Lance said. 'Well, he's not gonna get shit.'

So that was the end of Kevin Livingston. A few weeks later Frankie Andreu did the same thing, and he too 'was not gonna get shit'. Another old friend who had helped Armstrong win the Tour bit the dust. It was, says Hamilton, not personal but mathematical: loyalty was less important than freeing up salary money—'whatever it took to win'. He assumed that everyone else was also '100 per cent ruthless'.

The narcissists Kernberg met on his couch were 'devoured by envy of those who have food, happiness and fame'. Often, he says, the way a narcissist sees others is a projection of their own internal world, which is full of hatred. This can be seen in Armstrong's advice to a young US Postal rider: 'Remember these guys are stone cold killers.' When he saw British rider David Millar happily chatting to others at the back of the pack, enjoying the moment and their friendship, Armstrong ordered him to stop: 'Dave, this is the Tour de France ... at the Tour de France *you have no friends*.' 'It was a war for him,' Millar says.

Then there is narcissistic rage, especially when thwarted, where 'the brakes of empathy' as psychotherapist Eleanor Payson says, 'are well and truly off'. Hamilton writes of an incident on a training run with Armstrong:

> Lance had pulled the guy out of his car and was pummelling him, and the guy was cowering and crying. I watched for a minute, not quite believing what I was seeing, Lance's face was beet red: he was in a full rage, really letting the guy have it. Finally it was over. Lance pushed the guy to the ground and left him.

Armstrong later laughed it off as just another 'crazy-ass thing' he'd done in France.

Kernberg found his narcissistic patients engaged in splitting: rather than recognise that most people are imperfect but still loveable, or at least likable, and made up of many contradictory qualities, some good and some bad, they divided the world into all white and all black. When a child is very young they have trouble acknowledging that the good, loving mother who gives milk, nurture and nourishment is also the bad, cruel mother who frustrates and deprives. As the child matures, if all goes well—if they are secure enough—they integrate these different aspects as being part of the one beloved person. A narcissist remains at the stage of splitting. People are seen as all good or all bad. They divide the world especially into winners and losers, 'the famous rich and great people on the one hand and the despicable, worthless "mediocrity" on the other'.

Likewise, Armstrong divided the world: into those he called 'choads' and the rest. Choad is a vulgar term for a penis. Anyone who opposed Lance, ceased to serve his interests or threatened him in competition was a choad. Or they were 'fucking Goddamn little trolls', Armstrong's epithet for those journalists who tried to tell the truth. For Armstrong, he and his mother were on the idealised side, and pretty much the rest of the world sat on the other.

Finally, Armstrong utterly lacked empathy, and not only when in a rage. This is the affective or emotional core of narcissism, according to Jessica Tracey and her colleagues in the seminal article 'Inflated by Pride and Deflated by Shame'. This means that the 'narcissistic self is continually under construction, as if the construction site is on quicksand'. Baumeister described the narcissist as being 'addicted' to the sugar hit of pride, to feeling good about themselves. Yet they are also hypersensitive and easily shamed and humiliated. Anybody who arouses their shame is at risk of incurring their wrath. Hence the emotional roller-coaster around a narcissist. Anyone who lives for his carefully cultivated and inflated self-image is wildly dangerous when threatened.

Armstrong again fits the pattern. When on the attack against those who claimed he had doped, he had no empathy. Emma O'Reilly, his former favourite *soigneur*, who assisted the team with nutrition, clothing and massage, agreed to speak frankly to David Walsh for *L.A. Confidential* about the drug use she saw. A rider had died of an overdose and she felt giving evidence was the ethical thing to do. Armstrong went on the offensive, describing her as an 'alcoholic whore', forced to leave the team because of 'inappropriate behaviour', implying she had had sex with most of the men on the team. It was absolutely untrue. Much to the frustration of many cyclists, the very attractive O'Reilly was completely professional and had no relationships with any men on the Tour. Moreover, she left of her own volition to start a business. Armstrong knew that. But he lied. He lied because he knew just how to hurt and damage her as an Irish Catholic, working-class woman. O'Reilly felt so ashamed she found it hard to be in public in England or face her family—she feared that many people would think it unlikely that there was smoke without fire. If she sued for defamation, her innocence would be hard to prove, especially since none of the cowed (and cowardly) teammates disputed Armstrong's slur. Besides which she had few financial resources, whereas Armstrong was worth US$100 million, and how could she defend herself without drawing more attention to the defamation she found so humiliating? Meanwhile Armstrong sued her. For many years she did not know whether she would be ruined.

O'Reilly and Andreu were not the only people bullied. When the rider Filippo Simeoni spoke out against doping, Armstrong threatened to 'destroy' him. When Greg LeMond famously said Armstrong's Tour de France victories were either 'the greatest comeback in history or the greatest fraud' and then later publicly criticised his association with Michele Ferrari, Armstrong again resorted to threats. He told LeMond he would find ten people to testify that LeMond had taken performance-enhancing drugs. (It was later discovered Armstrong had offered a former teammate of LeMond's a bribe of US$50 000 to do just that.) Fearing he'd lose sponsorship and risk bankruptcy, LeMond—who had raced clean before the EPO era—backed down in order to save his business, offering a humiliating apology.

After Hamilton gave evidence to USADA, he felt he was being watched and followed. Then, after he appeared on *Sixty Minutes*, talking about the doping at US Postal, there was an ugly exchange with Armstrong. At a Colorado restaurant, a rage-filled Armstrong created a scene, abusing Hamilton: 'When you're on the witness stand,' he said, 'we are going to fucking tear you apart. You are going to look like a fucking idiot, I'm going to make your life a living … fucking hell.' Typical of the way Armstrong's bullying worked, the restaurateur sided with the more famous cyclist and demanded Hamilton never return. Hamilton backed down, apologised for the fracas, and shortly after left Colorado for good.

In the *Oprah* interview, responding to allegations that he was a bully, Armstrong finally admitted to having ruined many people's lives. Yet he swapped to the third person in speaking about it, distancing himself as if he was not really responsible, and used abstractions. Armstrong also conceded that he had always responded to threat and challenge in similarly aggressive ways, ever since his boyhood. It was 'controlling the message', he said. Emma O'Reilly was just one of those people 'rolled over'. He said to Oprah that in a telephone conversation 'apologising' to Betsy Andreu, he had asserted magnanimously, 'Listen, I called you "crazy", I called you "a bitch". I called you all these things … but I never called you "fat".'

The Making of a Narcissist

Not long after Armstrong's confession on *Oprah*, the psychologist Joseph Burgo wrote the perceptive article 'How Aggressive Narcissism Explains Lance Armstrong' in the *Atlantic*. Burgo's analysis is the classic 'behind the mask' psychodynamic view of a narcissistic exterior defending a vulnerable core self 'hurt deep down inside'. Armstrong's personality works, just as psychodynamic theorists like Kernberg and Kohut have argued, 'as a defence mechanism to ward off unconscious feelings of shame or inferiority'.

The Lance Armstrong story 'embodied a carefully constructed lie', in order to 'sustain the central lie of his existence', which was 'I'm a winner not a loser.' Underneath his braggart's exterior,

Burgo asserts, Armstrong had a spoiled identity, a shamed self, born of a 'chaotic early childhood which instils a basic sense of shame and unworthiness'. After all, his father, Roy Gunderson, had abandoned him when he was two, and then his punitive and authoritarian stepfather rubbed salt in this primal wound. 'Something went very wrong in these early years,' Burgo suggests, the kind of emotional trauma that can lead to a 'conviction, felt at the very core of one's being, a feeling that they are defective, abnormal, ugly or a "loser"'. As a result Armstrong craved admiration like an addict craves a hit.

It is precisely the unconscious, disavowed nature of such feelings that makes them so toxic. In other words, here is the highly unstable, fragile egotist that Baumeister spoke of, who has a high *explicit* sense of self-esteem, but a low *implicit* one. Hence his vindictive reaction when threatened. Most people handle criticism or insult by feeling upset or angry, but are able to control themselves, without becoming cruel or vindictive like Armstrong. But for the narcissist, the only way of being up is to lower someone else.

Burgo makes really good points. No one should underestimate the emotional significance of being rejected by his biological father and treated harshly by his stepfather. And the evidence that he felt shamed in front of his schoolfriends too, felt shunned and an outsider, is striking. Burgo zeros in on exactly the right quote: 'I had started with nothing. My mother was a secretary in Plano, Texas, but on my bike, I had *become something*. When other kids were swimming at the country club, I was biking for miles after school, because it was my chance.'

Burgo is astute in pointing out that this is 'about *feeling* as if you're nothing rather than *having* nothing'. It was winning at cycling that enabled Armstrong to transform his feeling of inferiority, from being a loser into being a winner. And in this rough start Armstrong does partially meet the requirements of the narcissist described so often in the clinical literature, who turns to self-aggrandisement—such as winning at any cost—in order to overcome a sense of shame. There are several accounts that point to Armstrong's vulnerability. Emma O'Reilly saw it:

> He would shoot me for saying this, but there is something vulnerable about him. You know it's because of baggage he's carrying. His father left before he knew him and he had a bad time with his stepfather. Because of this, he's on a mission to demolish every rival and anyone else who gets in his way.

Hamilton, too, noticed a vulnerable side, especially if someone made fun of him or mocked him: 'If you interrupted Lance, or contradicted him, you got the Look. But the thing which really set off the Look was if you made fun of him. Underneath that tough exterior was an extraordinarily sensitive person.'

Burgo points to Armstrong's deep-seated psychological need to win, and his 'swift brutality' when challenged, to ward off his sense of an inner defect, and 'prevent the return of shame'. Hamilton agrees: Lance was a bad loser. When Hamilton won a stage of the Tour de France and the US Postal team benefited, Armstrong was livid. While other team members celebrated his success that night, Armstrong 'would barely make eye contact. It was like he was having an uncontrollable reaction, like an allergy.'

These are all compelling points. But Burgo ignores the parent who actually raised Lance: his mother. And that changes everything. There is equally compelling evidence that Armstrong was not just deprived of love from his fathers, but also overvalued, indulged, worshipped and treated like a prince by his adoring and permissive mother.

It is only when taken together, combining the two accounts, that we can get the most accurate, plausible and precise rendering of 'the making of a narcissist'—at least in Armstrong's case. Rather than being simply 'deprived' and 'hurt deep down inside', or an indulged, entitled, spoiled child, he had *both* elements in his upbringing. He had parents who treated him very differently—with both grandiosity and savage deflation. The Armstrong case shows that not enough attention is given in the literature to the possibility that there might be two models operating here: one permissive adoring parent who overvalues and cultivates grandiosity and entitlement in the child, and another who is cold, punitive and cultivates anger, rage and frustration. The model is simultaneously one of deprivation *and* indulgence. In fact, Lance Armstrong would have had two competing internal working models of self and other. One came from his mother, of himself as special, entitled, able to do no wrong and hence be exploitative, with grandiose visions of a world without limits. The other working model came from his two fathers, a profoundly insecure attachment, as a boy not worth loving, not worth hanging around for, not worth caring for or, in the case of his stepfather, so unworthy as to be worthy of a beating. Hardly surprising he was not able to integrate both elements to find a realistic version of himself and others.

We also know that children can have very different attachment patterns with both parents. Disorganised and disassociated attachments are usually the consequence of abandonment and harsh treatment. Armstrong dismissed his biological father contemptuously as only 'his DNA donor' and refused all efforts from Gunderson and his paternal grandmother to contact him. When his brutal stepfather left, he described himself as 'joyful' and 'ecstatic'. He said of the Armstrongs: 'All I felt for them was a coldness, and a lack of trust.'

It is these patterns of early troubled attachments that are the most implicated in psychological problems later, including narcissism and lack of empathy. However, permissive parenting is also clearly part of the picture. Consider the evidence of Armstrong's mother in relation to the case made by Twenge and Campbell about indulgence and spoiling. Armstrong's tribute to his mother is at once moving and troubling. It is clear that Armstrong's mother had admirable courage, grit and determination. Under difficult circumstances she gave her son so much. Yet perhaps the problem is that it was too much. Armstrong describes his mother as his 'best friend'. He recounts intimate candlelit dinners with her, talking over her troubles. Psychologists wisely—and adamantly— warn against 'best friending' a child. It usually speaks of a role reversal where the child is treated like the adult intimate partner of the parent rather than as a child in need of nurturing; the child may feel extra special but that feeling comes at a cost. Parents should not treat a child as their confidante. Children need to be able to depend upon a stronger, older, more experienced adult, who takes responsibility for them, who has enough authority and, at times, willingness to be unpopular in order to correct character faults or teach right from wrong. Without being unduly harsh or authoritarian in the way Armstrong's stepfather behaved, parents have to call their children into line, or to frustrate their excessive demands. No good will come of giving in on everything. Kernberg wrote of how a narcissist will claim an admired other as if they are part of the self—not a separate person. Armstrong often describes Linda as if they were one person, as if there were no degrees of separation, and his will was her will. 'We understood each other perfectly and when we were together we didn't have to say much. We just knew,' he says. 'I was proud of her, and we were very much alike.' Despite her lack of money, she gave him anything he wanted: 'She always found a way to get me the latest bike I wanted, or the accessories that went with it.' She hoarded them all as they were so expensive she couldn't bear to get rid of them.

As a child moves from child to adult, there is usually at least some increase in conflict. This usually fulfils two important functions. One is that the child is separating, releasing the intense attachment of childhood, when the parent was their first love object. They oscillate between dependency (the need to be looked after) and independence, pushing parents away. There is a more intense focus on peer groups and friendships, and of course sexual relationships. All this 'detaching' is about the child becoming an adult, being able to step away from the beloved parent, to no longer be dependent on them and to move forward into the love relationships of adulthood. Otherwise they would stay locked in the mother–son embrace forever—as the 'sons and lovers' that D.H. Lawrence wrote so brilliantly about, remaining more important than any adult partner.

New York Times sports writer Daniel Coyle writes how, watching Linda's arrival at a race, everyone 'felt the Freudian buzz of being in the presence of the latest in the series of great American mother–son relationships'. Their extreme closeness was notable. Armstrong, as a teenager, rode in races with 'I Love My Mom' printed on his T-shirts. He describes his mother as dainty and slim, small and delicate, young enough to look like his sister, and so on. Armstrong relays a decidedly odd scene in *It's Not about the Bike*. Before his high school prom he hired a limousine and, rather than take a girlfriend, got his mother to put on a beautiful sundress that they always called her 'prom dress', and rode around for an hour together before the dance, toasting each other with champagne.

Part of the essential process of adolescence is usually some kind of de-idealisation: the mother and father are knocked off the pedestal on which they were placed during childhood, before a more balanced appraisal takes place in adulthood. But the key point is that adolescence is about separation, and conflict as parents set limits teenagers want to test. There is no evidence in *It's Not about the Bike* of such separation, or of any conflict. Yet, given Armstrong's behaviour, there should have been—it was very much a case of the child being in charge:

> My mother and I became very open with each other. She trusted me totally. *I did whatever I wanted*, and the

interesting thing is, whatever I did I always told her about it, I never lied to her. If I wanted to go out, nobody stopped me. While most kids were sneaking out of their home at night, I'd go out through the front door.

But then, if there is never any discipline or punishment or conflict, and the child can do whatever they want, why would they ever need to lie? The context for lying, for a teenager, is their disobeying or violating the limits set by parents. For Armstrong, there were no limits. Reflecting later on his dangerous behaviour, on risking death weaving in and out of traffic on highways, dodging cars, on his bike, Armstrong says, 'I probably had too much rope. I was a hyper kid and I could have done some harm to myself.'

Always a high-energy boy, getting into mischief, he became rebellious. He would dip tennis balls in kerosene and set them alight, batting them into the air and then catching them with gardening gloves. He once set the roof alight when he hit a flaming ball up there, and had to climb up to jump on it. Linda did nothing. After a car hit his bike at an intersection, Armstrong was too badly injured to compete in an upcoming triathlon. He had been knocked unconscious, suffered concussion, and been given stitches for a gashed foot. He had a badly sprained knee, which also had its flesh torn up, and it needed to be put in a heavy brace. The doctor said he couldn't compete six days later: 'Absolutely no way. You can't do anything for three weeks. Don't run, don't walk.' Lance was quickly bored by sitting around. So he left the house to play golf. It felt okay and so, against the doctor's instructions, he took the leg brace off. Then he decided he would compete. 'That night I told my mother: "I'm doing that thing. I'm racing." She just said, "Okay great."' Armstrong appeared to suffer no long-term damage to the knee, but he could have. Here was a moment when a parent might have tempered the competitive urge with prudence, and said, No way, wait and compete in the next one when your knee is recovered. He might have learned that as important as competing and striving and achieving are, other priorities—like good health—are more important than winning.

When he was fifteen and competing in triathlons, Armstrong and his mother befriended Rick Crawford, then the third-ranked triathlete in the United States. Lance had just hopped into the pool with two of the nation's top triathletes and said, 'Can I train with you guys?' Crawford was kind, and took the boy on. He taught Armstrong how to train, lent him gear and over several years became very close to both mother and son. 'When things were peachy they treated me like gold, and we were like a family,' Crawford says, adding, of Linda, 'She's queen of the universe and she holds him in such reverence. He was real fragile, just a raw nerve.' When travelling together he found Armstrong unmanageable; he just 'ran wild'. In Bermuda, he smashed some expensive dishes and crystalware in the house of Crawford's friend, where they were staying. When Crawford got angry and shouted at him, Armstrong yelled back, 'Fuck you, you're not my dad'. Crawford apologised for disciplining Lance, telling Linda he loved her son, but their friendship was over. 'I was never in their house again.'

Yet Linda was not the 'helicopter mother' either. Understandably, working long hours, she didn't have time to hover. Less happily, however, she imposed little discipline and few limits on his behaviour. The young Lance was often left to his own devices, and it fell to other adults to try—and fail—to discipline him. Whatever Lance wanted to do, he did, with only cheers from her. Linda's famous refrain about never quitting, is more ambiguous than it first looks. Lance thought quitting meant he was a loser: 'Pain is temporary ... If I quit, however, it lasts forever. That surrender, even the smallest act of giving up, stays with me ... which would I rather live with?' There may well be times in life when it is prudent, or even honest, to withdraw, like when confronted with the moral dilemma of doping and winning or racing clean and losing. In every life there are times when the saying 'discretion is the better part of valour' is true. Or when it is better to withdraw 'to face another day'. A child needs a dose of Freud's 'reality principle'. Turning every negative into a positive, as Linda advised, is not always realistic. 'If you can't give it 110 per cent, you won't make it' is easily translated as 'do whatever it takes'.

Consider how Armstrong made a name for himself and won his first major race in Europe. Bike racing, even when one individual wins, is actually a team sport, with carefully defined rules and codes of conduct. In a race, a team manager selects the rider who is thought the most experienced or talented of the team, and most likely to win, while the rest of the team support them as *domestiques*. The *domestiques* act like less glamorous servants or traditional wives, who support and protect the visible player, the chosen one, in the peloton, carry drinks and food to him, take on an attack to wear out a rival, conserve his energy by 'pulling' up hills at the front of the pack and allowing the rider-most-likely to follow in their slipstream. It is a sturdy, unglamorous but respected role, where the invisible ethic of care of the many helps one person from the team to win, to be the visible representative of a country or team.

Early on in his pro career, Armstrong was racing as a *domestique* in the pro Subaru–Montgomery team. In a major race in Europe, he was doing extremely well as an individual competitor. However, this caused a clash with the team manager, who felt Armstrong should not be putting himself in line for winning. Instead, he should be behaving like a proper *domestique*, using his talents to support the designated team leader, Nate Reese, to win. Armstrong was coming second but had a real chance of competing against Reese and winning. The manager pulled Armstrong aside and said, 'You are not to attack. You work for Nate.' Armstrong was incredulous: 'Surely he didn't mean I was to hang back and play the role of *domestique* to Nate? ... He told me straight out I was obliged to let Nate win.'

In fact, the situation was ambiguous, as domestically Armstrong rode for Suburu–Montgomery, but internationally he was riding for the US team under Chris Carmichael. He rang his mother to talk over the conflict of loyalties. After listening, she said, 'Lance, if you feel like you can win the race, you do it.' He told her he thought he could. 'To hell with them,' she said, 'you're going to win this race. Don't let anyone intimidate you—you put your head down, and you race.'

When he was faced with a conflict between loyalty to the team and his own individual self-interest, his mother told him that *it's all about Lance*.

The Degradation of Sport

Sport represents something more deeply symbolic and morally serious than physical skill: it always bears a relationship to honour, struggle and the strength of the human spirit. David Walsh, the journalist who has done most to expose the doping scandals of Lance Armstrong, writes of the proud history of the Tour de France, caught in old black-and-white photographs of the cyclists:

> pain etched in their faces ... images that defined the sport. The suffering was an offering, a gift freely given by sportsmen to their public. They drove themselves to God knows what lengths, endured the most terrible conditions, because at the end of the day, we would think more of them and more of ourselves, the severity of the sport examined a man's character, illuminating his nobility ... Perhaps most of all, it offered a challenge that allowed man to transcend his everyday self.

Christopher Lasch would have agreed with this account. Sport is play, he wrote, and yet it is also deeply serious. Reality is suspended in a spirit of 'childlike exuberance' and, with a fierce 'intensity of concentration', very difficult challenges are confronted and overcome. Yet at the same time, sport is simultaneously a drama, carrying intimations of life in a much deeper way. There are, he said, 'ancient connections between play, ritual and drama. The players not only compete, they enact a familiar ceremony that reaffirms common values.'

What common values can we see in the doping scandals of the Tour de France? Surely nothing can be further from the spirit of play than a modern professional racer hiding syringes in coke cans, lying on the hotel floor with bags of blood draped over picture hooks, dripping into his veins, or even dying from a bad bag of blood. What could be more distant from play than spending time figuring out how to get a supply of banned drugs, as desperate for the next fix as any heroin addict? There can be no sense of play in the fate of those talented cyclists who died when EPO caused their blood to thicken, triggering a heart attack. Nor for those like former Tour winner Marco Pantani, who moved from performance drugs to recreational drugs, and was found dead in a lonely hotel room from a cocaine overdose.

There was little of the spirit of play in fresh-faced boys like David Millar, whose ideals of racing clean were slowly undermined by the culture of pro cycling, and who ended up being labelled as cheats for the rest of their lives. 'I had believed I could exist in a morally corrupt world as long as I was strong enough to stand my ground and respect my value system,' Millar says. He deeply regrets succumbing to the lure of doping. So does Hamilton: 'I am not proud of that decision, I wish with all my heart that I'd been stronger. I wish I'd realised the path I was taking, wish I'd quit the sport ... had a different life. But I didn't. I took the pill.' Ironically it made him feel more 'professional'. To be professional in that era was to dope. One can admire absolutely the courage of those who chose not to, like Christophe Bassons and Filippo Simeoni.

Yet the reality was that they were beaten in the races by the likes of Armstrong, and ended up withdrawing from the sport altogether. The corrupt culture of the peloton, of pro cycling, of the Tour de France, allowed a narcissist—exploitative, entitled, aggressive, a domineering bully, a cheat, a bad guy—to become the winner who took all. For more than a decade, a man with Armstrong's character was not expelled; instead he triumphed. He was supported, protected and able to flourish, as did the culture of cheating and doping; his was the character type best able, for the short term at least, to succeed.

In the end it was less a human being who won the Tour de France than Roboracer. The corruption went well beyond the riders to the highest level. Armstrong alleged in late 2013 that Hein Verbruggen, president of the world cycling body in that period, the UCI, knew of his doping and helped him cover it up. The larger, invisible supporting 'team' of masseurs, nutritionists, doctors, trainers and physical therapists were all part of it. A team's access to performance-enhancing drugs or transfusions in the middle of the tour required collusion by the team management. And team managers were not just colluders; they were instigators, pushing the never-stated message of *dope and succeed, or retire*. Riders were treated like disposable objects, expected to race when they were beyond exhaustion, sick or injured—anything that bettered the leader's chances. Everything was about results— it was a results-based business. Winning meant money, fame and power. For many teams, any principled characters just got in the way. Cheats, on the other hand, fitted beautifully into the logic of the team, and of 'professionalism'; corrupting a young man's character was nothing. A new ethic of 'responsibility' emerged. The responsibility, as part of the team, was simply to dope if it meant winning.

When team doctor Pedro Celaya checked Hamilton's haematocrit, the exchange showed the rider he was a commodity with value. 'Not too bad,' he said, 'you are a 43.' Hamilton was struck by the wording: 'It wasn't "You scored a 43" or "your level is 43", it was "*you are a 43*." Like I was a stock, and 43 was my price.'

It's Not about the Bike ended up being a truer title than Lance Armstrong or his clever ghost writer could have guessed. Armstrong's story, from hero to villain, is about far more than the corroding influence of one man's character, or his malign effect on cycling. It is about more than the corruption of a sub-culture, the micro-society of the Tour. The title is also a metaphor for the relationship of the Tour to a deeper erosion of values in the society at large, deriving from the imperatives of the new economy. The corrosion of character, in this light, is an emblem of the wider social system in which the degradation of sport is both reflected and embedded. The narcissist has become the character for our times.

Part Two

Narcissism and Society

Chapter 7

The Goddess of the Market

I am done with the monster of 'we', the world of serfdom, of plunder, of misery, falsehood and shame.

And now I see the face of god, and I raise this god over the earth, this god whom men have sought since men came into being, this god will grant them joy and peace and pride.

This god, this one word:

I.

Ayn Rand

I T WAS 1981. An elderly woman stood at the lectern. She had deep-set eyes in which a flame of intensity burned. In a heavy Russian accent, she delivered her message to cheers from an ecstatic audience: Selfishness is good. Altruism is pure evil.

The speaker was Ayn Rand. The occasion was her last lecture, before an all-male business audience. The title of her address was 'The Sanction of the Victims', and the 'victims' were these well-heeled businessmen. (She did not seem to entertain the possibility that a woman might be in business.) They were, Rand told them, 'heroes'. They had the most socially useful occupation. Yet they suffered 'an unspeakable injustice': they were 'the most hated, blamed, denounced men' in the evil she called the 'humanitarian society'.

167

America, 'the greatest and freest example of capitalism man-kind has ever reached', was under diabolical threat. From within. It was not possible for an 'outside power' to destroy America. No. It could only be done by an 'inner power: the power of morality. More specifically, the power of a contemptibly evil idea accepted as a moral principle—altruism.' The strange figure continued, her eyes glistening:

> Altruism is a moral theory which preaches that man must sacrifice himself for others, that he must place the interests of others *above* his own, that he must live for the sake of others. Altruism is a monstrous notion, it is the morality of cannibals devouring one another. It is a theory of profound hatred for man, for reason, for achievement, for any form of human success or happiness on earth.

There was no place for altruism in capitalism. Businessmen, she said, had to profit and grow rich without apology. Whatever was good for them, in their self-interest, was good for the country—as in 'What is good for General Motors is good for America'. The enemy altruists were motivated by envy and a hatred of the successful. Evil theories, like altruism, must rely on evil means—in this case, guilt—in order to gain a hold over their victims. A businessman's guilt over his wealth was appease-ment. No, worse, it was treason. His worst enemy was ... himself: 'that self-destroying group is *you*, the American businessman.' In appeasing wicked altruists, by caring about the poor and under-privileged, they were carrying out Karl Marx's prediction, and triggering capitalism's suicide. The way to improve the lot of the poor, she said, was not to be one of them.

Doom was close: America was on the brink of capitulating to collectivism; altruism was turning men into 'abjectly help-less serfs of dictatorship'. Here Rand alluded to her follower

Leonard Peikoff's book, *The Ominous Parallels*, which alleged similarities between the United States in the early 1980s and pre-Nazi Germany. Rand's paranoia and hatred of statism, altruism and collectivism were not hard to understand. For her they were code words for communism. Her ideological hostility came from a story long ago, in the ashes of her past.

The intellectually precocious and spoiled eldest child of a prosperous Russian family, Rand was only twelve when her bourgeois lifestyle was shattered by the communist revolution of 1917. Communism changed her family's life forever. Her father was ruined. Previously a well-to-do pharmacist, he had his business confiscated by the state. Penniless, they were forced to flee to the Crimean region, then held by anti-communist forces. Four years later they moved to Petrograd. Conditions in 1921 were desperate. Like so many others, they faced conditions of terrible privation, cold, and hunger to the point of starvation. Just before graduating from Petrograd University, the brilliant student suffered again at the hands of the communists. All that hard work towards a degree looked likely to be lost when she and others of her social class were purged from the university for being bourgeois. It was only after the intervention of some foreign scientists that they were reinstated and allowed to graduate. The horror of her experiences was formative, decisive and never forgotten. Collectivism, the state—even a benign one like a social-democratic welfare state—seemed to Rand the epitome of evil. Sent to the United States in 1926 to visit relatives in Chicago, Rand made her escape. If Russia was the Evil Empire, America was the Promised Land. When she saw the Manhattan skyline, she 'wept tears of splendour'.

In Jennifer Burns' biography of Rand, *Goddess of the Market*, despite her scrupulous efforts to be fair, a portrait of a monstrously narcissistic character emerges: Rand 'saw herself as a genius who transcended Time ... the most creative thinker alive'. Rand never expressed gratitude or acknowledged her debt to other thinkers, despite being heavily influenced by others, especially Nietzsche. She was gracious enough to concede that Aristotle, and only Aristotle, *might* have been on her level: 'I inherit nothing, I stand at the end of no tradition but I may perhaps stand at the beginning of one.' As her biographer duly remarks, 'Apparently Objectivism sprang, Athena like, fully formed from the brow of its creator.'

Rand's narcissism was on display during her final lecture. When a photographer tried to take a photo of her, she stopped the speech and waved him away; she was too old. During question time her usual answer was to command, angrily, that the questioner 'read her books'. Her philosophy, Objectivism, had all the answers. There was apparently no one else worth reading.

Unsurprisingly, such greatness bestowed special entitlements. As Rand put it: 'The question isn't who is going to let me; it's who is going to stop me.' She practised what she preached. In her philosophy of selfishness, Objectivists are not meant to give way to human weakness like loyalty. Or jealousy. Like the heroes in her novels, they should take what they want. There can be no romantic triangles, according to Rand, because the 'loser' cannot have what the 'winner' has earned. At least, as long as Rand was the winner. Although married to Frank O'Connor, Rand became sexually attracted to Nathaniel Branden, her much younger and most loyal lieutenant at the centre of the cult-like group that had formed around her. She called Frank, Nathaniel and his wife Barbara to a meeting, and announced she would be having an affair with Nathaniel. Inequality of power had its ugly fingerprints all over the arrangement. O'Connor was financially dependent on Rand, besides which he was very much the dominated spouse. It need hardly be pointed out how we would regard a boss today who demanded sex with a much younger employee with the reluctant approval of both spouses.

Certain days of the week would be set aside for sex in Rand's apartment. Her husband would trail off to a bar to drown his sorrows while the lovers were together. He became an alcoholic. Barbara was made deeply depressed and anxious by the situation, but was powerless to do anything. Rand knew of her anxiety attacks but continued regardless. Whatever Rand wanted, no matter the consequences for others, she felt entitled to take.

When eventually the affair began to pall and Branden fell in love with a much younger woman, Patrecia Scott, Rand's reaction was anything but Objectivist. Instead she was rage-filled—as she was frequently—and vengeful. It turned out that being on the receiving end of a selfish individual, rather than being one, wasn't so great after all. Incandescent with fury, she discovered that desire could not be commanded or extracted by sheer force of will. Rather than admit that the rejection hurt, Rand wrote an article condemning Branden for such ideological offences as 'philosophic irrationality' and 'unresolved psychological problems'—an interesting way of saying that he no longer wanted to continue the affair. She demanded Branden and his wife be excommunicated from the group. Unaware of the affair and its demise, and its role in triggering the purging, other members of her inner circle obediently signed a letter denouncing the Brandens. One of the signatories of the Stalinist-style denunciation was Alan Greenspan, economist and future chairman of the Federal Reserve of the United States.

A few years after Rand gave her last lecture, I attended an Australian dinner where an American speaker preached the glories of the free market. High at the top of a city office building, people had gathered to listen. Waiters swanned about with white gloves, ceremoniously flushing crystal glasses with excellent wines. An elaborate sculpture of smoked salmon was followed by the finest cuts of beef. The speaker's eyes had that mysterious, haunted glow of the true believer. After the speech, a highly interesting conversation was conducted at the table. My ears pricked. Two businessmen were discussing, with considerable passion and a sense of aggrieved, thwarted entitlement, the perfidies of a tax system that prevented merely wealthy men becoming really rich. It was, they agreed, Australia's biggest social problem.

It was a conversation about entitlement that had suddenly become national and global, a preoccupation that was to dominate us for the next several decades: was the top end of town getting enough? Were any of us, for that matter, getting enough?

In many ways that conversation was very similar to another that society had been having ever since the 1960s, about unfair restraints imposed by a dour Christianity on sexual freedom: were people getting enough sex? In this new refusal of older moral restraints and obligations surrounding sexuality, according to historian Eric Hobsbawm's sober account of the cultural revolution of the *Sixties*, a new expressive, radical individualism was born. It was, Hobsbawm argued, a new libertarianism 'in the name of the unlimited autonomy of unlimited desire ... a self-regarding individualism pushed to its limits ... the world was now tacitly assumed to consist of several billion human beings defined by their pursuit of individual desire'. A new impatience with constraints and limits exemplified 'a triumph of the individual over society'.

When Margaret Thatcher made her famous remark that 'there is no such thing as society, only individuals', she was giving expression to a new kind of radical economic individualism. While Hobsbawm's remarks were primarily about the sexual revolution, he could equally have been speaking of the transformation from the old to the new capitalism, the great leap forwards into a neo-liberal, high-consumption society. The conversation I overheard among those businessmen in 1980s Australia was the flipside of such thinking, this time from the New Right. It was an outlook I encountered more and more. At a lunch in a fashionable suburb of Sydney, I listened as a conservative, staid-looking banker professed enthusiasm for the way turbo-charged economic change was creating rust-belt areas, where people would be forced to leave to find employment. 'Who cares?' he said, in rude defiance of those expressing concern around him. He was supremely indifferent to people being uprooted from their communities as manufacturing industries declined without tariff protection.

It was like stepping into the pages of the Dickens novel *Hard Times*, set in another period of laissez-faire capitalism, nineteenth-century Britain, and listening to Gradgrind expound that the only principle in life that matters is 'to buy cheap and sell dear'. Improved productivity and economic efficiency—the 'bottom line' as it came to be called—were all-important. It was not long before this stance was echoed in a value shift in core institutions. Of course new social programs have to be economically sustainable. However, instead of putting social justice issues like parental leave and disability insurance before the consideration of parliamentary committees, where economic efficiency might be one among many concerns, the government now often set them first before the Productivity Commission, where it was the paramount concern. Changes that were about *justice* had now to be about improving the nation's productivity or, however worthy, they would fail. This kind of thinking was new. As Michael Sandel puts it, this was a shift from *having* a market society to *being* a market society.

Australians soon invented a deft term for such thinking: economic rationalism. It was about the head and not the heart—the hard-nosed 'pointy heads' versus the 'bleeding hearts', as Don Watson calls them in his fine memoir of his time as speechwriter for Prime Minister Paul Keating during the 1990s. This New Right world view had nothing to do with a conservative's moderate, cautious temper, their sense that 'if it ain't broke don't fix it'. Instead it cast to the winds any respect for past traditions and established ways of doing things. It thumbed its nose at the conservatives' scepticism, their belief in the imperfectibility of human institutions, and their embrace of the rueful compromises and mutual accommodations necessary in politics. Now politics was aglow with a sense of the perfectibility of human arrangements if only the market principle was enshrined. The new movement also had nothing of the conservatives' deep suspicion of, and caution about, radical and rapid change. Rather, like the True Believers of communism, the new market fundamentalists elevated one principle above all others: economic freedom and the free market.

The problems Anglo-American democracies faced were real enough. The new economic libertarianism emerged against the backdrop of the moral bankruptcy of communism. But the golden age of capitalism had also ended, in the early 1970s, because of the West's own intractable problems. The old regime of a strong state regulating relations between unions and capital—the long-term outcome of the New Deal in the United States, and the establishment of post-war welfare states under Attlee in the United Kingdom and Chifley in Australia—had all fallen victim to the difficult, intractable problem of 'stagflation': simultaneous rising unemployment and inflation.

Into this moral and policy vacuum came the energising winds of neoliberalism, or free-market fundamentalism. This, as one commentator puts it, was the 'party in waiting'. The neoliberals shared Rand's hostility to communism and any form of collectivism, as well as her uncritical embrace of its radical opposite, the laissez-faire free market. More mainstream economists like Milton Friedman and Friedrich von Hayek had also responded deeply to the threat of communism with a counter ideology of economic freedom.

In many respects neoliberalism mirrored its enemy, the old creed of communism. If at the centre of communism was an idea of a state-controlled economy, which would bring the good society, this was the reverse: from the market all good things flowed. There was a dramatic revival of ideas, from those of Adam Smith to those of Friedrich von Hayek. This new ideology placed at the centre a vision of Economic Man, where the greatest good for the greatest number was based on a vision of a sovereign self, freely competing against others in the marketplace, pursuing rational self-interest, while entering and exiting contracts. If the *Sixties* questioned the limits to eros, the neoliberal era shrugged off limits to the radical energy of the free market, unleashing the 'animal spirits' of the new capitalism, shedding the shackles of concern for the consequences of such freedom for vulnerable individuals and their communities. Neoliberalism, too, offered a total explanation of how, if only one principle were allowed to reign, all would be well. If that principle in the case of Marxism was equality, with the state being the beneficent entity in ensuring the common good of the people, in the new capitalism it was freedom and faith in the beneficent power of the market to deliver wellbeing. The long shadow cast by communism, and by the fear of radical Marxist ideas about redistributing wealth, was caught in Hayek's statement: 'I have come to feel that the greatest service I can still render to my fellow men would be that I could make the speakers and writers among them thoroughly ashamed ever again to employ the term "social justice".'

In the great leap forwards into the neoliberal age, such ideas became part of the 'dominant common sense'. They spread across the West but especially in the Anglo-American economies of the United Kingdom, Australia, New Zealand and the United States. In the United Kingdom, Thatcher was making her radical pronouncement about the triumph of individual over society while smashing the exemplars of collectivism, the trade unions. Ronald Reagan, at about the same time, also declared that the free market 'held the key to prosperity and freedom', and set about reducing tax for the rich and ending progressive taxation aimed at redistribution. 'A rising tide lifts all boats' became the answer to earlier concerns over redistribution and the plight of the poor. Government spending was slashed, and 'small government' and 'surplus not deficit' became the new mantras. Privatisation—the selling off of previously government-owned institutions—proceeded apace. The golden words were 'private enterprise'; 'government' and 'state-owned' were the dirty ones. In Australia, protection and tariff barriers toppled with the embrace of the muscular ideal of a free market. The currency was floated and, as elsewhere in the world, the financial sector was in part deregulated.

A new social Darwinism helped justify the rapidly increasing levels of inequality. The words 'winners' and 'losers'—the latter a nasty epithet for anyone poor or on welfare—entered the lexicon. Welfare-to-work programs were undertaken and a new class of the undeserving poor created. Trade unions were weakened, allowing job losses. For employers, however, restructuring firms and downsizing the workforce usually meant a leap in stock prices and hefty bonuses for executives. Sociologist Richard Sennett, in his landmark study *The Corrosion of Character: The Personal Consequences of Work in the New Capitalism*, shows how the new economy had social consequences of a profound kind, transforming the lives of ordinary people. Efforts to raise productivity and constant labour shedding led to an intensification of work and a treacherous workplace culture of 'no long-term'. A hand grenade of insecurity was thrown into workers' lives, leading to a sharpened imperative to compete and a new high-risk society. Sennett's evocative book, based on interviews with displaced workers, describes an atmosphere of 'dull continual worry', which now replaced earlier assumptions about predictable, life-long careers. As a *New York Times* writer put it, 'Job apprehension has intruded everywhere, diluting self-worth, splintering families, fragmenting communities, and altering the chemistry of workplaces.'

As inequality increased, the labor market also began to split into two distinct groups. At one end was a highly paid, highly skilled group of well-educated 'knowledge workers' happily inhabiting a long-hours culture epitomised by the title of a book: *Better than Sex: How a Whole Generation Got Hooked on Work*. At the other were those affected by the 'Brazilianisation' of the labour market—a vast army of low-paid, insecure workers who serviced the highly paid as house cleaners, gardeners, and childcare and elder-care workers. If the recognisable human face of the old regime was a male factory worker, for the new capitalism it was a female service employee, like a childcare worker.

The changes went deeper than this. There was a shift not merely in economic activity but also in sensibility, away from the ethic of delayed gratification towards the 'hedonistic sensa- tion gatherer' of the consumer society. Until the global financial crisis, at least, neoliberal societies delivered remarkable economic growth and greater wealth. This was an era marked by 'affluenza', conspicuous consumption financed by unprecedented levels of debt. On the eve of the GFC, the average income in Australia was three times what it was in the 1950s. Although the point is rarely made explicit, the higher productivity delivered by employees resulted in higher profits, rather than more time with families, as it did in France with the 35-hour week. Instead, in neoliberal societies, more hours were worked per family per year to service the consumption habit. What was created was a relentless work- and-spend cycle, with more family hours going into paid work to service credit card debt and spiraling mortgages.

Those economic changes should not obscure, however, the role of a libertarian ideology centred on the untrammeled rights of the individual. Like the sexual revolution, but in many ways much more consequential and revolutionary, this too was about *desire*. The desire in question was not lust but greed.

Twenge and Campbell's emphasis on individual greed in creating the explosion of credit gets the cause and the effect back to front. As the very substantial literature on the global financial crisis unequivocally shows, decisions by government and financial elites to change the legislative and regulatory framework were the cause. Moreover the real excesses and most serious misconduct occurred among the financial elite. Just as a formerly faithful housewife exchanged fidelity for her neighbour's keys at a swingers' party, the sober, prudential figure of the banker of the golden age of capitalism was replaced with the manic recklessness of the high roller at the casino. The legitimacy of the old religious interdicts against greed and selfishness gave way. As economists Robert Shiller and George Akerlof say in their book *Animal Spirits*, 'the permissive-parent view of the role of government replaced the Keynesian happy home'. Or as George W. Bush quipped, 'Wall Street got drunk.' And, as with a bunch of drunken adolescents trashing the family home, all this could not occur except in the absence of good authority.

All intellectual revolutions, particularly those depending on the dry theories of dour economists, need their popularisers. Rand was the surprising but significant populariser of the radical new credo. And, like all popularisers, her message was starker, cruder and simpler. Her version of liberation was selfishness for all—or, simply, narcissism for all. But revolutions need more than that; theoreticians and visionaries need loyal apparatchiks who put their ideas into practice.

The Manchurian Candidate

The Manchurian Candidate is a 1962 thriller about a man who is captured and brainwashed by communists during the Korean War. He is programmed to infiltrate government and kill the President of the United States, to make way for someone sympathetic to communism. In a 2004 remake, the action is set in the Iraq War, and the 'Manchurian Candidate' is to be an agent of influence for a multinational corporation.

Journalist Gary Weiss mischievously describes Alan Greenspan, who rose to become the chairman of the Federal Reserve of the

United States, presiding over the neoliberal era, as Ayn Rand's Manchurian candidate. Weiss was just beginning his research into his lively and penetrating book on her influence when he came across an arresting photo of Rand and Gerald Ford at the White House. Standing between them was an unprepossessing fellow with oversized spectacles. It was Greenspan. His career in key government institutions was just beginning. He had left the hallowed world of private enterprise for the evil one of government at Rand's instruction, in order to spread her influence. 'I think it is an heroic undertaking,' Rand was quoted as saying in the *New York Times*. 'Alan is my disciple philosophically. He is an advocate of laissez-faire capitalism. But neither he nor I expect it to happen overnight. I don't believe he would stay if he was asked to compromise his principles.'

In the 1940s and 1950s Rand had been dismissed as a crank. Mainstream moral philosophers had never taken her Objectivism seriously, and her ideas about the virtue of selfishness were in direct contradiction to a tradition that includes Plato (whom she hated) and Socrates, which suggests that a good life is one in which it is better to suffer evil than to do it. Major religions, too, as they grappled with the mysteries of good and evil in human affairs, had a central mission to transcend human selfishness, not to celebrate it. Where there is a taboo, said Freud, there is a desire. In Christianity, *avaritia*—greed—is one of the seven deadly sins from which all other vices flow. Many famous biblical injunctions tell us that 'the love of money is a root of all kinds of evils'. Perhaps the best known is: 'And again I say unto you, it is easier for a camel to pass through the eye of a needle than for a rich man to enter the kingdom of God.' The converse is equally true. From the life of Christ and his teachings comes a very different ideal: 'If you would be perfect, go, sell what you possess and give to the poor, and you will have treasure in heaven.' Rand's new doctrine of selfishness overturned these deep traditions.

Given her extremism, it would have been easy to dismiss her as a loopy oddball at the margins of society. Easy, but wrong. The strength of Weiss' account is in showing just how deeply embedded in the neoliberal revolution her ideas became. If once her ideas had been marginal, the times they were a-changing, and after the social revolution of the *Sixties*, her moment had come. Her central theme, expressed in the title of one of her books, *The Virtue of Selfishness*, found a new cultural receptiveness. Her turgid, simplistic and extraordinarily long novels (*Atlas Shrugged* is over one thousand pages) became unlikely international bestsellers. There is no denying the popular appeal of the aggressive assertion of self in her novels. All her male heroes, with their excellent jawlines, are 'creators' and 'producers'—rugged individualists and loners who battle against being dragged down by the 'parasites', 'moochers' and 'looters', all the mediocrities of life. She described the poor as 'refuse'. By 2008 more than a third of Americans had read her novels. Around half of those readers felt it had changed the way they saw the world. Her popularity made her both an 'agent of influence', to use the concept from the Cold War, and a figure whose ideas expressed the Zeitgeist.

More than that, Rand had written the very first populist philosophy of narcissism. Consider the following statement from her novella *Anthem*:

> I am done with the monster of 'we,' ... now I see the face of god, and I raise this god over the earth ... this god will grant them joy and peace and pride.
>
> This god, this one word:
>
> I.

In 1938, when she wrote those words, there was not merely little receptivity to them; they would have been antithetical to the spirit of the times. Fast-forward to our current era, and a transformation has occurred; her words are a brilliant emblem of an era. She is one of the most important 'superspreaders' of the narcissism epidemic. Superspreaders of narcissism have an influence far beyond their small circle. Call it the contagion effect. British writer George Monbiot has noticed how Objectivist values are spreading to his side of the Atlantic, accepted even by people who have never read Rand. The result is:

> the clamorous new demands to remove the 50p tax band for the very rich, for instance; or among the sneering, jeering bloggers who write for the *Telegraph* and the *Spectator*, mocking compassion and empathy, attacking efforts to make the word a kinder place.

More importantly, however, her ideology of narcissism represents the interests of the most powerful, influential and wealthy of all societal groups: financial elites. At the centre of Weiss' account of Rand's influence is Alan Greenspan. In Greenspan's autobiography, published just prior to the great crash of 2008, he pretended to nothing more than a youthful enthusiasm for Rand. In fact, Greenspan was within the Randian inner sanctum—for over three decades. He never defected or repudiated her doctrines; he was always the 'loyal apparatchik'. Just as it is impossible to understand the GFC without taking into account Greenspan's role, so is it impossible to understand his role without her ideas. Greenspan was a true believer in Rand, one of the most ardent defenders of her creed. He ranked equal to her other trusted lieutenant, Leonard Peikoff. He wrote many Objectivist articles. He even went on to co-edit, with Rand, *Capitalism: The Unknown Ideal*, to which he contributed a number of essays.

Weiss describes Greenspan as a 'Ralph Nader in reverse', with a fervent, religious belief in laissez-faire capitalism. Any form of government regulation or protection of the consumer was seen as coercive, on a continuum with Stalinist Russia and the communist secret police. In 1963, in pro-business America, Greenspan warned darkly about the perils of financial regulation: 'The basis of regulation is armed force. At the bottom of the endless pile of paperwork which characterises all regulation *lies a gun.*'

This is no mere theory. As with all apparatchiks, Greenspan's task was a matter of translating theory into practice. It was Greenspan who presided over the deregulation of the financial sector in the United States. In 1995 he argued against safety regulations such as minimum capital requirements for derivatives. He intervened when there were attempts under Clinton in the late 1990s to regulate the high-risk derivatives market, which was to prove so fatally flaky in the crash of 2008. It was Greenspan, too, whose role was vital in reforming the Glass–Steagall Act in 1999. The reform removed a central barrier between the commercial and investment arms of banking, a key defence against banks holding insufficient capital, which dated from the Great Depression. Despite warnings about mounting risks, in 2003 Greenspan informed Congress, 'Market pricing and counterparty surveillance can be expected to do most of the job of sustaining safety and soundness.'

In reality, the global financial crisis developed in areas of the economy that were deregulated, and hence no longer under the careful oversight of financial authorities. Charles Morris, a banker, in his book *The Two Trillion Dollar Meltdown*, gives a sober account of the failure of regulators like Greenspan to control the speculation bubble that had formed and floated rapidly skywards. He writes of a 'relentless deregulation drive' that 'steadily shifted lending activities' to 'the less regulated part of the economy, until by 2006, only about one quarter of lending occurred in regulated sectors, down from about 80 per cent twenty years before'. No one was more enthusiastic than Alan Greenspan. In the face of rising concern, he remained blithe: derivative market participants, he said, 'seem keenly aware of the counterparty credit risks ... and take various measures to mitigate those risks'. Yet during the 1998 hedge fund collapse, Greenspan had acknowledged that without the intervention of the Federal Reserve, many economies around the world were at risk. As Morris says sharply, 'Counterparty surveillance works fine so long as you are willing to accept the occasional crash of "the economies of many nations" ... given the enormous rewards that accrue to top-of-the-food-chain players ... true market-believers may find that a cheap enough price.'

Deregulation and the new derivatives market were 'a new paradigm of active credit management', Greenspan purred. Which was one way of putting it. Because bank loans seemed 'insured' by complex new mechanisms like credit default swaps now permissible under deregulation, there were ever-riskier loans, and lower capital arrangements covering corporate loans. These risky, frighteningly complex and thus inscrutable devices had even financial whizzes like billionaire Warren Buffett baffled. They grew from US$1 trillion in 2001 to US$45 trillion in mid-2007.

Deregulation resulted in 'a wall of money'. Morris explains how it worked:

> Put up $1 billion. Borrow $4 billion more, snap up a healthy company for $5 billion (after making a very rich deal with its executives), vote yourselves a "special dividend" of $1 billion ... sell the company back to the public, pocketing another couple billion, all the while taking *no* risk.

Soon there was an even more ominous development in the scope of deregulation: in the huge housing market, loans became riskier and riskier. What came to be called the subprime mortgage market—where loans were made to people who were credit

risks—expanded rapidly. Greenspan continued to be an enthu-
siast. Mortgages were increasingly subject to predatory lending.
Greenspan's fellow Federal Reserve governor, the late Edward
Gramlich, reported that Greenspan had no interest in looking
into it. Subprime lending jumped from an annual volume of
US$145 billion in 2001 to US$625 billion in 2005, more than
20 per cent of total issuances. More than a third of subprime loans,
Morris points out, 'were for 100 per cent of the home value—
even more when the fees were added in. Light documentation
mortgages transmuted into "ninja" loans—no income, no job, no
assets. The industry's underbelly became viciously predatory.'

Ordinary people became victims of shonky lending practices,
duped into taking out high-risk, complex loans that started out
with low interest but rapidly escalated to usurious levels. Morris
cites examples of outright deception. This kind of cheating behaviour became entrenched in the culture of banking. 'Yield spread
premium', for example, meant fees for brokers who got people to
agree to high-rate loans when they actually qualified for better
deals. Loan sharks from apparently respectable institutions used
expertise and financial clout to exploit people. Foolish behaviour
by ordinary people in the subprime market would not have been
possible without irresponsibility from the top, without government
authorities and individuals like Greenspan relaxing regulation.
There was simply a lack of governance.

By 2004, neoliberal policies overseen by Greenspan had even
the *Economist* concerned:

> The global financial system ... has become a giant money
> press as America's easy-money policy has spilled beyond
> its borders ... this gush of global liquidity has not pushed
> up inflation. Instead it has flowed into share prices and
> houses around the world, inflating a series of asset-price
> bubbles.

Deregulation prompted the greatest real estate boom in world history, between 2000 and 2005, with momentous and harmful consequences for younger generations trying to get into the housing market as asset prices inflated around the world, Australia and the United Kingdom included. The value of homes grew by 50 per cent, and there was a 'frenzy of new construction'. More than half of all new private-sector jobs after 2001 were in housing-related activities. The housing boom led to speculation and to the widespread practice of investing in real estate and then selling at quickly inflated prices. Greenspan—who had earlier written that the greed of the businessperson was 'the unexcelled protector of the consumer' because 'the slightest doubt as to the trustworthiness of a broker's word or commitment would put him out of business overnight'—cheered it on.

When the catastrophe of the global financial crisis hit in 2008, Greenspan was called before Congressman Henry Waxman's Committee on Oversight and Government Reform. He made an admission that went instantly viral, reverberating throughout the world: that he had found 'a flaw in the model that I perceived as the critical functioning structure that defines how the world works, so to speak ... Those of us who have looked to the self-interest of lending institutions to protect shareholders' equity, myself especially, are in a state of shocked disbelief.'

It was less of a repudiation of free market ideology, however, than many people thought. Greenspan followed his 'flaw' statement with the rider, 'I don't know how significant or permanent it is.' He then gave a little lecture to the congressman on the importance of having an ideology, 'a conceptual framework with the way people deal with reality. Everyone has one. You have to—to exist, you need an ideology.'

As Weiss points out, this was vintage Rand, almost word for word: 'he wasn't repudiating his ideology, his faith, he was reaffirming it.' Moreover, apart from that one tiny admission of the *possible* flaw, Greenspan has gone on to argue time and again that he and Rand were right. The fault lies elsewhere. It was lack of faith in bankers, too little capital held, and too *much* regulation, not too little, that caused the crisis. In March 2011, Greenspan authored an article in *International Finance* saying government 'activism' was slowing recovery:

> I infer that a minimum of half and possibly as much as three fourths of the effect can be explained by the shock of vastly greater uncertainties embedded in the competitive regulatory and financial environments faced by businesses since the collapse of Lehman Brothers, deriving from the surge in government activism.

In the *Financial Times*, he again insisted that finance was too complex for government regulation to work, and there were only 'notably rare exceptions'—like the global financial crisis—to the rule of 'Adam Smith's invisible hand', delivering stable and prosperous economies. 'So the meltdown of the world,' writes Weiss wryly, 'the irreparable harm done to so many, was all a "rare exception, even a notably rare exception". Still the youthful acolyte, at the age of eighty-five.'

In 2010, at a rally organised by right-wing shock jock Glenn Beck, Tea Party activists waved Ayn Rand placards emblazoned with 'Rand Was Right' and 'Who Is John Galt?', the catch cry of *Atlas Shrugged*. Beck called the rally 'Restoring Honor'. It is hard to know what he meant—unless it was honour among thieves.

Trickle-up Economics: Inequality and John Thain's New Rug

Communism was indeed a monumentally cruel political system, built, as George Orwell said, on a pyramid of corpses. Yet at its deeply distorted centre was a powerful ideal that had inspired human civilisation since the Enlightenment, the French Revolution and later the industrial revolution in Britain: equality. It was a moral wrong, according to this ideal, for one class of human being to have so much more than others. How could a polity have legitimacy when it mainly served the interests of the powerful and wealthy class? Before the 1980s, communism, for all its evils, appeared a viable alternative to Anglo-American democratic capitalism. Here was an alternative philosophy, a competing form of governance, a set of questions raised about inequality and justice that had to be answered. And were answered, by the establishment of the modern social democratic welfare states. When social democracy was paralysed by the stagflation of the 1970s, and communism crumbled in the 1980s, the laissez-faire economics of the nineteenth century came out from the shadows and began reshaping our sensibility. The twentieth-century preoccupations with inequality, class and justice gave way. Communism, if you like, kept the bastards in Western democracies more honest, more responsive to the plight of the poor and underprivileged, than they might have otherwise been.

Neoliberal economics was, as J.K. Galbraith pointed out, legitimised by an unproven trickle-down theory, which depended on the 'less than elegant metaphor that if one feeds the horse enough oats, some will pass through onto the road for the sparrows'. It was very quickly apparent that CEOs and financiers were growing very plump on their oats. They began arranging matters for themselves so that they raked in salaries and share options to more than answer the prayers of those businessmen at the table I was sitting at, that wealthy men might become really rich. By the mid-1990s, Westpac's chief executive in Australia earned more than $50 000 per week, then around the average annual salary. Meanwhile, in the United States top financial traders did even better, taking home US$40–50 million a year, or $100 000—more than twice the average yearly salary—per week.

During the 1950s and 60s United States' CEOs earned about twenty-five to thirty times what their employees did. But in the neoliberal era their pay packet grew by 725 per cent. By 2008 they earned 300–500 times what their workers did. George Soros, for example, paid himself US$840 million.

Even these earnings look lean compared with those of the CEO of Walmart, who earned a cool 900 times what his employees did. His family was worth as much as the bottom 40 per cent of Americans. If in the 1970s the top 1 per cent owned 20 per cent of America, now they owned 40 per cent. Warren Buffett and Bill Gates now had fortunes worth billions: US$44 billion for Buffett and US$46 billion for Gates. The three richest people on earth now earned as much as the poorest 600 million people together.

Through its somewhat different Labor and trade union–influenced traditions, Australia did do more in the way of providing a safety net and redistributing the spoils of wealth created during the neoliberal era. Yet even here, as Fairfax columnist Julia Baird notes, from 1980 onwards the top 10 per cent raked in almost half of all the growth in income. And the top 1 per cent took almost one-quarter of all household growth from 1980 to 2008.

Meanwhile the sparrows did much worse. President Obama, in his 2011 and 2013 addresses on rising inequality in the United States, stated that between 1979 and 2007, according to the Congressional Budget Office, while for the top 1 per cent of American households income grew by 275 per cent, it grew by 65 per cent for the next 19 per cent, just under 40 per cent for the next 60 per cent, and a measly 18 per cent for the bottom 20 per cent.

Moreover, increases in labour productivity were progressively uncoupled from wage rises. In the United States, for example, unlike in the Keynesian period when the income of average workers grew by 2.5–3 per cent each year, under neoliberalism the income of the average American worker remained stagnant.

Only by sending women into the workforce in ever-greater numbers, and taking advantage of deregulated credit, could the American family keep pace with rising prices and skyrocketing mortgages. Under neoliberal economic policies, from 1980 to 2006, the wealthiest 10 per cent increased their share of the national income from 35 per cent to 49 per cent. Soon there was a jokey term that caught this new reality of wealth being transferred to the top: it was not trickle-down economics, quipped economist Joseph Stiglitz, but trickle-up!

Many in the financial elite began to live like the French nobility before the revolution. Take the fraudster Bernie Madoff. At the height of the success of his gigantic Ponzi scheme, swindling investors, he and his wife Ruth had a gross income of more than US$13 million. His salary was over US$9 million, and they collected tax-free interest of US$2.5 million from US$45 million in municipal bonds. The whole seventeenth floor of his building was devoted to making up the fictitious 'trades' that supposedly gave him the best record as an investor of anyone during the boom. There was so much cocaine snorted at Madoff Enterprises, insiders called it the North Pole. Wild sex parties were held at the offices, with employees taking particular delight in having sex on one of the Madoff family couches. Meanwhile, the Madoffs owned a number of multimillion-dollar palatial residences—a mansion at Palm Beach in Florida, a Manhattan penthouse, an ocean-front house at Montauk, and a house and yacht on the French Riviera at Cap d'Antibes—two private jets, and spent thousands on single dinners at the best restaurants in New York. Bernie wore trousers worth $2000 and dozens of $350 suede loafers, made just as he liked them. Every one of his houses held separate but identical sets of clothes. Holidays at resorts like Aspen and St Moritz completed the picture of conspicuous consumption.

Madoff's behaviour was extreme but by no means exceptional. Even those CEOs who were not, like Madoff, criminals and sociopaths, began to behave, the *Huffington Post* complained, like 'new rock stars'. As the GFC got worse, firms under siege began not so much to rearrange the deckchairs on the *Titanic* as to order expensive makeovers for their particular sinking ships. John Thain, CEO of Merrill Lynch, certainly didn't sit on his hands as the company suffered massive losses—$US19.2 billion, or $US52 million daily, in the year between July 2007 and July 2008—and faced liquidation from investment losses tied to the plummeting real estate market during the 2008 crisis. He redecorated. He spent US$90 000 on two new chairs for his office at its exclusive Manhattan address, while pulling Merrill Lynch's money out of other companies. As he slashed thousands of jobs, he hired the Obamas' celebrity decorator, Michael Smith, and spent US$1.22 million on refurbishing. He also spent almost US$90 000 on a new rug. He presided over the company's decision to give an extra 'performance' bonus, worth US$3.6 billion, to its executives, who had brought the company to the brink of ruin, before news got out about the firm failing—money that amounted to more than one-third of the government money given to bail them out.

If the neoliberal revolution created the ideological framework, it is narcissism at an individual level, which took root and flourished, that explains firms like Merrill Lynch and their behaviour during the GFC. Psychologists, pricking their ears, soon skilfully used the new work on narcissism to illuminate the CEOs' behaviour. As the *Huffington Post* reported, this new research into CEOs showed that narcissism was indeed a factor in their firms' success or failure. The research revealed that, just as in all other domains, finance narcissists are short-term strategists, but tend not to be successful in the long term. The more narcissistic the CEO, the more charismatic, arrogant, self-centred and entitled, the worse they perform. They do things like restructuring and cutting jobs to boost the stock price and their own bonuses in the short term, but at the expense of the long-term interests of the company. Narcissists are more likely to be convicted of corporate fraud such as insider trading or, like Bernie Madoff, fiddling the books to create fake financial reports. The *Huffington Post* warned:

> Interestingly, the detrimental effects of narcissism appear to be exacerbated when CEOs are charismatic, which is consistent with the idea that charisma is toxic because it increases employees' blind trust and irrational confidence in the leader. If you hire a charismatic leader, be prepared to put up with a narcissist.

Narcissistic CEO's create a culture that has a disastrous effect on employee morale and turnover: 'greed is not only contagious, but competitive and jealous too'. In contrast, leaders who lack hubris and have greater humility are better for employee morale, and are closer to the ideal that management consultant Peter Drucker outlines:

> The leaders who work most effectively, it seems to me, never say 'I'. And that's not because they have trained themselves not to say 'I'. They don't think 'I'. They think 'we'; they think 'team'. They understand their job to be to make the team function. They accept responsibility and don't sidestep it, but 'we' gets the credit.

Macquarie University's School of Management in Australia was soon using natural language programs to analyse CEOs' speeches: the number of times they used 'we' or 'team' compared with the degree to which the long shadow of the letter 'I' was cast over their speeches. They began publishing a league table of the ten best and least narcissistic performers. The CEO of Amcor, Ken MacKenzie, headed up the least narcissistic bosses in 2013.

Coyly, and perhaps unhappily for our nation's moral instruction, they refused to release a list of the ten *most* narcissistic CEOs. But they gave a broad hint: they usually worked in finance or mining.

Luxury fever and narcissism, however, did not only affect the wolves of Wall Street. If it was a case of trickle-up economics as wealth was redistributed from the middle class to financial elites, what was really trickling down to ordinary people, then turning into a torrent via easy credit, was conspicuous consumption. Worse, as matters turned out, Ayn Rand and her disciples could not have been more wrong in their assumption that a richer society is a better one. Instead, the evidence shows that, as people get more affluent, they can become more entitled, more grandiose, meaner and less charitable, and even more likely to cheat. Call it the asshole effect.

Chapter 8

Because I'm Worth It!

Affluence and the Asshole Effect

It's a bright, guilty world.

Orson Welles, *The Lady from Shanghai*

T HE SINGER'S BLONDE hair lifted gently in the breeze as she ended her rousing song. The crowds cheered. The contestants were as nervous as colts on Derby Day. Some looked about to cry. Months of hard work were about to be tested. The cameras whirred and the nation waited. It was about to begin.

The event in question was ... an auction. They were flogging some flats they'd fixed up. The competition—and it had been fierce—was over different window treatments, couch covers, kitchen sinks and toilets. And, ultimately, who could get the most money for their makeover. It was the finale to the first series of *The Block*, one of Australian TV's highest rating programs which continues to command good audiences many years later. So much misplaced emotion! So much intensity! So much eros attached to colour schemes and ornaments! To the ever-expanding category of reality TV celebrities a new type was added: the celebrity renovator.

Lifestyle shows since 1980 onwards have changed rapidly, reflecting a new society. First *Burke's Backyard* and *Better Homes and Gardens* began sprucing up our suburban traditions of rickety DIY. Let me make clear that my argument here does not reflect any disdain for suburban living. Playing in the backyard has been a glorious part of Australian childhood, while for adults, pottering and tinkering in the garden and shed have long been one of the deep pleasures of life in a country lucky enough to have spacious backyards, a cherished form of relaxation. Leisurely fix-it projects have the necessary weekend antidote to work (a collective family effort with no particular timetable).

In the neoliberal era, however, newer programs, like a mutant virus, have not only proliferated, but have absorbed the more ruthless aspects of their host culture. This is the era of the professional makeover. This is Work! The hopelessly inefficient householder is bundled out of the way, packed off for the weekend. This makes way for The Team. In programs with names resembling army offensives—*Backyard Blitz*, *Ground Force*—they descend, executing a makeover with the speed and precision of Operation Desert Storm.

Within minutes of their arrival it seemed, whole houses were ripped apart, gardens uprooted, paving stones slapped into place and instant turf hurled down, while fully grown shrubs and trees fly up into the air. The pace was manic. The Team scuttled about, paving, painting, grouting, hammering and drilling at breakneck speed, funnelling a motley house through a human conveyor belt. Out the other side emerged a gleaming house (resembling all the other made-over houses), much as a meal emerges from a McDonald's drive-through. Finally a submissive, pathetically grateful owner was led through the creation that they had played no part in, meekly uttering the words: 'Oh—My—God.'

The pursuit of these shows is of perfection. The ideal of self-improvement leaps clean over the mind–body divide and takes up residence in the architraves. Ordinary citizens have begun to relate to their houses the way that Michael Jackson did to his nose: there is always, to use the title of another show, *Room for Improvement*. Following the new tendency to resort to cosmetic surgery for flabby bodies and Botox for sagging faces, disguising the vicissitudes of ageing, our houses, too, are not to show any imperfections.

The new attitude is that every last corner of turf is on display and used for the purpose of self-enhancement. Like a nation of real estate agents, everyone seems to believe that presentation is now everything. Gone is the notion that, unlike the front parlour, the backyard might be resolutely not on show, not part of keeping up appearances.

Detaching renovation from living has gone one step further in *The Block*. All that furious work, the intensity over choosing every aspect of a living space, is not about making a home to live in but to sell, to make a profit. The sale price of the apartments—ranging from around three quarters of a million dollars in the first series and rising to around one and a half million dollars in 2013—would require a huge mortgage; with two people working such long hours to service it, it is hard to imagine them ever having time or energy for anything else. Freedom furniture might be the closest they get to freedom. Contra Karl Marx, the opium of the people might not be religion but renovation.

In consumer capitalism, there has been a seismic shift in sensibility: away from the ethic of thrift, of mending instead of discarding, of frugality and living within one's means and being careful about credit. There has been a movement from the delayed gratification of the industrial era, towards what sociologist Zygmunt Bauman calls the 'hedonistic sensation gatherer' of the consumer society. In the era of affluenza, based on high levels of debt, a 'positional arms race' over conspicuous consumption has occurred. Armed with new limits on our credit cards, our shopping sprees have become as competitive as they are profligate. As Karl Marx once put it:

> A house may be large or small; as long as the neighboring houses are likewise small, it satisfies all social requirement for a residence. But let there arise next to the little house a palace, and the little house shrinks to a hut. The little house now makes it clear that its inmate has no social position at all to maintain.

Our attitudes to spending and saving have reversed. 'Bank Day' in my old country primary school, when children brought along their carefully saved pocket money to deposit in a savings account, resembled a religious ceremony. Saving, like cleanliness, was close to godliness. If bank managers were respected as much as priests, then bank monitors had the holy mark of the novitiate. Children who saved their pocket money exuded the sober virtue and prosperity attached to future pillars of the community. Spend-thrifts who succumbed to small pleasures of the moment carried the whiff of a dark future: gambling, debt, bankruptcy, shame. The bank monitors were usually obedient blonde girls who folded their hands on demure laps.

Everything's changed. Nowadays those girls might be lolling on a sunlit beach ordering cocktails or a relaxation massage, or perhaps even waiting for their breast augmentation procedure as part of their 'Gorgeous Getaway' cosmetic surgery holiday in Thailand, paid for by rewards points accumulated by spending big on a credit card. The thing to be good at is spending, not saving. The Protestant ethic of postponing future gratification has gone. It is spend, spend, spend. And we receive 'rewards' for doing so: we earn points for spending on credit, even spending money we shouldn't.

The great game of points has a serious subliminal purpose. It integrates us into the new secular religion of consumerism.

It inculcates new values, creates new taboos and new forms of transgression. The logic of Flybuys and credit card rewards radically inverts old assumptions. It establishes a new moral order based on one's relation to consumption.

A consumer is the quintessential sensation gatherer. The new ethos is that to consume more is better than consuming less, from socks to electronic gadgets. Society's losers, the unemployed, transgress not only the work ethic but also the ethic of spending properly. Bauman aptly called them 'failed consumers'. Winners spend a lot; losers don't. Children absorb these lessons early. Long before they can read they know brands like McDonald's, Disney and even Toyota. By the time they are teenagers, they have been initiated by their elders not into the sobriety of thrift, but into the ethic of spending. They persuade their parents of their 'need' to keep up with the Little Joneses next door, splurging on expensive sunglasses, label clothing, the latest iPod, iPhone or iPad. These badges of belonging and worth signify acceptance into the cult of consumption. The formation of identity—who I am—becomes inseparable from what I am worth—what I can afford to buy.

Deregulation and the explosion of credit means new cards are offered even as the current one sinks under the weight of debt. There is a seemingly limitless array of goods to spend on. Houses—like our waistlines—have to expand to fit all the excess goods we are accumulating. Houses in the United States are now twice as big as in the 1950s and have twice as many bathrooms as in the 1970s. In Australia, the average house size swelled from 100 square metres in the 1950s to 250 square metres, while families shrank as fewer people wanted children. The average house in the baby-boom era housed five or six people with one bathroom. Now houses are two and a half times as big, with more than one bathroom but an average of only 2.6 people. There are fewer children but more televisions, as it has become customary for households to have multiple sets. Yet even with bigger

THE LIFE OF I

houses we do not have 'enough' room. One of the fastest growing markets in the United Kingdom, the United States and Australia is in self-storage sites. There are more than a thousand sites in Australia where we can stash our excess stuff.

Even climbing into bed is no longer simple, with the fashion for having multiple decorative pillows on a bed, which need to be dislodged before slipping between the sheets: the average sleeper has begun to resemble a mole burrowing underground. Beds are no longer made up with mattresses, sheets and blankets. They are fitted with 'Fine Linen Collections', hinting at nobility, such as 'The Manor Collection', or depicting elite accomplishment—a bed called 'The Ambassador'—while the humble mattress now bespeaks royalty, as in the Sealy 'Dynasty Series'. (There are always 'series' or 'collections', as if from high fashion, which somehow sounds better than just the one measly version.) The larger sizes of the old double bed are now called 'King' or 'Queen' as opposed to the humdrum but more informative terms 'large' and 'extra-large'. And the morning wash? Well, you can dry yourself off in the 'Monarch Series' luxury towel range, of course. As for using the toilet, there are even capsules you can swallow, at $400 dollars each, which will make your excrement sparkle, King Midas–like!

Fittingly, it is an advertisement for men's skin care, by L'Oréal, that catches the moment, becoming the emblem of an age of narcissism, entitlement and excess. The TV star endorsing the product range, Patrick Dempsey, represents neoliberalism's ideal type: the unencumbered, competitive, middle-class male who is one of life's winners. He exudes sex, power and wealth. Even his well-moisturised stubble looks expensive. In the closing frames he gazes into the camera: 'Because you're worth it.'

The Asshole Effect

The influential social theorist Slavoj Zizek argues that the new capitalism *creates* but also *needs* this new human type: the narcissist who fuels the consumption binge. If he was right—and I think he was—then all the tut-tutting and headshaking over the increase in narcissism pretty much misses the point. Just as early capitalism and the era of industrialisation had a predominant character type, so too do new capitalism and the consumption era need a new one. The narcissism epidemic *is not an aberration*. Without the narcissistic character, the new capitalism might collapse.

Consider. Max Weber in his classic essay 'The Protestant Ethic and the Spirit of Capitalism' showed how one variant of Christian religion, Protestantism, emerged as the key legitimating idea of early capitalism. With Catholicism, salvation was assured by submission to the church's authority. With Calvinist Protestantism, however, God's grace was less certain. Protestants could only fathom whether they were fulfilling God's will, and would become one of the elect, by measuring their progress in material terms. In this way, the pious felt vindicated and assured of heavenly reward when they achieved worldly success. Central to the Protestant ethic was the notion of work as a vocation. If work was part of God's great design, it was more than just a job: it was a calling. Work was thus imbued with a heavenly glow. It had a profound *moral* significance. In attaching a sacramental quality to the humblest occupations in the secular world, and to the most profane of tasks—making money—an extraordinary productivity was unleashed. Puritanism also forbade conspicuous consumption, and the ethos of delayed gratification gave a potent rationale for saving rather than spending. It encouraged the rational pursuit of economic gain and capital accumulation. Weber's thesis had a strongly paradoxical aspect: one system of ideas ends up fuelling the success of another, despite being foreign to it. While the development of capitalism was never the aim of Protestantism, as a belief system it fostered a unique constellation of human values and qualities that helped create the conditions for a capitalist economy to flourish.

If Weber were writing today, in the era of the 'selfie' snapped on an iPhone bought on credit, his title might be 'The Narcissistic Ethic and the Spirit of the New Capitalism'. In many ways the 'work is sacred' mantra of the older era has both continued and intensified as other, religious sources of esteem have vaporised under secularisation. For the new capitalism has also fostered a new psychology, a unique constellation of human values and out-looks, a 'thinking as usual' which has allowed the new economy to flourish. Even more than this, the new capitalism has created a new set of social relationships, a new ethos of spending rather than saving, of instant rather than delayed gratification, and a new, more narcissistic character type.

New work from Californian psychologist Paul Piff has deliv-ered a stunning finding: there is a tendency when people get richer to become more grandiose, entitled, exploitative, meaner and more likely to cheat—or more narcissistic. Piff is a former student of Michael Kraus, whose seminal work concerned the effects of social class and status on empathy and sense of self. In 2010, Kraus and his colleagues published a significant study, which showed that upper-class individuals were less empathetic— less able to accurately identify emotions—than individuals who were from lower socio-economic groups. This was connected with the way wealth inured people to the difficulties others might face: money allowed independent, self-sufficient lives, whereas poorer people had to be more interdependent, and orientated to the external environment to get by.

Piff, taking Kraus' work in a new direction, conducted a series of revealing experiments, which challenged the core assumption in Western societies, from Rand onward, that more affluent societies bring only good things. He discovered a paradoxical effect of wealth. Rather than people becoming more generous, altruistic and eager to share with the less fortunate as they become better off, as one might expect, the opposite is true. As people become more affluent, the counter trend—towards bad behaviour—can be found. The wealthier people become, the more narcissistic, selfish and mean they behave.

One experiment was remarkably simple. Piff positioned researchers at crossroads. They then waited, observing aggressive, selfish behaviour among drivers and then recording the make and model of the car. If you have ever driven along in an old bomb of a car and found yourself cut off by a new, expensive SUV or Mercedes and thought that drivers of expensive vehicles were more likely to behave like jerks, you were right. Piff found drivers of expensive, high-status vehicles *do* behave worse than those sputtering along in battered Toyota Corollas, and they are more likely to cut off drivers with lower status vehicles. Four times more likely, to be precise. As a pedestrian looking carefully left and right before using a crossing, you should pay attention to the make and model of the cars bearing down on you. Piff's research showed drivers of high-status vehicles were three times as likely to fail to yield at pedestrian crossings, even when the pedestrians had right of way. There was a direct relationship; fully 50 per cent of drivers of the most expensive vehicles failed to give way. In contrast, all of the drivers of the least expensive type of car gave way to pedestrians.

Fascinated by these results, Piff and his colleagues then looked at manipulating people's behaviour in the laboratory setting to see what it was that created these impulses to bad behaviour. They primed participants with status and wealth statements before getting them to consider 'stealing or benefiting from things to which they were not entitled'. The researchers discovered something intriguing: the richest of the college graduates in their study were much more likely to admit that they would consider it, compared with participants from a middle-class or lower-class background. In another study Piff showed that people primed to feel rich helped themselves to more sweets meant for children in a lab next door than those primed to feel disadvantaged.

The reason, it turns out, is that even thoughts of being wealthy can create a feeling of increased entitlement: you start to feel superior to everyone else and thus more deserving—a dynamic at the centre of narcissism. They found this was also true of people who were, in real life, better off. Wealthier people were more likely to agree with statements like 'I honestly feel I'm just more deserving than other people' and place themselves higher on a self-assessed 'class ladder' that indicated increasing levels of income, education and job prestige. This had straightforward and clearly measurable effects on behavior.

For example, when told that they would have their photograph taken, well-off people were more likely to rush to the mirror to check themselves out and adjust their appearance. Asked to draw symbols, like circles, to represent how they saw themselves and others, more affluent people drew much larger circles for themselves and smaller ones for the rest of humankind. If you think of yourself as larger than life, larger and more important than other people, it is hardly surprising that your behaviour would become orientated towards getting what you think you deserve.

Piff's studies show that it is not just the number of pillows on your bed or the size of your barbecue that grows with affluence, but it is also your ego and an unpleasant sense of entitlement. Journalist Maia Szalavitz interviewed psychologist Madeline Levine about her work with privileged adolescents in connection with Piff's studies. Levine could relate to Piff's work all right: one boy stormed into her office filled with rage because he had only his mother's Lexus to drive, as opposed to her BMW. Tellingly, his entitled attitude paid dividends: soon after his tantrum, they bought him a BMW!

Piff points to the wider social attitudes that might form as a consequence of the link between wealth and narcissism. One example is how greater feelings of entitlement might lead to the tax revolt by the upper classes. It is the logic of 'I've earned it', 'It's mine', 'Why should I have to use my hard-earned cash for those inferior scroungers, the poor?' and so on. Wealth cultivates attitudes that are against redistribution and for privilege. Piff says: 'The more severe inequality becomes, the more entitled people may feel and less likely to share resources they become. The wealthier [that] segments of society become then, the more vulnerable communities may be to selfish tendencies and the less charity the least among us can expect.'

In fact, Piff's experiments showed that as affluence increased, so did people's agreement with Gordon Gecko's idea that 'Greed is good'. One of them showed that in a simulated job interview, if given the position of prospective employer, wealthy people were more likely to trick the hapless interviewee. The study was set up so that the 'employer' knew that the job would end in six months. They also knew that the interviewee would be willing to trade a lower salary for job security. Hence a moral dilemma: honesty says you tell the interviewee about the temporary nature of the position; greed tempts you towards withholding this fact. Wealthier people of a higher social class, they found, were more likely to withhold the vital information from the job seeker.

This result was confirmed by another laboratory test, this time examining cheating in a dice game. The participants on this occasion were not college students; they were recruited from Craigslist, a major online advertising website in the United States. The wide and varied population that Piff studied gives even greater strength to his work. The participants were quizzed on attitudes to greed and on their backgrounds. Unsurprisingly, people who thought that greed was good were more likely to cheat. Piff and his colleagues also found that when people were simply primed with the benefits of greed, they were more likely to support bribery or to cheat unsuspecting customers, suggesting that people could be influenced by the excesses of Wall Street and the wider culture. If primed neutrally, with no benefits of greed suggested to them, participants were more likely to support ethical behaviour.

It would be reasonable to object here, and point to famous and inspiring examples of philanthropy by wealthy individuals like Bill Gates, who gives so much, especially to foreign aid, and Warren Buffett, who has promised to give away, during his lifetime and after his death, 99 per cent of his fortune to philanthropic causes. In making his pledge, Buffett acknowledged that since he is so wealthy, even in giving so much away he is not actually giving up anything he really needs, unlike poorer people who willingly give funds to the church collection plate that they could spend on their family. Nor is he giving 'the most precious asset, time'. He recognised that he had been rewarded by a market system that rewards a soldier with a medal, and a wonderful teacher with a thank-you note from parents, but rewards someone 'who can detect the mispricing of securities with sums reaching into billions. In short, fate's distribution of long straws is wildly capricious.' Philanthropy has been as deeply valued as the Scrooge-like behaviour of the very wealthy has been reviled. It inspires not only because of its usefulness to the needy but also because of the human qualities of generosity that it represents, and the voluntary nature of the giving.

Yet these well-known and justly admired examples can delude us into thinking that such generous philanthropy from the wealthy is the norm. It is not. In another arresting and counterintuitive finding, Piff discovered that the richer a person is the meaner they are—despite having more to give, wealthier people are less likely to be generous and give to charity. Well-off people were less likely to help a person who entered the laboratory in distress, unless they had just watched a video about child poverty. In a series of controlled experiments, lower income people and those who identified themselves as being on a relatively low social rung were consistently more generous with limited goods than upper-class participants were. 'There's this idea that the more you have, the less entitled and more grateful you feel; and the less you have, the more you feel you deserve. That's not what we find,' Piff says. 'This seems to be the opposite of noblesse oblige.'

Taking this investigation from the laboratory out into society, Piff also looked at who donated the most to charity. What he found was the opposite of what one might expect. The rich donated a smaller percentage of their wealth than poorer people. In 2011, the wealthiest Americans, those with earnings in the top 20 per cent, contributed 1.3 per cent of their income to charity, while those in the bottom 20 per cent donated 3.2 per cent of their income. 'The personal drive to accumulate wealth,' Piff concludes, 'may be inconsistent with the idea of communal support.'

Remember the person being primed by child poverty and behaving better? That finding was confirmed by research into different postcodes and charitable donations. If the affluent increasingly insulate themselves in the cloistered atmosphere of privileged suburbs or even gated communities, we need to pay heed to this research. In the richest, most homogenous postcodes, where the average annual income was uniformly at least $200 000, people were less generous than those who had similar incomes but lived in more socio-economically diverse areas containing poorer people: 'It seems that the insulation from people in need may dampen charitable impulse.'

The less affluent folk from the poorer end of town were also more likely to give to those servicing the genuinely needy—social services or charities—while the rich gave to high-status institutions such as already well-endowed art galleries, museums and universities. Many of these already cater to the nation's elite, like Harvard and Yale. Indeed, *The Atlantic* noted that more gifts in this wealthy group went to elite preschools than to any charities supplying social services to the poor. Feeding America, which deals with the nation's poorest, got nothing.

The fact that the affluent are quite easily influenced by videos of child poverty shows that these qualities are not set in concrete. 'We're not suggesting rich people are bad at all,' says Piff, 'but rather that psychological effects of wealth have these natural effects.' It is, he says, a function of greater prosperity, rather than innate qualities of rich people. Moreover, 'there are simple things you can adjust, which suggest rich people are fairly sensitive and just need little reminders'. However, as our society gets wealthier, we need to pay attention to his sober observation: 'While having money doesn't necessarily make anybody anything, the rich are way more likely to prioritise their own self-interests above the interests of other people. They are more likely to exhibit characteristics we would stereotypically associate with, say, assholes.'

The Devil Wears Prada: The Consumer Self and Narcissism

The Devil Wears Prada, a bestselling book, and later hit movie, is about a young wannabe writer, Andrea, who takes a job as assistant to the ruthless and powerful head of a New York fashion magazine, based on the real-life editor-in-chief of American *Vogue*, Anna Wintour. The characters are obsessed by their own and everybody else's appearance, and remain impossibly thin in order to wear the designer clothing they regard with the same intensity that a famine victim regards food. Designer clothing bestows *status*. New fashion trends are treated with the seriousness of an announcement of war. Their work world is bitchy and hyper-competitive: every person for themselves. One reviewer in the *New York Times*, who had worked in the industry, said the film's depiction of the fashion world

> moves beyond the myth of its practitioners as visionaries, revealing them instead as the exacting functionaries they are: those who live and dress and think according to the

seasonal edicts of global conglomerates ... no one wears square-toed shoes in the presence of someone who might disapprove of square-toed shoes. A fashion editor might not genuinely crave the new pump of the hour, but she worries how devalued she'll be if she doesn't get it.

Slowly Andrea not only begins to wear designer clothes but is transformed inwardly too: she begins more and more to take on her surrounding values and resemble her boss in putting ambition and work before her boyfriend and family, before finally seeing the emptiness behind the logos.

The Devil Wears Prada is a light-hearted portrayal of a very serious business practice extending far beyond the fashion industry. Whereas once companies used to compete over efficiencies of production, now they are more likely to compete by product differentiation, by selling an embellished, enhanced identity allegedly bestowed by a product from a designer brand like Prada. In a world of heightened individualism, we find appealing those products that confirm our success, but also differentiate us from others. Indeed, so much in advertising is now about symbolic associations and selling us a better version of ourselves, it is often hard to work out what on earth it is they are selling until the tagline and a new car or gadget pops into view.

Tom Wolfe, in his 1976 essay 'The Me Decade', writes: 'The new alchemical dream is: changing one's personality—remaking, remodeling, elevating, and polishing one's very *self* ... and observing, studying, and doting on it. (Me!)' Advertisements now routinely pander to this new narcissism in selling something. An advertisement screening in Australia showed a 'Modern Man' or 'Modern Woman' bounding along busy city streets, talking rapid-fire, rapper-style into the camera about themselves, listing their own virtues. The man boasts: 'I'm a barbecuing, meat-eating, sausage-sizzling, prawn-peeling salad lover ... I push the envelope, push a button, push a pram ... push 'em real good. I wear the pants, I wear aftershave, I wear the blame ... and I wear it well.' The woman brags: 'I'm texting, typing, LOL-ing, OMG-ing, I'm digitally in touch, but not retouched. I'm a storytelling, canteen-helping, fundraising, muffin-making, party-going yoga lover.' The product being sold by this all-about-me display? The humble and unglamorous Kia, one of the cheapest cars on the market. The advertisement did not list a single quality of the product.

As Naomi Klein shows in her powerful critique of brand name consumerism, *No Logo*, selling self-enhancing identities along with a product also has a deeper economic logic. Sneakers might cost $20 to make in a developing nation with sweatshop labour, but once associated with sports stars like Tiger Woods or Rafael Nadal, the humble rubber shoe acquires the lustre of success (one can almost hear the roar of the adoring crowds) and can be sold in the West for $200. People will pay that much for a humble sneaker, because it confers a worthwhile—better—identity on the wearer. It is by deploying these symbolic associations with high status that many firms now compete.

Once again, it is increased narcissism that has greatly helped the new business strategy along. Constantine Sedikides, a leading scholar in narcissism at the University of Southampton in the United Kingdom, has shown that the higher a person is on the narcissism scale, the more orientated to high-status brand names they will be. Or, to put it another way, selling the Ralph Lauren/Armani/Gucci/Prada identity would not succeed as it does on such a widespread scale without growing narcissism. Narcissists, Sedikides points out, have a psychological profile that empirical research has shown to be 'self-centred, self-aggrandising, show-offs, and prone to illusions of superiority and specialness'. Prime targets, surely, for brand-name consumerism

One of Sedikides' studies in 2007 showed that narcissism is directly related to materialism, the desire for material possessions, and compulsive buying, as well as the desire for fame and wealth. Not all people are equally susceptible to the allure of high-status brand names; Sedikides says the 'particular type of self that is likely to be enhanced through conspicuous consumption ... is the narcissistic self'. Scholars have shown that across a range of domains, narcissists are 'addicted' to boosting their self-esteem by constant self-enhancement. They cannot control their egocentrism, and have a 'strong need to validate themselves in the presence of others'—a polite way of saying they love an audience. They are power-hungry, status-driven and 'persist with shameless self-promotion despite its long-term personal and occupational costs'. They don't just want to feel *good* about themselves; they want to feel *great* about themselves. Hardly surprising, then, if, for the narcissist, acquiring high-status luxury goods is taken to a whole new level. Conspicuous consumption, especially of prestige 'brand names', is a form of potent self-enhancement in a materialistic society, and one of the easiest to engage in.

Narcissists, we know, like to perform and compete only when there is an opportunity to be observed, when there is a chance of self-enhancement. And what better way to do so than to have the visible symbols of success—the latest BMW, a large house, opulent lifestyles of travel and designer clothing. Money is used by narcissists, Sedikides notes, as a form of self-enhancement to maintain a grandiose self-image, as an indicator of status and power. And we do actually often misjudge books by their attention grabbing or glamorous covers: 'affluent individuals are judged as capable and intelligent, self-disciplined and cultured'. All these are the very traits of success, competence and achievement—not altruistic or communally orientated traits—which narcissists are known to value. And again the effect flows causally from riches to narcissism—a continuation of the asshole effect. Sedikides' research shows that even thoughts about money can make people feel more self-sufficient, making them less pro-social, and decreasing their desire to help others.

There is more. The susceptibility to buying brand names is not only related to the look-at-me style of the grandiose narcissist. It may be part of a defensive stance against fragile, low implicit self-esteem. Narcissists on the 'inflated by pride, deflated by shame' roller-coaster are more susceptible to the competitive nature of consumption as they do not have egos that can easily withstand the bruising realisation of others having more and better posses-sions. Just as aggression in narcissists can be triggered in the lab when they are primed with feelings of worthlessness, in the real world, so can feelings of insecurity lead to a shopping spree!

As Yi-Fi Tuan has remarked, 'Our fragile sense of self needs support, and this we get by having and possessing things because in a large degree, we are what we have and possess.' Intriguing experiments have borne out this sense of fragility: when people focused on their sadness, for example, they were willing to spend relatively higher amounts of money for product consumption. A number of studies have tracked the relationship between insecurity and greater materialism.

The bulk of research establishes that self-doubt and insecurity predict materialism. Sedikides found that individuals with narcis-sistic fragility turn to brand names and status-enhancing products 'for the reparative effects such a consumption pattern has on the self'. Both chronically and momentarily insecure people are more materialistic and more likely to take their material success in life as a sign of a verdict on them. When people agreed with such items as 'I often wish I felt more certain of my strengths and weaknesses' and 'Sometimes I feel I don't know why I haven't succeeded at something', they were also more likely to agree with measures of materialism, such as 'Buying things gives me a lot of pleasure' and 'The things I own say a lot about how well I am doing in life'. If participants in a lab setting were primed with words suggesting self-doubt, they immediately rated higher on materialism. It also worked the other way. In one study high self-esteem and psychological security *reduced* materialism. Thoughts of death—the ultimate ontological insecurity—also markedly *increased* materialism.

This suggests that narcissistic consumption of brand-name products can be changed or rehabilitated. Like the 'rich and mean' hypothesis, people's behaviour is open to influence. A more altruistic, more equal, less competitive and more nurturing society could help people overcome their addiction to consumption. When people received self-affirming messages or self-threatening messages, their attitude to paying more for a brand-name watch changed. Those whose self was affirmed were willing to pay less for the flashy watch, meaning they were able to resist its self-enhancing properties. Those whose self-worth felt threatened, in contrast, were willing to pay *more*. Even something as simple as negative feedback on performance made people willing to pay more for a photograph when it was described as rare, unique and infused with high status. The scholars concluded that 'motivation to increase self-worth then, is what drives brand name consumption'.

Make that an insecure, narcissistic devil wearing Prada!

* * *

There is another startling aspect of neoliberalism and the new culture of narcissism. Social science now solidly shows that cheating—like that perpetrated by the worst of the companies on Wall Street—occurs more in this kind of winner-takes-all society, where books like Rand's *The Virtue of Selfishness* express the Zeitgeist. Neoliberal societies are more likely to include people who endorse the value of cheating.

The research began when social psychologists, with their usual eagle eye for social change at the level of the individual,

THE LIFE OF I

began to notice a number of cheating scandals—in business, obviously, but also in sport and even academia. A lot of frauds were
hitting the headlines all at once. Carolyn Pulfrey and Fabrizio
Butera, from Lausanne in Switzerland, examined whether prevailing values of neoliberalism—self-interest, the desire for material
goods to consume, and individual competition—might be resulting in unethical business practices and cheating more generally.

One cross-national study of twenty member nations of the
OECD had decisively shown that the degree to which a nation
pursues this 'most extreme form of competitive capitalism', neoliberalism, as opposed to coordinated capitalism, determines
the degree of unethical behaviour. Here's how the connection
works. Under the new capitalism, a neoliberal consumer society
correlates positively with national aggregates of individual-level
adherence to self-enhancement values. Put simply, *more* people in
these societies self-enhance, or present themselves as better than
they really are. Next, the psychologists found that adoption of
such narcissistic self-enhancement values meant that people were
more likely to condone cheating. When they primed people with
a pep talk redolent of values like ambition, success, influence,
achievement and power—all self-enhancing values—individuals
were more likely to condone cheating. However, when primed
with self-transcending values and words like loyalty, trust, honesty, broad-minded, helping, care, equality, peace, protecting
the environment, wisdom and beauty, people did not condone
cheating. Pulfrey and Butera observe:

> the first and most noteworthy finding is that it establishes
> for the first time a direct relation between adherence
> to individual level self-enhancing values of neoliberal,
> free market capitalism and both condoning of cheating
> and engagement in cheating behaviour. Robert Merton
> argued that the 'cultural exaggeration of the success goal

... and the extreme emphasis upon the accumulation of
wealth, combined with restricted access to wealth, lead to
deviant behaviour like theft ...'

The focus on material success, they found, intensifies unethical
behaviour by leading to an 'end justifies the means' and 'whatever
it takes' mentality.

The research suggests the pathway between neoliberal life
goals and the condoning of cheating operates via an excessive
pressure to work, succeed and win. This goes far beyond the very
normal desires to do well in a chosen profession, and the willingness to work hard. It comes closer to the idea at the centre of the
doping scandal in cycling—other values like honesty and integrity,
which might act as moral counterweights, shrink in comparison
to the all-important goal of success in a winner-takes-all culture.
Nothing else matters. Performing well because of inner goals, like
the aim of testing oneself against one's own standards, gives way
to self-enhancing performances orientated to impressing other
people in an audience.

On Haemorrhoids and Vegemite Jars
Tom Wolfe's essay begins with a woman lying with her face
down in a carpet, as a self-help guru exhorts those attending a
life-coaching weekend in Los Angeles to share what they are
thinking about at that moment. All the woman can think about
is the hard little pea of a haemorrhoid impressing unpleasantly
on her consciousness. In a single paragraph, Wolfe captures the
myopic self-absorption and the self-regarding obsession of an era.

Australia's haemorrhoid moment, I think, came in the 2013
election, when, as the catastrophe of climate change loomed, then
Prime Minister Kevin Rudd held up a Vegemite jar, in one of
the richest nations on earth, and with great moral indignation
bemoaned the likely increase of a few cents under an Abbott

government. Our world of abundance and self-indulgence—the consumerist world—was recast into one of self-pitying deprivation and grievance. The ripe soil for such a sense of grievance is created not by the 'cost of living', as journalist George Negus has shrewdly pointed out, but by the 'cost of a lifestyle'. It is usually rooted not in material deprivation but in temporal poverty. People go into heavy debt and must work many hours per family in order to finance the large houses and the three- or four-car garages and the rest.

Alongside the cultivation of a sense of entitlement—the 'right' to luxury goods—is an additional 'right' to receive tax cuts every year. In reality, we have one of the lowest percentages of tax to gross domestic product in OECD countries, yet our commonsense thinking is how hard done by we are by the taxman. It was not difficult for Tony Abbott to urge inaction over climate change with his slogan on the carbon tax, 'No new tax'. Nor, incredibly enough, to advocate 'compensation' for the tax that no longer existed.

It is important here to be precise. The implications of all this work by social scientists is that there will be increases in the sense of entitlement and in narcissism as a society grows wealthier. Yet this self-orientated state of mind is quite fluid—nothing like the rigid coping patterns of someone with a full-blown narcissistic personality disorder—and hence is able to be changed. When the affluent are primed with images of vulnerability, their better self comes to the fore. On the other hand, when primed with examples of people behaving in self-interested ways, where greed or ruthless behaviour is legitimated or rewarded, they can be tempted.

It is easy enough in Australia to see both impulses. There was a tremendous outpouring of generosity and empathy among the citizenry when a deadly tsunami struck on Boxing Day in 2004 and killed over 230 000 people in fourteen countries. Likewise when the now opposition leader Bill Shorten, along with disability activists, achieved a transformation of attitudes towards our current support for people with a disability and their families: many Australians responded to the plight of these people with empathetic understanding, and a willingness to do more for them. In practical terms it meant popular support for a new $6 billion program and a new increase in the Medicare levy to pay for a National Disability Insurance Scheme (NDIS).

Yet in other ways we have become richer and meaner. As Bob Brown ruefully observed on retirement:

> In the Howard years Australia became a much meaner and more self-interested country ... We are the richest people per capita in the world, if you just look in material terms, and we are the richest people ever to live on the earth ... Yet there's this air of dissatisfaction and a feeling that we are being cheated, and that is a cultural shift that came out of the Howard years and has been promoted mightily by the Murdoch media—and that flows on through the ABC and all the other radio shock jocks and so on.

Despite being one of the richest nations on earth, we have thought of refugees as 'illegals' and queue jumpers and treated them with astonishing cruelty; we have become impatient with the fragile efforts at reconciliation with Indigenous people; we have been miserly with our poorer neighbours and cut foreign aid while, locally, welfare recipients, including sole mothers caring for children, are increasingly considered, as Rupert Murdoch colourfully put it, 'scroungers'.

Every election since the mid-1990s has been a competition that might once have been called 'appealing to the lowest common denominator' but now, following the research above, might be called 'priming for narcissism'. Politicians have reminded us of how much we deserve. How hard done by we really are. How the cost of living pressures are killing us. The tabloids have reminded us how someone else—some fat, grubby welfare cheat—is trying to get something for nothing, get one up on us, and spend *our* money. One headline at the *Daily Telegraph* thundered, 'Fat People, Drug and Alcohol Addicts Paid to Stay Home'. Yet the article in question pointed to a small number of morbidly obese people, who usually suffer related serious health issues, on the Disability Support Pension, but offered only anecdotal evidence to support the claim about drug and alcohol addicts. As support for the NDIS grew, so did the portrayal of many people on the DSP as lazy, fat bums rorting the system.

Politicians competed over who could appeal to the paradoxical but growing sense of grievance over taxation being too high in one of the lowest-taxing OECD nations. Billionaire mining magnate Gina Rinehart did her bit, railing at the fact that over 60 per cent of Australians were, allegedly, on welfare. Unsurprisingly, all kinds of essential aspects of life that should not be so difficult to find the money for in such a wealthy country —health, education, support for Indigenous people, aged care, providing for refugees, care for people with a disability, and so on—were under siege.

Politicians did not stand brave and bold, or appeal to our better natures. They no longer addressed just the 'Australian people', or the 'men and women of Australia'; they invariably addressed '*working* people', or 'working Australians', or 'hard-working Australians', always said with the hint of a whine. It was the official cultivation of resentment: the constant talk of the long-suffering *working people*, Australians *doing it tough* out there, with all those cost-of-living pressures.

We need to ask of ourselves whether, as the writer David Foster Wallace observed of America:

> We've changed the way we think of ourselves as citizens. We don't think of ourselves as in the old sense of being small parts of something larger and infinitely more

important to which we have serious responsibilities ... We think of ourselves now as eaters of the [American] pie.

Narcissistic Society and the Care Deficit

Narcissists, says psychiatrist Glen Gabbard, do not age well. Ayn Rand is a case in point. She spent her life preaching a gospel where life was seen from the point of view of the ruthless and the strong, never from the perspective of the vulnerable. She hated dependency, which she confused with passivity. Her heroes are all young, male, wealthy and without any responsibilities for inconvenient dependents like children or the elderly. Real human beings in all their frailties simply do not exist in her novels.

Yet as age caught up with her and she contracted lung cancer, she realised that not even bestselling authors, indeed no one except the fabulously wealthy, could afford sustained medical treatment in the neoliberal United States. Greed no longer looked so good either, as she bitterly decried the 'greed' of the doctors who cared for her. So Rand—self-interested to the end—took help from the government she had despised all her life. She ended her life on Medicare and social security. Which raises the question of care in a narcissistic society.

Chapter 9

The Care Deficit

Ayn Rand: 'Do you know what a baby's saying when she reaches for a bottle? She's saying, "I am a leech." Our aim here is to develop the bottle within.'

From the fictional Ayn Rand School of Tots in *The Simpsons*

IN A COMMENCEMENT speech to an Ivy League college, the writer David Foster Wallace told a story:

> There are these two young fish swimming along and they happen to meet an older fish swimming the other way, who nods at them and says, 'Morning, boys. How's the water?' And the two young fish swim on for a bit, and then eventually one of them looks over at the other and goes, 'What the hell is water?'

'The point of the fish story,' he went on, 'is merely that the most obvious, important realities are often the ones that are hardest to see and talk about.' In a consumer society, he continued, the 'deep belief that I am the absolute centre of everything' is the 'default setting, hard wired into our boards at birth'. It is very easy in such a society to worship all the wrong deities, like money, sexual allure, power or being cleverer than others, but in the long run all these forms of narcissistic supply only bring a sense of emptiness and unhappiness.

This mode of being is insidious because it is unconscious, leaving us haunted by 'the constant gnawing sense of having had, and lost, some infinite thing':

> The really important kind of freedom involves attention and awareness and discipline, and being able truly to care about other people and to sacrifice for them over and over in myriad petty, unsexy ways every day ... awareness of what is so real and essential, so hidden in plain sight all around us, all the time, that we have to keep reminding ourselves over and over. This is the water.

So what is this invisible 'infinite thing' all around us, so omnipresent that we don't see it? The water that Wallace spoke of is care. And if he was even half right about the default setting of narcissism, then care—*giving* attention to others rather than pursuing and *getting* it for oneself—is going to be much more difficult.

The Invisible Heart

In his 'Because You're Worth It' advertisement for L'Oréal, Patrick Dempsey briefly fondles a baby before a pair of obliging hands whisks it away. Dempsey represents an ideal male type who, in reality, is able to be successful precisely because he has the care work done for him. The carer of the baby remains invisible. It is not only the slogan that is emblematic of an era. So is the invisibility of the shadow world of care upon which every visible achievement and market enterprise rests.

Nancy Folbre has called the world of care 'the invisible heart'. Folbre, a feminist economist, has done some hard-headed thinking about why this might be so. She argues that the eighteenth-century writer Adam Smith, whose idea of the invisible hand of the market has so enchanted neoliberals, had a blind spot. Smith was not at all like Ayn Rand, preaching a doctrine of virtue in selfishness. When he extolled the virtue of self-interest it was only meant to operate in the impersonal world of the marketplace. At the heart of his *Theory of Moral Sentiments* was the old gender contract. He assumed that there would always be an altruistic private realm presided over by women, who would go on selflessly delivering care. It was women who, prevented by law, custom and a lack of education, would be forbidden from any public or working role in the marketplace, and would buffer those muscular, animal spirits by providing them with a haven in the heartless world. Neoliberalism is based on the model of the self-interested rational individual, *homo economicus*. There is nothing wrong, in this vision, with exploiting others for economic advantage—after all, the theory goes, people can always exit the contract and take their business or labour elsewhere. Yet applied to the relational world, *homo economicus* would be a self-interested, affectionless, ruthless narcissist.

At the centre of this invisible world of care is a willingness to give time and attention to others. It requires a connected, communal self, cooperating with others for purposes larger than the self. It is not a competitive self, bent on gaining advantage over others and exploiting them out of self-interest. An important part of being a mother, a father, an adult daughter or son of an elderly parent, and so on, is the capacity to decentre from self, to swing one's full attention to others when needed. All care is like this. Yet in a narcissistic society such a person seems more and more like a strange island of selflessness in a sea of selfishness.

Hardly surprising then, that this 'invisible heart' is under pressure. The neoliberal ideal does not really account for care, or for who does it or how it is paid for. On top of that, neoliberalism brings, as Richard Sennett observes, a new character ideal: of the unencumbered, economically self-sufficient individual. He vividly describes this new ideal as a cruelty. This is because for so many it is an impossibility; too many are excluded from it.

This economic self-sufficiency is now meant to include women, who are supposed to work too, as well as manage household and family care. Yet here we strike another aspect of neoliberal societies: the new family is not yet fully supported by new work-place regulations, or the kind of funding necessary for high-quality care services. If you believe that markets are better than gov-ernment, that good governance means small government, then reducing taxation is the logical result. Yet taxation is precisely how we fund care services for families to replace what women used to do, as they take their position in the workplace. Neoliberalism desires the deregulation of the labour market, with fewer, not more, protections for workers. Yet the new gender contract, where two wage earners are juggling both care and work, requires a thoroughgoing transformation: an updated, *re-regulated* labour market to reflect modern realities, such as job-protected, extended parental leave; leave to care for sick children or the elderly; and the right to part-time work. Such changes maintain a caregiver's attachment to the workplace, while also making care possible.

Folbre openly and honestly acknowledges that patriarchy was a reasonably effective means of ensuring, however unfairly, a system of caring for dependents. When we transform patriarchy, then, we must take care how we do it. Fighting patriarchy with individualism runs the danger that we will all become too selfish, unleashing the 'war of all against all'. Much ink has been spilt on getting men to do their fair share of care, but individualism and the new capitalism as value systems give men no real incentive to change. Instead, all the incentive is on the side of remain-ing competitive in the workplace and in life, by devolving care responsibilities onto others. Yet the needs of the sick, the young and the elderly remain, competing with an ever–more demanding workplace that requires a player 'off field' looking after the needs of every player 'on field'. This can leave working mothers with insoluble problems in balancing care and work.

The 'care penalty' for doing the right thing by others—the earnings foregone, the opportunities lost, the poverty in old age in the event of divorce, even the loss of esteem in the eyes of the world—is harsher than ever. It has been estimated that a well-educated American woman with a college degree who stays home to look after the kids can expect to forego up to one million dollars of potential earnings. Working mothers also suffer a care penalty, in terms of promotions, being available for the plum jobs and so on. In order to care for their families well, they rush around after work and cut back on sleep and leisure, making it look more like the road to exhaustion than emancipation. The difficulties faced by both at-home mothers and working mothers have the same source: the devaluation of care. The devaluation of that non-market work, and ideal worker norms based on the old male breadwinner with no responsibilities allow employers to be unsympathetic or even puni-tive towards those with significant caregiving responsibilities. In such a world, children, in particular, can be treated not as a part of the 'commons', with all adult citizens having a stake in their being raised well, but more like pets, and their rearing as a hobby of a strangely selfish kind with little sense of its larger social purpose.

Meanwhile, the rewards for behaving selfishly have also increased. Elite professions all too often function under the old assumption that the worker has someone else in the background doing all the care work, so as to let them hit the ground running each morning, no distractions or interruptions from needy chil-dren or sick old mothers. The ideal worker is an unencumbered one. Under patriarchy, both social norms and laws enforced women's dependency. Legislation like the marriage bars, which banned female employment after marriage, ensured that women were available to care for others. Because women had no other choice, we became accustomed, Folbre argues, to 'free riding' on women's caring labour. We are used to getting it done for us, free of charge, in close to a non-reciprocal manner. And we expect it to continue much the same even when many women work full time. Both men and society, Folbre suggests, have come to like it that way. The problem, however, is that once women invest large amounts of time, energy and effort into training and developing skills, we can no longer assume a universal supply of free caring labour. Too many women find themselves in the grip of the 'nice person's dilemma'. Their sacrifices on behalf of others go unrequited, and make them vulnerable to exploitation and, in the event of divorce, to poverty. Opportunists in an individualist paradise can take advantage of those who are generous and cooperative. 'Nice gals and guys,' says Folbre ruefully, 'come last.' Women are too often presented with an impossible choice: sell your soul to the work ethic and succeed, or continue to honour the ethic of care but at increasing personal cost.

Folbre's work spells out with analytic clarity a framework for understanding the problems we face. It is also true that the values of the marketplace, with the emphasis on the agentic aspects of achievement, competition, besting others and ruthless striving, cannot be cordoned off and made to stop at the doorstep of the private realm. Rather such values can begin to colonise the life world, even transforming the most intimate of relations, like that of mother to child. More deeply, as Michael Sandal observes, turning too much over to the market can profoundly affect the social world. Markets don't only allocate goods and services; they also express and promote certain attitudes towards the goods being exchanged, and whether it is appropriate to treat them as commodities, as instruments of profit and use. Like care. But we should never treat other human beings like this. Sandal suggests that outsourcing some things 'is to demean them, to value them in the wrong way ... some of the good things of life are corrupted or degraded if turned into commodities'.

With respect to care, the risk is that intimate life is commercialised, turned into a commodity, and in the process emptied of the close human bonds that enrich it and bestow meaning. Even love can be made over into a market relationship. Sociologist Julie Stephens, in her insightful book *Confronting Postmaternal Thinking*, gives a telling example. Just like a bull's semen, colostrum, the highly nutritious substance secreted immediately after birth before a mother starts lactating milk, is now available for sale on the internet, under enticing titles like 'Buy 1 and get 1 free'. Stephens also cites a description of US academics lining up at a human milk station:

> Duck into the ladies room at a conference of say, professors, and chances are you'll find a flock of women with matching 'briefcases' waiting none too patiently and trust me, more than a little sheepishly for a turn with the electric outlet. Pumps come with plastic sleeves like the sleeves in a man's wallet, into which the mother is supposed to slip a photograph of her baby, because, Pavlov-like, looking at the picture aids 'let-down', the release of milk normally triggered by the presence of the baby, its touch, its cry.

This image is redolent of an assembly line; the breast is being industrialised. The emotional closeness of the breastfeeding relationship is erased, and a mother's milk reduced to its physical properties. Stephens links the new market ideology to the transformation of an emphasis on *'being with'* a child—giving responsive, loving care—into a new ethos of *doing something to a child*, in order to winch out more productivity and create a better child product.

Tiger Mother: The Iron Lady of Neoliberal Parenting

In her controversial and bestselling book *Battle Hymn of the Tiger Mother*, Amy Chua extolls the virtues of a 'tough love' regime in order to get her daughters to not be 'soft entitled children' but driven high achievers. Although at times tongue-in-cheek, there is no mistaking the message. It boasts of extreme parenting practices aimed at instilling high-performance norms in her daughters. She institutes draconian music practice regimes on top of expectations that they succeed brilliantly at school. They must not only get straight As, but be the top students in every class except gym and drama. They must practise a classical musical instrument two hours a day and perform brilliantly at concerts. Social life is the enemy of achievement, so there are no sleepovers or play dates. Or time relaxing watching TV, or holidays not pressed into the service of performance. If they fail at a performance, they are called 'garbage', or 'fat' and 'ugly'. She tells them they will be 'losers' if they are second best.

When one of her children gives her a handmade birthday card not to her satisfaction, she hands it back and demands a better effort. When younger daughter Lulu had trouble learning a difficult piano piece:

> I hauled Lulu's dollhouse to the car and told her I'd donate it to the Salvation Army piece by piece if she didn't have 'The Little White Donkey' perfect by the next day … I threatened her with no lunch, no dinner, no Christmas or Hanukkah presents, no birthday parties for two, three, four years. When she still kept playing it wrong, I told her she was purposely working herself into a frenzy because she was secretly afraid she couldn't do it. I told her to stop being lazy, cowardly, self-indulgent and pathetic.

Chua continues to shout at her daughter, and the house becomes a war zone. They work right through dinner. Her daughter is not allowed to get up, 'not for water, not even for bathroom breaks'. The daughter finally manages to learn the piano piece. In another incident concerning a failed performance, Chua threatens to burn all her child's soft toys. (She later claimed this was a joke—some joke!) The older daughter, Sophia, is generally compliant, despite her father finding marks in the piano where she has sunk her teeth, a sign of her extreme stress. On the cusp of adulthood, Sophia fulfils her mother's dreams and goes to Harvard, but also joins the army. Lulu, however, rebels. A defiant spirit, she actually manages to defeat her mother's desires and asserts some independence. Or at least sort of—she opts for high-performance tennis instead of the violin.

Chua's memoir gives a more precise understanding of the derogatory term 'helicopter parent', but also shows up the mis-apprehension and confusion in the widespread view that it is synonymous with the 'smother mother', whose excess of nur-turance prevents children ever taking responsibility. Chua is hovering, all right, but her over-concern is about her daughters' future material and worldly success, gaining attention and admira-tion in the eyes of others. Indeed, of her own relationship with her daughters, she says, 'I'm happy to be the one hated.' It is the only time the word 'happy' occurs in the entire book.

Chua looks at the landscape of childhood rather like a mining engineer looks at a pristine landscape—ripe for the excavation of talent. Her success as a parent is contingent on her daughters' success, which will reflect back on her. It is All About Amy. *She* was raised to feel a failure unless she was a high achiever, with her Chinese immigrant father humiliating and punishing her if she came home with less than an A. Now a Yale law professor, Chua ratchets up her own demands for perfection from her daughters, and it does not appear to have dawned on her that she may have paid the most terrible price for worldly success: the loss of empathy.

Her book includes nothing about raising children who have a capacity for love, empathy, kindness and care for others. Although she invokes her own childhood, it is likely that the older generation of immigrants, for all their desire for children

to work hard at school and succeed in an alien land, also emphasised countervailing virtues: less on piano practice and more
on observing family rituals and contributing chores and help to
the household. Discipline and character-building in her memoir,
however, are about performance and future productivity for
oneself, not about how to act in the relational world, about behaviour to *others*, loyalty, trust, sharing, defeating selfishness in one's
nature, kindness, charity or developing loving relationships.

Chua's version strips away those communal aspects and
leaves a pushy parent on steroids. In fact the *only* values that are
endorsed are the narcissistic ones: agentic achievement-orientated
values to the exclusion of communal ones. Most importantly, the
potent moral authority of the adult, internalised as the new super-
ego, is not about one's moral behaviour to others. It is not about
the development of a conscience, teaching a child to master what
Iris Murdoch called the 'fat relentless ego'. Instead there is a new
and persecutory super-ego based on achieving social dominance
through high achievement, bettering others and gaining a competitive edge. The parental imperative is to create a winner who
takes all. If you are not perfect, you are a *loser*.

Battle Hymn of the Tiger Mother caused great outrage. 'Parents
like Amy Chua are why Asian-Americans like me are in therapy',
wailed one much-discussed blog post, by a woman who had
suffered a similar parenting regime. Widely denounced for her
cruelty, Chua even received death threats. The uproar, however,
was by no means one-sided. Others cheered her on as an antidote
to the 'soft', permissive parenting norms based on trying to build
a child's self-esteem.

Where that support came from was revealing. The neoliberal
flagship, the *Wall Street Journal*, published the book's first extract
and gave it the headline 'Why Chinese Mothers Are Superior',
guaranteed to arouse not just American, post-GFC anxieties
about economic decline and China's rise, but also envy in the

toxic Motherwars territory of the US upper middle class parenting. The neoliberal think tank the American Enterprise Institute was enthusiastic. Charles Murray, the writer whose work on the alleged bell curve gave justification for entrenched African-American disadvantage, loved it: 'large numbers of talented children everywhere would profit from Chua's approach, and instead are frittering away their gifts—they're nice kids, not brats, but they are also self-indulgent and inclined to make excuses for themselves'. Even after reading the extract, two-thirds of the *WSJ* readers polled were in favour of the 'Demanding Asian' style of parenting over the 'Permissive Western' model. Chua was invited to speak to the global economic elites at Davos, where she addressed the World Economic Forum, extolling to a rapt audience the virtues of her harsh business of parenting and its two child products. This performance and the support she garnered in neoliberal circles tell us about the deeper cultural importance of Chua's book.

The novelist J.M. Coetzee once said that some words carry the freight of a whole civilisation. Surely this is true of the word 'mother'. In that one word come memories of our first love, of milk, nurture, and the distant memory of the sound of a mother's voice in the dark as we cried out to her at night for comfort. The words 'mother', 'mum', 'mom', '*mutte*', 'mama', remain a potent verbal reminder, a symbol of nurture and unconditional love. Yet here, in *Tiger Mother*, we see that symbol transformed. The phrase 'tiger mother' has all the comfort of the sound of a whip cracking.

Chua is an extreme case, but her mothering style exemplifies the hardnosed, hyper-competitive values of the new capitalism; the winner-take-all society has penetrated, colonised and transformed even intimate relations. Success, defined in conventional terms, *is everything*. Mothering is reduced to something like a business, a hard-driving process with a sharp eye on the bottom line. Chua's children are her products. They must be 'stars', bright and shining people who beat other people's children in the competitive game of life. We should be grateful to Chua for showing us with such unflinching, unvarnished honesty where we might be headed.

High Expectations: Poor Little Rich Kids

Soon Chua was spruiking a new book on what it takes to be successful, this time penned with husband Jed, highlighting the different qualities that they allege belong to high-achieving racial and cultural groups in the United States. Right about the same time, there was a headline in the *Australian*: 'Pushy Parents Damage Rich Kids'. The article reported an important new study from an Arizona University psychologist, Suniya Luthar.

Luthar, a professor of psychology and education, was reporting the latest in her studies dating back to the 1990s. Luthar stumbled upon her life's work by accident. In the 1990s she went looking for a control group—children of white, affluent, two-parent families from America's north-east—to compare poor, inner-city kids with. Most of the psychological research of 'at risk' children—those for whom there is a statistically higher risk of problems—has understandably concentrated on those in poverty.

What Luthar found stunned her. She expected these well-off youngsters, attending some of the best schools in the country, to have *fewer* problems. Instead, she found they had more. In a disturbing but counterintuitive trend, these well-off kids, who seemed to have it all, were more depressed and anxious, and had more problems with substance abuse, than inner-city children: 'Something fundamental has changed: evidence suggests the privileged young are much more vulnerable today than in previous generations.' Many other studies since Luthar's early work, as well as her own further research, have confirmed her conclusions. In late 2013 Luthar reported her latest findings in the *Journal of Development and Psychopathology*, in an article entitled 'I Can, Therefore I Must: Fragility in the Upper Middle Class'.

Depression and anxiety occurred at twice the rate for children in families earning over US$170 000, along with cheating in school work, binge drinking and substance abuse. So why all the problems among these children of privilege? 'The evidence,' Luthar says, 'all points to one cause: pressure for high octane achievement.' These children are expected to excel at everything. This results in a 'crippling' fear of failure. Little wonder then that these children suffer from depression and resort to substance abuse to relieve the 'relentless sense of pressure'. It is critical to note that the pressure to succeed comes not just from parents but as much, if not more, from outside the family. Schools, coaches and arts teachers, for example, can be highly invested in the performers' star status, setting exacting and sometimes extreme standards in quests for their team's distinction at district, county and state levels.

Luthar is unusual in refusing to simply blame parents for inculcating the idea that success is the measure of all things. She is right. After all, modern society immerses children in institutions and their peer group—day care through to university—from a very early age. Typically children spend more time with peers in such settings than with their families. Schools are intensely aware that competition for higher education places is fierce, because many more children now attempt to get there than in previous generations: 'by secondary school, these youth think there is one path to happiness—having money—which in turn requires attend-ing a prestigious university.' Top-tier colleges have received double or treble the applicants over the past five years. These children of the affluent, post-GFC, are for the first time in generations *less* likely to do better economically than their parents. Yet one boy said, 'I want to make what my dad does, so I must get into Wharton. By 30 or 35, I should be making at least a quarter of a million a year.'

There has been a profound shift towards materialism: in 1967, 86 per cent of US freshmen rated 'developing a meaningful philosophy of life' as an essential life goal. In 2004, only 42 per cent of freshmen felt the same. Instead, over the time period, values such as 'being well off financially' and 'attaining prestigious jobs' rose equivalently in importance. The desire for fame also rose dramatically. The outcome is that children become extremely orientated to competition for star status, and begin to treat themselves as marketable commodities. They become walking résumés, focused on what makes them look good on paper.

Parents make 'excessive demands', according to Luthar, which are 'over the top'. Children have to be not just high achievers but, like Chua's children, 'stars'. Yet Chua, at least, was a constant presence in her children's lives. In Luthar's study, these affluent children had money and access to cars, and were more frequently left at home alone after seventh grade than similar-aged children in less affluent groups. If both parents had demanding careers, but little in the way of family-friendly workplaces, an ideology of 'self-care', consistent with the core neoliberal value of self-sufficiency, can take the place of parental presence. In reality this 'laissez-faire' monitoring was more likely to lead to vulnerability; to problems like depression, anxiety and involvement with drugs.

The parenting style among some of Luthar's subjects is a paradoxical one: punitive attitudes around success in competition, but lax attitudes to supervision, and permissiveness around moral conduct. Surprisingly, a 'non trivial' number of teenagers said they would 'face few repercussions' if parents found excessive substance abuse, and even that parents would 'actively bail them out if discovered by authorities'. Children often scored high on the perception of parental criticism, but the nature of the criticism was revealing. It was about the quest for perfection in performance. It was not about their moral character or how they behaved with others; hence their 'self-worth rests largely—perilously—on achieving and maintaining "star status"'. When these children go off the rails, Luthar says, there is a plea: 'Please give me a break. I can't handle this all.' Competitiveness can undermine the important solidarity of adolescent friendship: 'After every test I've taken someone has asked me how I did,' one child said, 'and to be honest, I've asked the same myself ... I don't particularly like the notion of competing but I do want to get into certain schools and to win certain awards.' This endless ranking of each other means core questions of identity in adolescence become 'What happens to me if I fall behind? I'll be worth *nothing*.'

Gender shapes how a child will experience the toxic aspects of affluence. Girls, to whom care obligations have traditionally fallen, find themselves in a double bind. Old assumptions are not so much displaced as slotted in alongside the new. Like their mothers, girls are meant to compete in the traditionally male domains, adopting the hard-driving qualities it takes to succeed. But they're also simultaneously meant to compete on traditional female turf: being pretty, polite, likeable and popular. For all the children in Luthar's studies, those rated as more attractive were more popular. But for girls, this effect was twice as strong. 'Daughters of the rich, therefore, strive for effortless perfection—which is ... ultimately soul-draining.' The fallout is 'multiple forms of maladjustment', about which Luthar says drily, 'They have it all.'

Luthar mapped the same demographic shown by Twenge and Campbell to have higher and rising scores of narcissism than previous generations. She found that 'narcissistic exhibitionism scores were twice the average across a more diverse sample'. Boys also show characteristics consistent with greater narcissism; pursuing alpha male status, they are 'disturbingly preoccupied with gaining power in the peer group, which becomes tied, by late adolescence, to grandstanding via money and sex'. Substance abuse is seen as 'the "cool factor"'. Such values mean 'limited compassion and kindness', and attitudes to women that can be as chauvinistic as they are lacking in empathy. Being a 'baller'— someone whose high status in society has been earned by one's possession of 'game' (using girls for sex)—was seen by some of Luthar's male subjects as desirable. The excessive valuing of competition undermined for these affluent children one of the most important aspects of life, the deep social connectedness of friendship. 'We never talk about it openly,' one child said, 'but we're constantly weighing our own chances of beating them and getting in.' More cheating occurs too: in 2013, Harvard University reported expelling seventy students (a quarter of a lecture class) in 'its largest cheating scandal in history'.

Parents themselves could be struggling; long working hours for fathers left many mothers, both in and out of the paid workforce, unsupported and isolated in their task of childrearing. After-school and extra-curricular activities can simply add demands to an already busy schedule, and eat into relaxed and nurturing family time, where feelings and anxieties can be heard and processed. Home can seem less a haven in a heartless world than Grand Central at peak hour, all moving trains headed in different directions.

The very idea of 'quality time', sociologist Arlie Hochschild says,

> is a way of transferring the cult of efficiency from office to home. Instead of nine hours a day with a child, we declare ourselves capable of getting the 'same result' with one more intensely focused total quality hour … our family bonds are being recalibrated to achieve greater productivity in less time.

We should care about such children and their parents, Luthar says, not only for their own sake, but because their values and life patterns have a disproportionate influence over the generations to come, in all walks of life: 'At a societal level, people who are unhappy and have a fragile sense of self can be more acquisitive than philanthropic, more focused on gaining more for themselves than on improving the lot of others.' Or more narcissistic.

Canadian Member of Parliament Chrystia Freeland put her finger on the nub of the problem: 'the truth is these parents or children are responding rationally to a hyper-competitive world economy ... subject to increasingly fierce winner-take-all forces, which means the winners' circle is ever smaller, and the value of winning is ever higher.'

Freeland is right. John Gray, writing in *Psychology Today*, adds an important factor. Alongside the rise in adult-controlled, structured and often competitive activities, there has been a decline in unstructured free play. After all, playmates are 'on an equal footing' and do not treat you as better than others, as precious or in need of special treatment. Behave like a prince or princess and your ego is likely to be punctured by being tossed out of the game. Free, unstructured play helps children to learn how to control their emotions in order to get along with others. They must learn to modify any tendencies to imperiousness if they want to stay in the game.

Gray is saying something important. Play *is* essential. Childhood is now increasingly seen as preparation for something else, where children are better off in structured institutional settings from infancy, where investment in brain cells now brings later returns. New parental anxieties centre, from infancy onwards, on preparation for success at a working life. And in that we can see how the imperatives and values of the more visible economy are transforming how many of us see and act in the shadow world of care. Childhood has become *work*.

Howareyoubusy? The new sacred of work

The astute Australian commentator Hugh Mackay has noticed that Australians have developed a new way of greeting each other. Whereas before it was 'How are you going? All right?' now it is 'How are you, busy?' Busyness, he says, 'is the new badge of honour, if you're not busy you must be dead, or on the scrapheap. If you're not busy you must have fallen victim to the demon drink or gone to the dogs. Not busy? Good grief, what a loser.' It is usually asked so quickly—we are, after all, so busy we do not have the time to spend on these questions—that it is said in a rush, the words run together as *Howareyoubusy?*

In my grandparents' era, both parents worked hard, but the gender division of labour and fewer material expectations meant 'only' forty hours of paid work for the family were done each week. In total, they did about a hundred hours of paid and unpaid labour: fifty hours of unpaid housework and care by my grandmother, forty hours of paid work and ten of unpaid household labour by my grandfather. Now both parents are more likely to work outside the home: 59.1 per cent of Australian parents with children under fifteen do so. Australians also work longer hours. Alongside the United States and New Zealand, Australia now puts in among the longest hours of the OECD nations. More than one-fifth of workers work long hours. In contrast, in social democratic Sweden and Finland, the figure is less than 5 per cent. France has a 35-hour week. Since 1978, the percentage of the Australian workforce working between forty-five and sixty hours has increased by almost 100 per cent. The 'land of the long weekend' has been rapidly transformed. The result is a whole new outlook on time. The new sense of time is related to hierarchies of paid labour and the old idea that time is money. The higher the financial remuneration, the more a day at the beach or caring for your family might cost you. If you are a top-flight business executive or working in finance, or a highly paid professional, you are busy. If you work part time, or ordinary hours, let alone if you are outside the paid workforce doing care work, achieving the much-desired 'busy' state is less certain. Having 'time on your hands' is the mark of a 'loser', to use the harsh designation attached to the unemployed. To be working and managing a family is increasingly accompanied by boasts of busyness, 'juggling', keeping many balls in the air. Being outside the labour force, even if working very hard caring for a needy infant or old person, you have the whiff of idleness, and lack of productivity; the insinuation of parasitism, passivity and 'doing nothing' hangs shamefully over you; you are not busy. Even retirees, who, one might think, have earned their leisure after a long working life, seem anxious to defend themselves against the charge of not working, as discussions mount over raising the retirement age. 'I've never been busier,' said one new retiree to me defensively, listing a punishing round of social activities and hobbies.

What Mackay captures is a new social norm based on a deeper structural aspect of the new capitalism: paid work has been given an enchanted value. It is a new kind of sacred, especially among elites—people who seem to live for work rather than work in order to live. As Ulrich Beck writes in *The Brave New World of Work*, the 'dominion of work' has triumphed to the exclusion of all else. It is unhindered 'to such an extent', Beck argues, 'that almost no alternative remains ... only those who work are truly human'. This may sound extreme, but look at what two powerful male representatives of the Zeitgeist in Australia have said about work. One might think that Don Edgar, former head of the Australian Institute of Family Studies, could be counted on to put forward the value of the loving but unpaid care work families do. But no: 'We have to work, to make us fully human.' In 2009, the tabloid headline 'Treasury Gets Tough on Bludging Soccer Mums' expanded to report that Ken Henry, then Treasury Secretary, had suggested cuts to family tax benefits for at-home mothers: 'Treasury ... has as its goal supporting a society that allows individuals *lives of value*.' He did not even genuflect towards the idea of choice. The economics columnist Ross Gittins noted bemusedly of Peter Costello's 2007 Budget, in an opinion piece entitled 'Work: Less an Ethic, More an Order', that it was all about 'Work. Work and more work. The budget was obsessed by work. Those who aren't working, should be. Those who *are* working, aren't working hard enough. And those considering retirement should resist the temptation.'

In 2014, the discussion has intensified, with new preoccupations about keeping older citizens in work until they are seventy years of age, and getting more mothers of young children to work. At the centre of this new emphasis on work is a growing intergenerational economic problem for many countries: the large baby boomer cohort is reaching or already in their sixties, but due to their own lower birth rates, they will be supported in old age by the taxes of a much smaller group of workers. As a consequence, a whole new attitude has become entrenched in governments and international bodies like the OECD, the World Bank and the International Monetary Fund, and among treasury officials around the world. It is what scholar Ann Orloff has called the 'farewell to maternalism', the withdrawal of old policies that supported maternal care. Now policy-makers, both conservatives as well as progressives, want women to work. It is not surprising that the simultaneous sacralisation and destabilising of work security has demanded a new family type, with female employment as a 'hedge fund' against the risk society. Women's paid work in 'flexible capitalism' is seen as a crucial family safety net and 'self-insurance' against the loss of a male earner. One OECD publication makes this particularly clear, declaring that 'social policies based on the male-breadwinner model of the family have become outmoded'. Because of this new emphasis, and the neoliberal definition of human worth as being based on work, only one voice from the vibrant feminist movement has been selected as 'representative'. Compared with Sheryl Sandberg, Anne-Marie Slaughter and Anne Summers, some of the most important voices working in the area of justice and the shadow world of care—Nancy Folbre, Eva Kittay, Sara Ruddick—are hardly known in the mainstream press.

Their voices are not those we usually associate with feminism. Rather only those concentrating on careers and the public realm are publicly understood to 'represent' feminist concerns. There is a reason. The prevailing culture is much more receptive to it. The women's movement's long-overdue struggle to open up equal opportunities in the workplace, as Australian academic Barbara Pocock argues, 'found its happy co-conspirator in a market greedy for women's labour, its "flexibility" and enthusiasm for the spending power of women's earnings. Of all of feminism's goals, entry to paid work has been the most compatible with the globalising market.' As Hochschild notes, for an increasing number of women too, the 'emotional magnets between home and workplace are in the process of being reversed'.

In this atmosphere it is hardly surprising that women might feel shame at being an at-home mother. One mother told a sociologist: 'For that six hours that they are at school, I don't sit down. I feel anxious. I have to be productive.' Men, too, as much as they are exhorted to do more at home, experience the devaluation of care; one 65-year-old man looking after his elderly mother said, 'If a man is caring for others, calling, shopping, visiting, it shows the world he has failed as a man.'

In the new capitalism, universal forms of regard coming from an older Christian culture—Weil's 'respect is due to the human being as such and is not a matter of degree'—are giving way to a near 'exclusive reliance' on the dignity and value bestowed by paid work. According to historians Linda Gordon and Nancy Fraser, the worker has become 'the universal social subject: everyone is expected to "work" and to be "self-supporting". Any adult not perceived as a worker shoulders a heavier burden of self-justification.'

The New Capitalism and the Survivor Ethic

One of the achievements of Richard Sennett's book *The Corrosion of Character* was to show that the new capitalism is not just a set of *economic* relations. It brings with it an accompanying *cultural logic*, with new social and intimate relations as a consequence, which in turn have an effect on forming new—worrying—ideals of character. Many of these changes propel us towards greater narcissism. A considerable amount of this narcissism centres on our identity at work. There is an old adage that on your deathbed you will never say, 'I wish I spent more time at the office.' Yet is this, especially among elites, really still true? The saying tugs us towards 'proper' priorities, reassuring us that neither work nor worldly success, but rather family, friends and love, ultimately matter. Few of us would disagree. Yet, watching contemporary behaviour, how many of us act as if it were true? If we take 'the office' not to represent just the humdrum location itself, but all work and, even more broadly, all our worldly accomplishments in life, we are rather more dependent on 'the office' than we care to admit. Workaholism has become a badge of honour. 'I work sixteen-hour days,' bragged a high-flying man whose wife was about to give birth. There was no sense that this might spell problems for their stated ideal of gender equality if he continued to work these long hours after the child's birth. A few years later they were divorced.

People compete over who has it hardest and have resentful bragging competitions over who works the longest hours. Australia has even instituted a 'Go Home on Time Day' to combat the new workaholic tendencies. Job insecurity has its effect too. One young woman working in the finance industry told me why she only took two weeks of vacation per year, and only one week at a time. If she was away from work longer, her job might not be there when she got back. Loyalty to one's worker was a thing of the past, and the new workplace, Sennett says, is marked by more fleeting relationships and 'the strength of weak ties'. In this hyper-competitive society, while CEOs are bestowed with astronomical salaries, the unemployed are humiliated by the charge of parasitism. The gloves are off.

239

As workplaces in the neoliberal era have become harsher environments, something very interesting happened in popular culture. New reality TV and game shows, like *The Weakest Link*, *The Mole*, *Dog Eat Dog*, *Survivor*, *Big Brother* and so on, have proliferated. All the games have an eerie similarity to the new workplace relations.

In the new TV shows there is not even honour among thieves. Forget fair play. The path to victory is via betrayal: forming short-term alliances with the 'team' before shafting former allies. Here, too, is a culture of 'no long-term'. The much hyped drama centres each week on which player will face expulsion. One by one, in rituals often involving abuse and humiliation, they are voted off. Self-interest is pursued shamelessly. Even lying and cheating are not out of bounds. Behaving badly fulfills the norms of the game—because the only thing that matters is winning. In the older ethos of sports, solidarity, trust, loyalty and the cooperation of teamwork were considered essential to success. Everybody put in, and everybody benefited. In such reality TV shows, there is 'teamwork' but with a twist. Housemates, tribes or teams work together to boost the stake. In reality, however, it's everyone for themselves. Everyone puts in, but only one individual benefits. As one host chanted triumphantly: 'It's tough, it's unfair, it's *Dog Eat Dog*!'

These games of the winner taking all bear an uncanny resemblance to the company executives who award themselves obscene bonuses just before going into receivership, while employees are shafted. Game contestants scream, shout, leap and applaud themselves in an ecstatic display whenever the prize money is mentioned. Greed is a kind of vocation. Meanwhile, the loser loses all. Even dignity. Old-fashioned games like *Sale of the Century* operated a little like unemployment benefits in the old welfare state. Losing players clutched consolation prizes like board games, which buffered against the indignity of failure. In the new games, compassion for the vanquished is a thing of the past. Losers are publicly humiliated with glee; it is part of the fun. In the game show *The Weakest Link*, the dominatrix host intoned coldly to the newly expelled: 'You are the weakest link. You go home with *nothing*. Take the Walk of Shame!' The newly ejected contestant then received an invitation to self-blame, rather like Tony Abbott's pious homilies to the unemployed. The loser's fate, in the game as well as in life, is a cautionary tale to remaining players.

Jokes, Freud observed long ago, bear a revealing relationship to our unconscious. Psychological tension over dark, uncomfortable matters lurking beneath the surface of polite society is released and defused by a joke. In games and sport, too, in the spirit of play, we face and defeat challenges confronting us in the more serious business of life. Popular culture is clearly playing with the harsher aspects of contemporary working life, and reflects the way our sensibility is being reshaped by the new capitalism. Instead of compassion and generosity towards vulnerability, the strong all too often 'take aim against the weak'. A kind of defensive narcissism, defined by survival of the fittest, has seeped into other aspects of contemporary life. Motorists living in inner cities around the world have begun to purchase ominous-sized SUV vehicles resembling armoured cars, with names like Outlander, Pathfinder, Wrangler, Trooper, Defender, Shogun Raider and Crossfire. 'Not only did the popularity of SUVs suggest a preoccupation with looking tough,' sociologist Richard Wilkinson notes, 'it also reflected growing mistrust, and the need to feel safe from others.'

The theme of mistrust and self-defence also shows up in women's changing sense of self. In Hochschild's account of the 'cool modern' ideal of self in contemporary women's advice books, she found a pronounced shift from an older traditional self, embedded in relationships with others, however hierarchical, to a new and very different ideal. Now the self is conceptualised as a solo enterprise. Women are advised against depending on others, and the virtues of emotional and financial self-sufficiency are extolled. The new ideal is a 'post-modern cowgirl', the contemporary female version of the old male fantasy of the American cowboy who lives 'alone, detached, roaming free with his horse', free of any permanent ties or responsibilities, unattached to any other human being.

Of particular interest is a new attitude towards dependency, in themselves and others. Hochschild found that advice books depicted any emotional needs within oneself, or the need when ill to be taken care of, as frightening examples of weakness. Acting as canny emotional investment counsellors, they advise against getting involved with needy people, and caution against reliance on others. Encouraged to 'rely on emotional asceticism', women should 'expect to give and receive surprisingly little love from other human beings'.

This defensive narcissism arises from a conception of self as a *survivor* in a regime of threat and uncertainty. The survivor self has her wits about her, is alert to danger and the main chance, relying on no one. 'The only person you can rely on is yourself,' is the bleak counsel of the mother to her daughter in the film *American Beauty*. 'Lead weights in the worker's saddle bags' was how former treasurer Wayne Swan described family responsibilities. The survivor self cannot allow the vulnerability of dependency.

The whole neoliberal trope about self-sufficiency carries overtones of the narcissist who doesn't think he needs to rely on other human beings. In truth, human beings are neither totally independent nor totally dependent. As psychiatrist John Bowlby once said, 'the truly self-reliant person proves to be by no means as independent as cultural stereotypes suppose'; in adult life a healthy self-reliance includes the capability of depending on others when needed. Across a lifespan of childhood, adulthood, sickness and old age, every person will be dependent and independent, reliant

on others and relied upon, vulnerable and strong. Given that—
and the fact that the ideal of independence and self-sufficiency can
only be achieved by the very few—we should relinquish our false
opposition of independence and dependency, and instead talk of
human interdependence. Care in such a world would not be seen
as time taken from more important activities, but a natural part of
the very fabric of existence.

In the short term, a society that punishes vulnerability and
penalises care can survive. In the long term, many potential caregivers will begin to recognise what is valued, where benefits are
directed, and where the care penalty lies. The problem, according
to Folbre, is that we are increasingly creating a world not just with
a new 'economic environment' but also a 'new social ecology', one
where 'individualistic competition for wealth offers no rewards
for the work of care'.

Care, however, need not only be about people. Robert
Macfarlane, the environmental writer, points to how much the
moral philosopher Iris Murdoch's thinking about love and care
could be also applied to the environment:

> 'Attention', Murdoch proposed, is an especially vigilant
> kind of 'looking'. When we exercise a care of attention
> towards a person, we note their gestures, their tones of
> voice, their facial expressions, their turns of phrase and
> thought. In this way, by interpreting these signs, we pro-
> ceed an important distance towards understanding the
> hopes, wishes and needs of that person. This 'attention',
> Murdoch noted, is the most basic and indispensable form
> of moral work. It is 'effortful', but its rewards are immense.
> For this attention, she memorably wrote, 'teaches us how
> real things can be looked at and loved without being seized
> and used, without being appropriated into the greedy
> organism of the self'.

Could we not give such attention to our non-human environment, to the habitat we all depend upon? Given the impending
catastrophe of climate change, surely he is right.

Chapter 10

Narcissism and the Commons

But the fear of death grew ever darker upon them, and ... those that lived turned the more eagerly to pleasure and revelry, desiring ever more goods and riches.

J.R.R. Tolkien

THE AUSTRALIAN SUMMER of 2013–14 was one of the hottest and driest on record. My specially purchased iPhone pinged regularly and alarmingly with fire alerts, warnings from the Country Fire Authority of new fires breaking out all around us. Since 7 February 2009, now called Black Saturday, everything has changed. On that terrible day, 173 people died in fires that raged across Victoria. One hundred and twenty of those deaths occurred just to our north, in the most deadly firestorm, which burned from Kilmore through Strathewen and St Andrews to Kinglake. Whole townships were destroyed, leaving behind horrifying blast zones resembling bombsites. In Marysville, only fourteen houses were left standing. Around the state, 2000 homes burned down. The amount of heat released from the 400 fires was the equivalent of 1500 Hiroshimas. Warnings are now much better than in 2009. We hear no more of foolish slogans such as 'Houses protect people and people protect houses'. The official policy has changed from Stay and Defend to a much wiser, if bleaker one: Leave and Live.

In 2013, the record-breaking temperatures required a whole new colour chart to be registered. In the same year, the CSIRO confirmed that Australia was getting hotter: average temperatures have risen almost one degree since 1910. Heatwaves are more frequent and more intense, and so too are the inevitable fires that follow them.

It seems astonishing to recall that in childhood summer used to be, even in the country, a time of ease, of holidays, a welcome end to the year's work, a chance for dreaming, relaxation, forgetfulness and even joy. Country people now talk of experiencing summer differently. Our consciousness has changed; now the threat of fire presses upon it. Summer is a grim time of anxious vigilance, on high alert, of watching, waiting, watching, waiting, until the season is over. Country Victorians are hardly alone, as all over Australia, and all over the world, more extreme weather events multiply with devastating effects, like the 2013 typhoon in the Philippines.

Climate change is not a *future* threat. It is already here.

* * *

'Why,' asks social theorist Ulrich Beck, 'is there no storming of the Bastille because of the environmental destruction threatening mankind, why no Red October of ecology?' The problem, as he sees it, is that dealing with climate change 'would require the public to loosen their attachments to their lifestyles, consumption habits and social status'. Hannah Arendt once said about another catastrophe, the totalitarianism that overtook the twentieth century:

All this was real enough as it took place in the public, there was nothing secret or mysterious about it. Yet many of these events were mysterious to people, by no means visible, for until the very moment when catastrophe overtook everything and everybody, it was covered up not by realities but by the highly efficient talk and double talk of nearly all the official representatives who, without interruption and in many ingenious variations explained away unpleasant facts and justified concerns.

As I argued in my essay 'Turning the Sky White', in *State of the Nation*, we are now at another globally historical moment when the catastrophe of climate change threatens to overtake everything and everybody. There is nothing 'secret or mysterious' about it, yet it is obscured by camouflage from the public realm, the reality covered up by the highly efficient doubletalk of governments explaining away unpalatable facts.

The former Labor government was preparing to allow huge new coalfields to open up in Queensland's Galilee Basin. Now, with the Abbott government, all brakes are off on such developments. What matters is the illusion, a reality carefully constructed of 'doing something'—like Abbott's Direct Action—when we are in fact doing almost nothing, or nothing that really matters.

This camouflage extends beyond that used by the 'establishment', as Arendt called it. Popular culture, in its relentless embrace of the addictions of consumerism, seduces ordinary people. It also tempts them to be complicit in the looming catastrophe, to be in denial about the reality of their consumption and about climate change.

In his *States of Denial: Knowing about Atrocities and Suffering* Stanley Cohen draws on an illuminating moment in a Saul Bellow novel. One of the characters, a doctor, is facing imminent death: 'Did he know this? Of course he did. He was a physician so he must know. But he was human, so he could arrange many things. Both knowing and not-knowing—one of those frequent human arrangements.'

'A frequent human arrangement indeed,' remarks Cohen. It is this fertile soil of ambiguity, of both knowing and not knowing, in which denial flourishes: 'we are vaguely aware of choosing not to look at the facts, but not quite conscious of what it is that we are evading.'

The 'facts' on climate change could not be clearer. There is a consensus among the climate scientists on the International Panel on Climate Change that human activity, especially burning fossil fuels, is contributing to climate change and global warming. While there may be differences in the estimates of the timing of the effects of climate change, there is a scientific consensus about the threat to the planet of warming. There is overwhelming evidence that we need to act to reduce emissions, that we need to act now, and that we also urgently need leadership from the developed world—especially the United States but also Australia, Europe and the United Kingdom—who have contributed most of the carbon in the atmosphere by their emissions thus far, and whose wealth and technological sophistication mean they are best able to make the necessary changes. And yet as the situation has worsened, so too has the politics of irrationalism. The newly elected Abbott government—led by a man who once declared climate science 'crap'—has scrapped funding for the Climate Commission, put a denialist, Dick Warburton, in charge of a major review of renewable energy, and promised to repeal the modest carbon tax as a major election plank. At a time when we need to leave coal in the ground, if we want to meet the necessary targets to avoid a catastrophic increase in global temperatures higher than 2 degrees, new coal fields are opening up and it is business as usual on behalf of the powerful fossil fuel lobby. The problem is much larger than this government, however.

In Anglo-American societies especially—those most committed to a neoliberal ideology—even as the evidence daily mounts,
belief in, or commitment to doing something about, climate
change has been getting weaker. Even as the imperilled planet
grows closer to the tipping point of no return, climate change
denialism has been on the rise. Overall, US citizens' belief in
global warming has declined since the mid-2000s. In Australia,
in January 2014, a CSIRO survey showed more than 80 per cent
of respondents thought climate change was happening, similar to
previous surveys. On average, respondents estimated that human
activity accounted for about 62 per cent of changes to the climate.
Only a small number of people—8 per cent—believed climate
change was not happening. However, this small group vastly
overestimated the number of Australians they thought shared
their views. People who disagreed with the denialists also believed
denial was more widespread than it is, no doubt fuelled by the
prominence given to these views by Murdoch-owned media.

People also overestimated how much they did, compared
with others. More than 90 per cent of respondents estimated
they engaged in the same or more environmentally responsible
behaviours than other Australians. Less than 7 per cent thought
they did less than other Australians. Even of the people doing
very little, only 10 per cent of them thought they did less than
the average Australian. The CSIRO found that direct experience
of climate change, feelings of ethical and moral responsibility
for the environment, and personal relevance were the strongest
predictors of behaviour.

With widespread belief in climate change, how do we explain
the election of the Abbott government and public passivity over
their dismantling of climate change policy? Most crucially, the
survey showed that in Australia climate change 'ranks low in
importance when compared to other concerns. Respondents
ranked climate change as the 14th most important concern among

16 general concerns, and 7th out of 8 environmental concerns.' Such a combination of high belief in climate change and denial or passivity leading to inaction needs explaining.

One explanation is simply the sense that this is too large for human beings to cope with. What can *I* do? Too large and too difficult to contemplate and comprehend; the doctor in Bellow's novel was evading what was unbearable: the stark truth of his own death. In her arresting book *Living in Denial: Climate Change, Emotions and Everyday Life*, Kari Norgaard gives a sensitive and nuanced account of how denial in everyday life operates with respect to the looming threat of climate change. She also shows how the people she interviewed resorted to cognitive dissonance, defined by Inga Clendinnen as 'an uncomfortable condition as a mind veers and twists as it strives to navigate between essential but mutually incompatible beliefs'. Rather than admit to the inconsistency, people preserve a sense of self-worth by denying the consequences of their behaviour.

Consider, too, the notion of the self-serving bias. People almost universally think of themselves as a little better than they are, and they do not respond rationally but irrationally to the facts, distorting perceptions and rationalising to preserve a favourable sense of self. Usually moral action carries with it a financial cost, as it does in this case: a carbon tax, or higher electricity prices, or the unpleasant prospect of reducing consumption. Moral self-enhancement—the selective presentation of self in everyday life as being virtuous—is one effort at gaining the social kudos of appearing moral while actually being self-interested. Or gaining the social credit for moral behaviour while not paying the cost of moral action.

The many fine scholars studying narcissism have shown that these 'ordinary' forms of self-enhancement and the inability to face the truth of things are much worse in people who have a more narcissistic disposition. For example, even among people they know, they will self-enhance and distort reality to a degree that offends their relationship partners. Moreover, they discern threat to their desired superiority even in innocuous or neutral statements. Criticism is more likely to provoke rage, as the threatened egotist scrambles for the higher ground to stand on. In the long trail of furious comments on almost any article claiming there is climate change, there is a predominance of men, and the degree of rage displayed is startling. Why? Rage is a hot emotion, as we have seen, usually resulting from a threatened ego, when someone feels they are not getting the respect they deserve. Could rising levels of narcissism, and a more narcissistic culture, be in play here?

At the heart of narcissism is hubris. This hubris is not just pride and self-confidence; a grandiose, self-enhancing image of oneself can also extend to a group—one's political tribe or nation. It depends on denial, distorting and representing things falsely, avoiding the sobriety of the reality principle and the pain of truthfulness. By no means does such hubris reside exclusively on the political Right. Let's briefly consider for a moment the hubris displayed by the political Left over the utopian project of communism. In the late 1970s, for example, the murderous nature of the Cambodian revolution was clear to anyone who wanted to look. Yet the catastrophic extent of Pol Pot's killing fields was continually disputed, even derided, among a large swathe of left-wing intelligentsia as either a CIA fabrication or a product of the fevered imagination of anti-communist scaremongers—a terrible, direct example of the consequences of this hubris and the distorting effects of ideology. One young academic I knew so fervently believed in the glorious Kampuchean revolution that he encouraged several of his Cambodian students to return to support it. There was a strong possibility that they went back to a horrible death. Few on the Left really wanted to talk about the case of the young, pro–Pol Pot academic or the fate of his students. Anyone who pointed to their likely fate was resented. The whole tragedy did not dent their imperturbable air of piety in the slightest. No one wanted to wrestle to the end the larger question of how a well-meaning ideology could so distort reality. Finally one said, irritably but loftily, 'Well, at least *he* is on the side of humanity!', as if good intentions resolved the matter.

What was at stake for that young academic and many others was not the truth about the nature of communism. It was something much closer and more real to them—their own sense of self, their own identity. The deaths of millions in the far-off killing fields were experienced as quite unreal. What was much more real was not just the mundane immediacy of domestic politics, but the 'politics of the warm inner glow', as one sharp Labor politician put it. Belonging to a political tribe bestowed a moral superiority by virtue of its relationship to a transformative, utopian project. That identity—of 'being on the side of humanity'—offered a protective halo that floated above the holder, exonerating, absolving, excusing. To accept the truth about the regimes they were supporting would usher in chaos, a kind of mental agony as they reordered their universe. Instead they opted for self-preservation. Rather than submit to the humiliation of being wrong, they denied all the evidence and thereby maintained their high opinion of themselves. It was my first puzzling encounter with what we might call political narcissism.

This is a political version of Nietzsche's idea that 'when pride and memory collide, it is memory which yields' as in 'when ideology and truth collide, it is truth that yields'. Human beings struggle to make meaning and sense of an anarchic and savage universe. To base a whole life around certain values and beliefs and then to see your reality tilt sideways is terrifying. This kind of terror was caught in the post-hoc explanation once offered to me by a long-time communist. 'Oh,' he said, 'you see, you kept on believing because you felt you just couldn't be *that* far wrong.'

* * *

The God that Failed was the perfect title of one of the best books on the communist delusion. But could there be another ideal of progress gone wrong, another god that failed, another case where there was motivated cognition among those refusing to face the darkest of prospects, the destruction that will be wrought by climate change? What appears to be threatened is a sense of self and identity tied to a belief in the Promethean thrust of our technological civilisation and human omnipotence—our capacity and right to control nature. This goes far beyond any just pride in our technologically sophisticated civilisation, to a point of dangerous hubris about a utopian project.

Sociologists Riley Dunlap and Aaron McCright found that those least likely to deny the risks of climate change are women and non-whites. In contrast, denial is strongest among conservative white men, who are confident in their scientific knowledge (even when they are ignorant), have strong beliefs in technological progress and are sceptical about environmental risk. Dunlap and McCright call them 'Cool Dudes'.

Myanna Lahsen, an anthropologist, interviewed three such 'Cool Dudes'—denialists from the highly influential George C. Marshall Institute, an anti-environment think tank—for her seminal 2008 study, 'Experiences of Modernity in the Greenhouse: A Cultural Analysis of a Physicist "Trio" Supporting the Backlash against Global Warming'. Lahsen's analysis evolved from her observation that we tend to ignore the deeper sociocultural roots of debate—specifically, a backlash against the environmentalist movement's questioning of beliefs in progress and the power of humankind to subdue, master and exploit nature for mankind's benefit. Lahsen conducted 'remarkably frank' interviews with three prominent members of a 'physicist elite' that emerged during the heyday of the nuclear age—Frederick Seitz, Robert Jastrow and William Nierenberg from the Marshall Institute, who together have lent status and credibility to the anti–climate-change backlash—as well as with those who worked with them. She presents a fascinating picture of the interactional style, world view and ideology of these elite representatives of Dunlap and McCright's Cool Dudes.

Lahsen describes the trio's style as 'self-confident, sceptical and confrontational'. She argues that it is important that the trio rose to prominence during the nuclear age. After the splitting of the atom, with its strategic and military significance, physicists were at the apex of science. Reflecting an era when anything seemed possible, the trio showed a fervent belief in progress, in humans' ability to master technologies and create social benefits for all. They believed that knowledge and expertise could prevent risks and unintended side effects. The trio 'enjoyed great privileges' of 'status, influence and funding' and were 'honoured and empowered' as they 'dominated the science–government interface in the US for most of the twentieth century'.

In the 1970s, with the rise of the New Left, environmentalism and the anti-nuclear movement, the status of such pro-nuclear physicists was challenged. They were even depicted as 'a symbol of all that was wrong with society'. Lahsen showed that 'the trio's engagement with the backlash can, in part, be read as a reaction to a loss in privilege and a general decline of physics'. But her case gets even more interesting. A strong sense of a crisis in self and identity was precipitated for them by the growing environmental critiques of long-established views about the unquestioned benevolence of science and technology. Seitz, for example, wrote of his depression at the emergence of such critiques, which challenged the dominance of his (and the others') own world view, which is 'characterised by strong trust in science and technology as providers of solutions to problems ... [and] an understanding of science and progress that prevailed during the first half of the twentieth century'.

The counterpoint to masculine self-assertion and belief in the invulnerability of a world under the rubric of scientific progress is the repudiation of ideas of vulnerability, whether in human beings or nature. Both Nierenberg and Seitz 'implicitly reject[ed] the notion of nature as fragile'. Redolent of the 'confident white male effect', in interviews Nierenberg also rejected evidence on the link between melanoma and ultraviolet rays, and between DDT and human health effects, or on the dangers of nuclear power. Climate change was 'nothing serious'. 'No big effects' would happen for 150 years. Government intervention was not needed to ensure alternative energy technologies; societies should rely instead on the market and technological innovation.

The culture among physicists, studies have found, requires a macho (or highly competitive and confrontational) style of self-assertion, even bravado, while disdaining and being contemptuous of the work of others—or, one might say, given the centrality of aggression, competitiveness, arrogance and a need to feel superiority over others, a culture that rewards narcissistic behaviour rather than punishes it: the 'desired presentation of self can be characterised as competitive, haughty, and superficially nonconformist ... One group leader said that to convince others of the validity of one's work one had to have great self-confidence and be very "aggressive"; he added that one needed a "son-of-a-bitchiness"'.

Moreover, the weapons research facilities and laboratories where such physicists work 'inculcate an atmosphere of expert rationalism that encourages the suppression of emotions, learning not to attend to particular fears, feelings and questions, while also reviling the anti-nuclear environmental activists' 'emotionalism'.

There is hubris too: often the physicists expressed over-confidence in their knowledge about other scientific areas, even feeling themselves to be 'experts on everything', and not recognising or showing the humility to see the limits of their expertise. Such an outlook and style were reinforced by the centrality of physicists to the prestigious government nuclear weapons programs.

One climate scientist said of the trio:

> I know all of these guys. They are all good scientists—they were: They are all retired, and they have a kind of hubris—an arrogance ... [They think these] global environmental problems can be handled by a good physicist on a Friday afternoon over a beer. That is the attitude they have ... They downplay the science of any other community. And they are really arrogant.

Another physicist remarked that 'this is a problem with physicists': 'Scientists working in the area of climate change do not appreciate the Marshall Institute scientists' confident assertions about climate reality, especially when such large assertions categorically dismiss the importance of large research efforts in climate science.'

Nierenberg 'sweepingly dismissed' the work of thousands of top climate scientists around the world and the International Panel on Climate Change, as well as the central technology used in that discipline, which was not his own. Instead

> he favoured his simple 'back of the envelope' calculation, which placed the likely degree of warming at half a degree Celsius over the next century. He did not find it necessary to rely on 'those giant computers which have all those facts in them ... As far as I am concerned, the situation [predicting future climate change] is fairly simple. The science has been simple.'

The problem goes far beyond these purveyors of denialism, however. Given that the overwhelming consensus of scientific opinion is against these views, for denialism to spread, these scientists need popular support for their opinions, so as not to be marginalised. Conservative think tanks, media like Fox News, large corporations, industry associations and the fossil-fuel industry are all institutions that are dominated by conservative white males, according to Dunlap and McCright's research. This 'key vector of climate change denial' also has a wider receptive and significant audience in the Cool Dudes outside scientific elites, among the general public.

These Cool Dudes are an influential subset of men who are dismissive of environmental risk. They are also more likely to be 'system justifiers', who are content with the existing social and political order in which they have a dominant place. Studies show they are less democratic, less egalitarian and more hierarchical in outlook, and that they have more trust in the powers that be. Like the elite cadre of denialist scientists at the Marshall Institute, they show a degree of hubris. Such men are more likely to report that they understand global warming well, perhaps better than the climate scientists. On the basis of this hubris, almost half of these 'confident white men' believe that global warming will never happen. Only 19 per cent of other males and a tiny 7.4 per cent of female adults believe this. Conservative confident white males are three times more likely to be denialists. One theory is that such white males may see less risk in the world because they are less vulnerable in the world they have created. Women and non-white men, less system-identified men, less confident 'masters of the universe', are more likely to perceive risk. The Cool Dudes' denialism is a form of what Yale legal scholar Dan Kahan calls 'motivated cognition', 'through which people seek to deflect threats to identities they hold, and roles they occupy'. Kahan and his colleagues call this identity protective cognition. It serves to protect the status and self-esteem individuals receive from group membership. Just like those academic supporters of Pol Pot.

These are the wider preconditions and cultural context of climate change denial. However, none of the Cool Dudes have ever been studied *specifically* in relation to narcissism and the NPI. Even if Seitz, Nierenberg and Jastrow display no small measure of arrogance as leading denialists, even if conservative white men use 'motivated cognition' to repel information that threatens the status quo, we still need more *direct* evidence that rising levels of narcissism can affect willingness to act on climate change. As it turns out, that is just what we have.

Narcissism, the Commons and Climate Change

In an extraordinarily important contribution to the literature concerning narcissism, entitled *Understanding the Social Costs of Narcissism: The Case of the Tragedy of the Commons*, Keith Campbell and his colleagues present direct evidence of the impact of narcissism on the debates over climate change. Let's review for a moment the core elements of narcissism.

First, narcissists distort reality into a form that is conducive to self-enhancement; they do this by inflated global self-evaluations, their ratings of their performances of tasks, and in their fantasy life. Second, 'they need to seek out positive feedback and disparage or attack those who provide negative feedback'. Third, narcissists often perform badly over the long term, when their self-centeredness, their illusion-filled world and their fantasies of success interfere with the grinding hard work and ability to get on with colleagues usually entailed in achievements in the real world. Fourth, narcissists are willing to experience 'significant personal costs in the pursuit of status and esteem', trading 'interdependence and closeness for individual status and esteem'. They make a good impression first up, but over time diminish in likeability in the eyes of others. They make difficult relationship partners. These are people who favour short-term gain over long-term investments; when they have alienated a new crop of people, they just move on.

But what effect, ask Campbell and his co-authors, do these individual aspects of narcissism have on the broader social or common realm? To study the effect empirically, they tested those higher in traits of narcissism (subclinical, not as extreme as NPD) in relation to the classic 'commons dilemma'. It was a good choice. Garrett Hardin's 1968 essay in *Science* magazine, 'The Tragedy of the Commons', looked at the conflict between the common good and individual self-interest. To illustrate his point, he invented a hypothetical herdsman, whose self-interest is to add as many beasts as he can to his herd. Yet if every herdsman does this, then soon the land they all hold in common will be overgrazed and degraded. The way of life for the many will be destroyed by individual decisions for gain. The problem, said Hardin, is that there is no counter-principle that defends the common, shared heritage against the depredations of self-interest. Global warming might be seen as the fulfilment of Aristotle's dictum: 'That which is common to the greatest number has the least care bestowed upon it.'

What Campbell and his colleagues show is that rising levels of narcissism may well be a key component in the 'tragedy of the commons'. Take a few of the key aspects of narcissism: a competitive orientation that includes focusing on one's own needs at the expense of others, a willingness to exploit others for short-term gain and, consistent with an inflated sense of oneself as special, a sense of overweening entitlement. Consider, too, that narcissists are less motivated towards caring and lack empathy for others. Given all this, Campbell's study suggests that they may also be 'more willing to exploit the commons'.

Until this study, empirical evidence had indicated that individuals who are high in competitive and individualistic orientation, and those who report higher extrinsic values (success, fame, status, money, outward physical appearance, brand name goods and so on) are *more* likely to be willing to exploit the commons. In contrast, people who are empathetic towards those they share the commons with are *less* likely to exploit it. No study had directly examined narcissism's exact relation to exploiting the commons, though, or to an unwillingness to do something about climate change. Given that narcissism is all about self-interested behaviour when 'the needs of the self are pitted against the needs of others', the Campbell study set out to examine the possible connection. Subjects were tested using the NPI and the Rosenberg Self-Esteem Scale. Then they were given a resource dilemma over how much forest they could harvest, as part of a 'company', knowing that three other 'companies' were also going to harvest. They were told resources were finite; the forest was 200 hectares and they could choose how many hectares they might cut down.

The study found that narcissists reported greater acquisitiveness than non-narcissists. Narcissists, as predicted, harvested much more in the first round than non-narcissists, with male narcissists harvesting more than female ones. Narcissists simply harvested more than others. The reason was that they desired more profit, especially in the first round of harvesting, suggesting they approached the task with an already acquisitive outlook. Short term they got *more* timber, but long term they, like everyone else, got *less*, because they so rapidly depleted the common resource. A second study, this time with competitive dyads (pairs), also found that those with a higher percentage of narcissists 'rapidly destroyed the common resource'. They reliably harvested more than non-narcissists, and because they competed so hard against others, they rapidly depleted the forest. Narcissists scored a 'clear victory' over the others in their group or dyad, yet the cost of this victory was carried by others and the common resource, which suffered. The study's foreboding conclusion has alarming implications for climate change, given narcissism is on the rise: 'In all narcissism is linked to individual gain but also to significant costs ... those competing with the narcissists suffered the most, reporting the lowest harvest amounts. Second, the commons was exploited and destroyed more rapidly when narcissists were involved.'

Then the authors say something to pause over: they urge us to consider how swiftly and ruthlessly narcissism is dealt with in hunter-gatherer societies:

> It is plausible that the long-term good is for societies to develop strategies for minimizing narcissistic behaviour and reinforcing egalitarian behaviour. Indeed this may have been the case throughout human history, even to the extent that these strategies have been selected genetically.

Likewise, the authors of this study assert, modern society has its own version of this: dishonest CEOs who fill their own coffers at the expense of the company 'are fired, fined or imprisoned'.

If only this were always true! In reality, while in the hunter-gatherer society such character types were regarded as the enemy, in our society they can still be hailed as heroes. We continue to reward narcissistic behaviour in every field. Far too many destructive CEOs in the global financial crisis survived or retired with golden handshakes. Very little has been done to transform the rapaciousness of the ideology of greed that produced the GFC. Worse, given Campbell's clear evidence, growing narcissism will reduce our willingness to act on climate change. So much in our contemporary world constantly primes us for extrinsic values. Sociologists have a useful concept—'thinking as usual'—to describe the way patterns of thought and action tend to remain within the existing paradigms and trajectories of the civilisations from which they come. The omnipresent danger, the implication of a more narcissistic society, is that rather than change direction, questioning the way we live now, we will prefer a technological fix consistent with preserving the life of the consumer.

Just such a fix has emerged. The big new idea to avert the consequences of climate change is to play God, or to become what Clive Hamilton calls 'Earth Masters'. In the face of inevitable catastrophic warming from inaction on climate change, radical programs of geo-engineering are now being proposed. These would try to counteract global warming by changing the composition of the atmosphere by pouring huge quantities of sulphur into it. The idea derives from the observation that following a large volcanic eruption, the sulphurous ash that enters the atmosphere briefly cools the temperature of the earth slightly. Geo-engineering offers to emulate this process by human hand. Because there is no international law or treaty governing geo-engineering, any nation or combination of nations could decide to use the method unilaterally. No one really knows what will happen if we start sending jets into the air to spew sulphur, especially what such actions on a large scale might do. What is known, however, is that once you begin this course of action, you will have to continue it in perpetuity. And that one consequence would be that our sky—that beautiful blue, so deep in human consciousness, from religious practices in antiquity to the contemporary artistic images of our painters and words of our poets—would be transformed into a sulphurous, yellowish white.

There is a clear choice: social, economic and cultural change, or potentially dangerous and radical measures to continue business as usual. One path is to open ourselves to 'the winds of thinking', to the voices of those women and men in *this* dark time who face the inconvenient truth of climate change, and who as Arendt eloquently put it, can 'shake us from our sleep and make us fully awake and alive'. The other path is to be deaf to such voices, and instead reach for a solution from inside the Cool Dudes' paradigm. Rather than accept limits to our galloping ambitions for ever more freedom to consume energy and goods, the great advantage of geo-engineering, despite its extraordinary risk, is that such a course of action is within the existing trajectory and value system of continued high consumption and growth. Geo-engineering excites the Cool Dudes, despite it being a solution to a problem the confident white males deny exists. Others, too, are climbing on board. Bill Gates has already sunk an enormous amount of money into it. Clever scientists like David Keith in the Applied Physics Department at Harvard are working on it. 'Thinking as usual' involves technology solving all our problems for us, and the sense that Earth has no limits. Our Cool Dudes perpetuate such thinking. They are certain that our technological and industrial civilisation, as we know it, just couldn't be that far wrong.

* * *

But what if it's all a great big lie?

One of the really interesting things is that the underlying utilitarian assumption of the neoliberal era, of the consumer society as it spreads around the world, is that it brings greater happiness for the greatest number. What if … it never brings happiness, but its opposite? Could it be that we are engaging in a labour of Sisyphus, as Hamilton once put it, working in order to 'buy things we don't need with money we don't have in order to impress people we don't like'?

It is the strangest social conundrum. While all our efforts are directed towards increasing wealth, the research is extremely solid in showing that beyond a point of real deprivation, the correlation works in the opposite direction. When GDP increases and takes a country beyond poverty and bestows moderate prosperity, increasing income does indeed bring greater happiness. Poverty isn't good for anyone. Yet beyond that quite modest level, scholars time and again do *not* find that with ever greater material prosperity individuals or nations become happier. Instead the correlation starts to go into reverse, with people reporting more stress and psychological problems such as depression and anxiety, more obesity and more lifestyle diseases.

One of the most important scholars investigating the connection between levels of materialism and wellbeing, questioning the direction of consumer capitalism, is psychologist Tim Kasser. Kasser has consistently found that more materialism is linked to greater unhappiness. People who are more materialistic have lower personal wellbeing and life satisfaction, more depression and social anxiety, more troubling physical symptoms like headaches, and worse psychological health, such as personality disorders, including narcissism, compared with those who think materialistic pursuits are relatively unimportant. They value extrinsic goals as opposed to intrinsic ones. The more narcissistic they are, the more they want 'flashy clothes' and expensive possessions, and value being pretty or handsome. This is in contrast to wanting, for instance, 'to be a really good person', 'to do what God wants me to do', 'to understand myself'.

Materialistic people are more possessive, and are less generous, unwilling to share with others. They tend to covet what other people have. One study of adolescents' mental health showed those who were materialistic were one and a half times more likely to have narcissistic personality disorders. In Australia, Shaun Saunders and Don Munro found that a materialistic outlook in Australian students was associated with increased feelings of anger, anxiety and depression, and with decreased life satisfaction. Similar results were found both among teenagers and the elderly, in studies of China, Turkey, Australia, Canada and the United States.

Kasser's work links back into the origins of narcissism: he also found the link between narcissism, materialism and cold parenting combined with grandiose expectations. He discovered that the more insecure the child in their primary attachment relationships, the more susceptible they are to materialism. Mothers who are less nurturing and more likely to express hostility, disapproval or criticism have more insecure children who are more materialistic. He also found that children of divorce also may be more materialistic via the link of insecurity. But it is insecurity rather than any one family situation that is crucial. Children who grow up poor, with too little in the way of resources, can also be more materialistic. Kasser concludes that:

> When family environments poorly satisfy needs for security, many children respond by adopting a value system that emphasises wealth and possessions ... children who feel insecure about themselves may be more likely to look for approval from other people in order to feel better about themselves. Because they are exposed to frequent messages in society glorifying image, fame and wealth, they may strongly pursue materialistic aspirations as a way to obtain that approval.

Kasser also found that the more people endorse extrinsic values like fame, money, status, power, image—all the things narcissists prioritise—the worse their environmental attitudes are. This works at the individual and national level. Countries like the United States, for example, which prioritise wealth and power, have higher carbon emissions even after controlling for population size. People with higher levels of intrinsic values—such as helping other people, having close relationships and growing as a person—are far more likely to hold positive ecological values, and to engage in more sustainable environmental behaviours. Moreover, such values clash; it is hard to have close relationships or help other people while relentlessly pursuing fame and money. In an intriguing 2011 study, Kasser found that when American college students were shown a paragraph appealing to pro-social, intrinsic values and endorsing an identity based on those values, they were much more willing to do something about climate change. The paragraph designed to activate intrinsic values read:

> Now we would like to know more about you as an American. The American people are known around the world for their generosity, and their willingness to pull together in times of need. Americans are also known for their ideal of self-expression and personal development, and for their strong family values.

The next statement, designed to activate extrinsic values, read:

> Now we would like to know more about you as an American. The American people are known around the world for their focus on wealth, financial success, and material gain. Americans are also known for their competitiveness, and for their movie industry with its Hollywood ideals of beauty, celebrity and fame.

Then the students were told that 'researchers who believe that human activity is partially responsible for Earth's ecological problems have found that the behaviours and lifestyles listed below have a particularly important influence on the environment ... materialistic consumption and lifestyle choices ... people's "ecological footprint" may be too large for a sustainable planetary ecology.' They were asked to imagine themselves in charge of setting goals to produce more environmentally friendly behaviours and lifestyle choices, and asked to recommend specifics—for example, an average house size from 500 to 2500 square feet; how far average Americans should travel by car, 0–400 miles, and how often; whether they should consume locally grown and unprocessed produce or processed packaged goods from far away.

While the identity statements above did not explicitly refer to the environment or global warming, Kasser found a powerful effect. When primed with a consumer, capitalist, 'extrinsic' identity, emphasising fame, money and ambition, the ecological footprint they recommended was higher. Bigger houses, more private-car and air travel, more processed and packaged food from far away, and higher consumption patterns were favoured. In contrast, when students were primed with an 'intrinsic' American identity, emphasising caring for others, families and generosity, the ecological footprint they recommended was lower: smaller houses, less car and air travel, more public transport, and more locally grown produce. In an even more worrying finding, when students were primed with a non-specified, general American identity, the results were indistinguishable from the identity based on extrinsic, materialistic values.

These robust findings about the kind of identity we adopt and its impact on our behaviour raise the question of whether we should appeal to self-interest or to pro-social values when we urge people to reduce their ecological footprint. Kasser also found that when people were primed with thoughts about death by writing about it, they were more materialistic in how they might use the commons. In a 2009 study, Kasser raised this question of whether the 'green consumer' approach—emphasising extrinsic values of self-interest like financial savings, status and image, and contributions to economic growth—really helps our commitment to the environment. Given also that people claim, notwithstanding the seductions of a narcissistic society, that intrinsic identities are more important than extrinsic ones, 'it seems likely communications based on intrinsic values may be fundamentally more appealing than are extrinsically based communications'. What is certain is that those values are consistently shown to be associated with higher levels of wellbeing than the extrinsic values of consumer capitalism.

The myth of Narcissus, who becomes so enchanted by the beauty of his own image reflected in the water that he cannot bear to leave the lily pond, is well known. He pines away and dies of thirst. All that remains of the beautiful youth is the white flower, narcissus. Less well known is that the fate of Narcissus is delivered by Nemesis, the much feared Goddess of Divine Retribution. She has been angered by the cruelty of Narcissus. Nemesis punishes arrogance, hubris, those who commit crimes with impunity. She is the restorer of the proper order of things. In the form of climate change, Gaia, our planet, is presently delivering a warning, as if from Nemesis, the dark-faced goddess of balance and fortune, daughter of Justice, puncturer of hubris and greed, who restrains 'the frivolous insolences of mortals'. Will we, like Narcissus, go on gazing at the lily pond, enchanted and intoxicated by all that we see there, all those things of the consumer good life, which reflect us back so much larger and more dazzling than we really are, all the way to disaster?

Or will we recognise that the solution to the impending tragedy of the commons that is climate change is ultimately a *moral* issue, not just a problem with a *technical* solution. In the end, it relies not just on individual (or country) restraint, but on different values, and a different politics expressive of a new social and political imaginary. In Freud's era of bourgeois security, order and repression, civilisation's discontent—its longing and hunger—centred on what was denied: sexual freedom. Is it possible, in the era of the selfie, when narcissism reigns supreme, our longing and hunger might end up centering on *caritas*—loving kindness—altruism, generosity and care for each other and purposes larger than the self? It is these human values that are beginning to look precious.

Notes

Chapter One: The Chosen One

p. 3   **Paranoia is the self-cure for insignificance:** Adam Phillips, *Side Effects*, Hamish Hamilton, Penguin, London, 2006, pp. 265–73.

p. 4   **And he shot each person multiple times:** This account is compiled from many press and eyewitness accounts. Here is a small selection: Kathryn Westcott, 'Norway Attacks: How will Experts Assess the Killer's Mind?', *BBC News*, 26 July 2011; BBC News Eyewitness Report, 'Tell the Police to Hurry. People are Dying Here!', 23 July 2011, *BBC News*; Spiegel Online, 'The Trail of Evil: Can Europe's Populists Be Blamed for Anders Breivik's Crusade?', *Spiegel Online*, 1 August 2011; Guy Walters, 'Breivik is not a Madman', *New Statesman*, 27 July 2011.

p. 5   **Just before his crimes:** Breivik's manifesto can be accessed at <www.fas.org/programs/tap/_docs/2083_-_A_European_ Declaration_of_Independence.pdf> (accessed 2 June 2014).

p. 5   **As one of the bloggers on *PI-news* admitted:** Spiegel Online, 'The Trail of Evil'.

p. 7   **'I do not approve of the super-liberal …':** Daily Telegraph, 'Norway Killer, Anders Behring Breivik was a Mummy's boy', *Daily Telegraph*, 25 July 2011.

p. 7   **These carefully stage-managed photos were also posted on Facebook:** For images of the self-decorated Breivik from his Manifesto see BBC News, 'Profile: Anders Behring Breivik', *BBC News*, 12 May 2012. See also BBC News, '"Breivik Manifesto" details Chilling Attack Preparation', *BBC News*, 24 July 2011, quoting Breivik on feeling great before the massacre, intention to use prostitutes before the attack, and his 'perfect body' due to steroid use.

p. 8 **By his early twenties he had gambled in the stock market:** Richard Orange, 'Anders Breivik was Victim of "Blood Diamond" Scam', *Telegraph*, 30 May 2012.

p. 9 **'On this day, I was waging a one-man war …':** Spiegel Online, 'The Trail of Evil'.

p. 9 **They argued he was in a state of psychosis:** Daily Telegraph, 'Norway Considers Fresh Exam of Anders Behring Breivik', *Daily Telegraph*, 22 December 2011; BBC News, 'Norway Massacre: Breivik Declared Insane Manifesto', *BBC News*, 29 November 2011.

pp. 9–10 **For the victims' grieving families, it seemed:** Liss Goril Anda, 'Norwegian Disbelief at Breivik "Insanity"', *BBC News*, 29 November 2011.

p. 10 **This argument was perhaps best expressed in the e-book *On Utøya*:** Tad Tietze, Guy Rundle and Elizabeth Humphreys (eds), *On Utøya: Anders Breivik, Right Terror, Racism and Europe*, Elguta Press, 21 October 2011 (Kindle edition).

p. 12 **There was a much better case, she said:** Spiegel Online, 'The Trail of Evil'.

p. 13 **'Breivik must be a narcissist':** ibid.

pp. 13–4 **Psychologists have found that subjects:** Dennis E. Reidy, Amos Zeichner, Josh D. Foster and Marc A Martinez, 'Effects of Narcissistic Entitlement and Exploitativeness on Human Physical Aggression', *Personality and Individual Differences*, vol. 44, 2008, pp. 865–75. Narcissists also are the most aggressive and deliver the loudest blasts of aversive noise to someone who has shamed them by judging their performance harshly. See Sander Thomaes, Brad J. Bushman, Hedy Stegge and Tjeert Olthof, 'Trumping Shame by Blasts of Noise: Narcissism, Self-Esteem, Shame, and Aggression in Young Adolescents', *Child Development*, vol. 79, no. 6, November/December 2008, pp. 1792–1801.

p. 14 **He wrote a letter to several Norwegian newspapers:** Reuters, 'Norway Killer—"Insane" Diagnosis "Worse than Death"', *Reuters*, 4 April 2012.

p. 14 **The second and final psychiatric evaluation:** Richard Alleyne, 'Anders Breivik the Norwegian Mass Killer Found Sane', *Telegraph*, 24 August 2012.

p. 14 **Expert witness Ulrik Fredrik Malt:** Richard Orange, 'Anders Behring Breivik is Lying, not Delusional', *Daily Telegraph*, 11 June 2012; Lars Bevanger, 'Breivik Trial: Psychiatric Reports Scrutinised', *BBC News Europe*, 14 June 2012.

p. 14   **There seem to have been a number of:** Richard Orange, 'Anders Behring Breivik's Sister Warned Mother about his Behaviour Two Years Ago', *Telegraph*, 4 December 2011.

p. 15   **Wenche dismissed her friend's comments:** Spiegel Online, 'The Trail of Evil'.

p. 15   **Elisabeth was more blunt:** Mark Lewis and David Jolly, 'Norwegian Defends Shooting and Regrets Death Toll Wasn't Higher', *New York Times*, 19 April 2012.

p. 15   **He refused to eat anything she cooked:** Aage Borchgrevink, *A Norwegian Tragedy: Anders Behring Breivik and the Massacre on Utøya*, Polity Press, Cambridge, 2013 (English translation by Guy Puzey); Mark Lewis, 'Norwegian Mass Killer Breivik's Mother Reveals He Terrified Her when He was Just FOUR Years Old ... and Tried Kissing Her when He Moved Back Home Aged 27', *Mail Online*, 15 June 2012; Richard Orange, 'Anders Behring Breivik's Mother "Sexualised" Him when He was Four', *Telegraph*, 7 October 2012.

p. 17   **He was sufficiently neglected that social welfare workers:** Borchgrevink, *A Norwegian Tragedy*.

p. 17   **'He should have taken his own life, too ...':** Lucy Carne, 'Killer Should Have Shot Himself: Dad', *Courier Mail*, 26 July 2011 (my emphasis).

p. 19   **The proliferation of visual and auditory images:** Christopher Lasch, *The Culture of Narcissism: American Life in the Age of Diminishing Expectations*, W. W. Norton & Co., New York, 1991 (1979), p. 239.

p. 20   **Psychotherapist Eleanor Payson's:** Eleanor Payson, *The Wizard of Oz and Other Narcissists: Coping with the One-Way Relationship in Work, Love and Family*, Julian Day Publications, 2010 (Kindle edition).

p. 20   **In *Why Is It Always About You?*:** Sandy Hotchkiss, *Why Is it Always About You? The Seven Deadly Sins of Narcissism*, Simon & Schuster, New York, 2003.

p. 22   **'He was really intent ...':** Telegraph, 'Anders Behring Breivik "Asked for Band-Aid when Arrested"', *Telegraph*, 25 May 2012.

p. 23   **Describing his act as 'spectacular':** Helen Pidd, 'Remorseless and Baffling, Breivik's Testimony Leaves Norway no Wiser', *Guardian*, 18 April 2012.

Chapter Two: Just a Jerk?

p. 24   **'The narcissistic self is perpetually "under construction" ...':** Carolyn C. Morf and Frederick Rhodewalt, 'Unravelling the

Paradoxes of Narcissism: A Dynamic Self-Regulatory Processing Model', *Psychological Inquiry*, vol. 12, no. 4, 2001, pp. 177–96.

p. 24   **Yet the empirical data simply wasn't available back then:** Jean Twenge and W. Keith Campbell, *The Narcissism Epidemic: Living in the Age of Entitlement*, Free Press, New York, 2009, pp. 5–7. See also more the scholarly volume: W. Keith Campbell and Joshua D. Miller (eds), *The Handbook of Narcissism and Narcissistic Personality Disorder: Theoretical Approaches, Empirical Findings, and Treatments*, John Wiley & Sons, New Jersey, 2011.

p. 24   **Now young academics, Twenge and Campbell:** Discussed in Twenge and Campbell, *The Narcissism Epidemic*. See also Jean Twenge and W. Keith Campbell, 'Increases in Positive Self-Views Among High School Students: Birth Cohort Changes in Anticipated Performance, Self-Satisfaction, Self-liking, and Self-Competence', *Psychological Science*, vol. 19, November 2008, pp. 1082–6; J. Twenge, S. Konrath, J. D. Foster and W. Keith Campbell, 'Egos Inflating Over Time: A Cross-temporal Meta-analysis of the Narcissistic Personality Inventory', *Journal Of Personality*, vol. 76, no. 4, August 2008, pp. 875–901.

p. 25   **'It was then we realised we had hit a nerve':** Twenge and Campbell, *The Narcissism Epidemic*, p. 6.

p. 25   **'"Narcissist" is among our current favourites …':** Jan Hoffman, 'Here's Looking at Me, Kid', *New York Times*, 20 July 2008. This article is also cited in Twenge and Campbell, *The Narcissism Epidemic*, p. 3.

p. 25   **It is easy to see the phenomenon they were talking about:** Some of these examples are taken from Twenge and Campbell, others are my own.

p. 25   **Preston Sturges once quipped:** Preston Sturges, *A Great Moment*, Paramount Pictures, Los Angeles, 6 September 1944.

pp. 25–6 **Lena Dunham, the clever and creative writer:** Kase Wickman, 'Talking to Lena Dunham about being a "Girl"', *The Awl*, 6 April 2012.

p. 26   **In a seminal article:** Roy Baumeister, R. F. Smart and J. M. Boden, 'Relation of Threatened Egotism to Violence and Aggression: The Dark Side of High Self-Esteem', *Psychological Review*, vol. 103, no. 1, January 1996, pp. 5–33. See also Brad J. Bushman and Roy Baumeister, 'Threatened Egotism, Narcissism, Self-Esteem, and Direct and Displaced Aggression: Does Self-Love or Self-Hate Lead to Violence?', *Journal of Personality and Social Psychology*, vol. 75, no. 11, November 2006, pp. 219–29.

p. 27   **As Baumeister concluded acidly:** Baumeister, Smart and Boden, 'Relation of Threatened Egotism to Violence and Aggression: The Dark Side of High Self-Esteem'.

p. 27   **Think of the Wizard of Oz:** Eleanor Payson, *The Wizard of Oz and Other Narcissists*.

p. 28   **All the couch pillows were decorated with her photo:** Tina Dirmann, 'Paris Hilton's Higher Aims', *LA Times*, 30 May 2011.

p. 28   **Although she seems confident:** Twenge and Campbell, *The Narcissism Epidemic*, p. 25.

p. 29   **They focus on narcissists who are confident:** ibid., p. 26.

p. 29   **'"I have done that," says my memory …':** Friedrich Niestchke, *Beyond Good and Evil*, p. 91.

p. 30   **They are less concerned with accuracy:** Constantine Sedikides, W. Keith Campbell, Glenn D. Reeder, Andrew J. Elliot and Aiden P. Gregg, 'Do Others Bring Out the Worst in Narcissists? The Others Exist for Me Illusion', in Y. Kashima, M. Foddy and M. Platow (eds), *Self And Identity: Personal, Social and Symbolic*, Erlbaum, Mahwah, p. 104.

p. 30   **Academic psychologist Cordelia Fine:** Cordelia Fine, *A Mind Of Its Own: How Your Brain Distorts and Deceives*, Icon Books, Cambridge, 2007.

p. 30   **Their self-serving orientation:** Sedikides et al, 'Do Others Bring Out the Worst in Narcissists?', pp. 103–23.

p. 31   **They hog the conversational limelight:** The best and most serious analysis of widespread narcissism in conversation is in Charles Derber, *The Pursuit of Attention: Power And Ego in Everyday Life*, Oxford University Press, Oxford, 2000 (2nd edition). He links it to individualistic competition and lack of social support. It is also discussed widely in the popular psychology books.

p. 31   **Others bring out the worst in them:** Sedikides et al, 'Do Others Bring Out the Worst in Narcissists?', pp. 103–23.

p. 32   **Twenge and Campbell take aim:** Twenge and Campbell, *The Narcissism Epidemic*, p. 27.

p. 34   **But they are also 'materialistic …':** ibid., pp. 24–30.

p. 34   **Keith Campbell:** W. Keith Campbell, *When You Love a Man Who Loves Himself*, Casablanca, Sourcebooks, Illinois, 2005.

pp. 35–6   **'To understand narcissists' approach to relationships …':** Twenge and Campbell, *The Narcissism Epidemic*, p. 213.

p. 36   **… Sam Vaknin described as narcissistic supply:** Sam Vaknin, *Malignant Self-Love: Narcissism Revisited*, Narcissus Publications, Prague, 2007.

pp. 36–7 **Studies showed 'narcissistic men felt less empathy …':** ibid., p. 71.

p. 38 **Sociologist Zygmunt Bauman:** Zygmunt Bauman, *Post Modernity and Its Discontents*, Polity Press, Cambridge, 1997. See also Zygmunt Bauman, *Life in Fragments*, Polity Press, Cambridge, 1995.

p. 38 **'I don't think I am attached at all':** Twenge and Campbell, *The Narcissism Epidemic*, pp. 214–5.

p. 38 **'Overall, we've seen a massive increase …':** Sandy Smith, 'Narcissists Anonymous or the iGeneration', *Sydney Morning Herald*, 31 July 2012. Australians also debate this question. In the same piece, Dr Helen McGrath, a senior lecturer in the School of Education at Deakin University, disagreed with Wyn, arguing that younger generations were more narcissistic.

p. 39 **… not all US scholars agree:** K. H. Trzesniewski, M. B. Donnellan, and R. W. Robins, 'Do Today's Young People Really Think They Are So Extraordinary? An Examination of Secular Trends in Narcissism and Self-Enhancement', *Psychological Science*, vol. 19, no. 2, February 2008, pp. 181–8; J. M. Twenge and J. D. Foster, 'Birth Cohort Increases in Narcissistic Personality Traits Among American College Students, 1982–2009', *Science*, vol. 1, no. 1, January 2010, pp. 99–106; for counter view see Donnellan, Trzesniewski, and R. W. Robins, 'An Emerging Epidemic of Narcissim or Much Ado About Nothing?', *Journal of Research in Personality*, vol. 43, 2009, pp. 498–501, and B. W. Robert, G. Edmonds and E. Grijalva, 'It is Developmental Me Not Generation Me: Developmental Changes are More Important than Generational Changes in Narcissism', *Perspectives in Psychological Science*, vol. 5, no. 1, January 2010, pp. 97–102.

p. 39 **Even collectivist China:** see J. Twenge, 'Narcissism and Culture', in Campbell and Miller (eds), *The Handbook of Narcissism and Narcissistic Personality Disorder*, p. 204. Usually the United States ranks highest among nations in narcissism, but it has also been found to increase elsewhere, including in Norway; see H. E Nafstad, R. M. Blakar, E. Carlquist, J. M. Phelps and K. Rand-Hendriksen, 'Ideology and Power: The Influence of Current Neo-liberalism in Society', *Journal of Community and Applied Social Psychology*, vol. 17, 2007, pp. 313–27; and in China, V. S. Kwan, L. L. Kuang, and N. H. H. Hui, 'Identifying the Sources of Self-Esteem: The Mixed Medley and Benevolence, Merit, and Bias', *Self and Identity*, vol. 8, 2009, pp. 176–95.

p. 39   **By 2004–05, a national US survey:** J. Twenge, 'Narcissism and Culture', in Campbell and Miller (eds), *The Handbook of Narcissism and Narcissistic Personality Disorder*, p. 204.

p. 40   **Or, as psychologist Dan Kindlon says:** quoted in Twenge and Campbell, *The Narcissism Epidemic*, p. 76.

p. 40   **Preschoolers in the United States:** ibid., p. 77.

p. 41   **In one 1997 survey:** These figures cited in Jean Twenge, *Generation Me: Why Today's Americans Are More Confident, Assertive, Entitled—And More Miserable than Ever Before*, Simon & Schuster, New York, 2006, p. 87. She is citing figures from Walker J. Smith and Ann Clurman, *Rocking the Ages: The Yankelovitch Report on Generational Marketing*, HarperCollins, New York, 1997.

p. 41   **By 2006, 51 per cent:** Twenge and Campbell, *The Narcissism Epidemic*, p. 93.

p. 42   **The youngsters all returned home:** Robert Frank, *The Darwin Economy: Liberty, Competition and the Common Good*, Princeton University Press, Princeton, 2011, p. 60.

p. 43   **Against this infantile paradise:** Twenge and Campbell, *The Narcissism Epidemic*, p. 127.

p. 43   **In a British study:** L. J. Otway and V. L. Vignoles, 'Narcissism and Childhood Recollections: A Qualitative Test of Psychoanalytic Predications', *Personality and Social Psychology Bulletin*, vol. 32, 2006, pp. 104–16.

p. 44   **As well as tracking all the brash:** Twenge, *Generation Me*, p. 107.

p. 44   **'For many in GenMe ...':** ibid., p. 111.

p. 46   *Habits Of The Heart:* Robert N. Bellah, Richard Madsen, William M. Sullivan, Ann Swidler, and Steven M. Tipton, *Habits of the Heart: Individualism and Commitment in American Life*, University of California Press, Berkeley, 2008 edition, pp. 108–9.

p. 46   **'Offering praise has become a sort of panacea ...':** P. Bronson, 'How Not to Talk to the Kids: The Inverse Power of Praise', *New York Magazine*, 3 August 2007.

Chapter Three: Inside the Mask

p. 48   **'These children get what they do not need and do not get what they do need':** J. Fiscalini, 'Interpersonal Relations and the Problem of Narcissism', in J. Fiscalini and Alan Grey, *Narcissism and the Interpersonal Self*, Columbia University Press, New York, 1993,

p. 82. Fiscalini gives a brilliant account of three paths to narcissism, the 'shamed', 'spoiled' and 'special' child.

p. 48   **In the Age of the Brain, we are all Mr Spocks now:** Adam Gopnik, 'Mindless: The New Neuro-skeptics', *New Yorker*, 9 September 2013.

pp. 48–9   **The narcissist lacks the 'double-minded ...':** Simon Baron-Cohen, *Zero Degrees of Empathy: A New Theory of Human Cruelty*, Allen Lane, London, 2011, pp. 10ff.

p. 49   **In a striking result:** Lars Schulze et al, 'Gray Matter Abnormalities in Patients with Narcissistic Personality Disorder', *Journal of Psychiatric Research*, July 2013.

p. 49   **So even while snoozing:** Tong Sheng, Anahita Gheytanchi and Lisa Aziz-Zadeh, 'Default Network Deactivations are Correlated with Psychopathic Personality Traits', *PLoS One*, 7 September 2010; Laboratory Equipment, 'Narcissism Prevails in Sleep', *Laboratory Equipment*, 20 September 2010; Carl Marziali, 'No Rest for the Narcissist', *University of Southern California News*, 17 September 2010.

p. 49   **Or is it that they use their empathy circuit:** Given what Norman Doidge argues about the brain's plasticity, in Norman Doidge, *The Brain That Changes Itself: Stories of Personal Triumph from the Frontiers of Brain Science*, Penguin, London, 2007.

p. 51   **A narcissistic personality disorder:** American Psychiatric Association, *Diagnostic and Statistical Manual of Mental Disorders (DSM-5)*, American Psychiatric Publishing, Washington, pp. 669–72.

p. 52   **In those revisions:** Ronningstam is much more hopeful about the chances of positive and negative life events, age, therapy and other encounters to change the narcissist. Elsa Ronningstam, *Identifying and Understanding the Narcissistic Personality*, Oxford University Press, New York, 2005.

p. 52   **Like all of Freud's work, 'On Narcissism':** Sigmund Freud, 'On Narcissism: An Introduction' in Andrew P. Morrison (ed), *Essential Papers on Narcissism (Essential Papers in Psychoanalysis)*, New York University Press, New York, 1986, pp. 17–43.

p. 53   **The self was taken as the love object:** He thought some people treated their *own* body as if it is their object of desire.

p. 53   **For Freud, the great antidotes to neurosis:** Freud, 'On Narcissism: An Introduction', pp. 17–43.

p. 53   **'We must love in order not to fall ill ...':** ibid., p. 28.

p. 53   **This is the opposite of a narcissistic state:** ibid. (my emphasis).

p. 53   **'If there is too much self-love ...':** This pithy summation of Freud's view is a quote from Otto Kernberg, psychoanalyst and professor of psychiatry at Weill Cornell Medical College, in an interview with Susan Bridle. He goes on to question Freud's view: 'Now, the dominant psychoanalytic thinking is that the loving investment in self and in others occurs simultaneously and that under normal conditions, self-love and love of others go together. Those happy natures who have been treated well are at peace with self, can be very secure, love themselves and at the same time be very committed to others.' Otto Kernberg, 'The Sense of Self: An interview with Susan Bridle', *EnlightmentNext Magazine*.

p. 54   **Likewise criminals and comics fascinate us by holding away:** Freud, 'On Narcissism: An Introduction', p. 32.

p. 54   **'Women, especially if they grow up with good looks ...':** ibid., p. 31.

p. 54   **All modern research shows that both genders can be narcissistic:** The DSM-5 estimated between 50 and 75 per cent of NPD sufferers are male, American Psychiatric Association, *Diagnostic and Statistical Manual of Mental Disorders (DSM-5)*, p. 671. It is not argued that any disparity is innate. Rather that culture still encourages women to exhibit attributes like modesty, self-deprecation and being caring, while discouraging qualities of aggression. In contrast, males are encouraged from an early age towards agentic achievement orientation, independence, and aggression.

p. 55   **There was a small army of family women:** Elizabeth Lunbeck, *The Americanization of Narcissism*, Harvard University Press, Cambridge, 2014.

p. 56   **'Parental love ...':** Freud, 'On Narcissism: An Introduction', p. 34.

p. 56   **We should not confuse ordinary:** Neville Symington, *Narcissism: A New Theory*, Karnac Books, London, 1993. See also his brilliant essay, 'Narcissism and the Human Condition', in Neville Symington, *Emotion and Spirit*, Karnac Books, London, 1994, pp. 116–23.

p. 57   **One of the most famous and influential:** Heinz Kohut, *The Analysis of the Self: A Systematic Approach to the Psychoanalytic Treatment of Narcissistic Personality Disorders*, International Universities Press, New York, 1971. See also Heinz Kohut, *The Restoration of the Self*, International Universities Press, New York, 1977; Arnold Goldberg (ed), *The Psychology of the Self: A Casebook*, International Universities Press, New York, 1978; and a wonderful biography of him by Charles Strozier, *Heinz Kohut: The Making of a Psychoanalyst*, Other Press, New York, 2001.

p. 59   **Permitting regression and dependency:** Kohut was similar to Donald Winnicott, a British psychoanalyst, in this respect.

p. 59   **'It hurts when you are not treated the way you feel you deserve to be treated':** Glen Gabbard, *Psychodynamic Psychiatry in Clinical Practise*, American Psychiatric Publishing, Washington, 2005, p. 497. Gabbard has an illuminating discussion of narcissism and key theorists like Kohut and Kernberg. Gabbard also thinks that some of his patients do not fit into either Kohut or Kernberg's view of the failures in parental empathy, rather they are spoiled, indulged, treated in ways that cultivate grandiosity as special and gifted. Hence they are 'repeatedly shattered because others do not respond to them as their parents did' (ibid., p. 502).

p. 60   **'secret preciousness which made her vastly better than anyone else':** Kohut, *The Analysis of The Self*, pp. 116–8.

p. 60   **What struck Kohut was not so much the *content* of what she said:** ibid.

p. 61   **Often she would skip home from school:** ibid., also quoted in Strozier, *Heinz Kohut*, p. 208.

p. 62   **Kohut was 'invited to participate in the child's narcissistic pleasure and thus to confirm it':** Kohut, *The Analysis of The Self*, pp. 116–8.

p. 62   **'Diddle diddle ... dum ...':** Heinz Kohut, 'Forms and Transformations of Narcissism', in Morrison (ed), *Essential Papers on Narcissism*, p. 69.

p. 65   **'People get mad at me saying that I am a creative genius ...':** Kayne West, 'Kayne West: The Man, The Myth, The Legend Part 1', *Philly's Morning Show*, radio program, 25 November 2013.

p. 66   **He explained: 'You have these patients with severe distortions ...':** Chandra Rankin, 'An Interview with Otto Kernberg, MD', 2006. See also for my discussion, Otto Kernberg, 'Further Contributions to Treatment of Narcissistic Personalities', in Morrison (ed), *Essential Papers on Narcissism*, pp. 213–44; Otto Kernberg, *Borderline Conditions and Pathological Narcissism*, Aronson, London, 1975; M. Cohen, 'Love Relations, Normality and Pathology: Otto Kernberg', *Journal of American Academic Psychoanalysis*, vol. 28, 1995, pp. 181–4.

p. 66   **Pathological narcissism is an 'ego trip':** Kernberg, 'The Sense of Self: An Interview with Susan Bridle'.

p. 67   **'A good number of them ...':** Kernberg, 'Further Contributions to Treatment of Narcissistic Personalities', p. 220.

p. 67   **Instead of aspiring to acquire the qualities of admired others:** Kernberg, *Borderline Conditions and Pathological Narcissism*, p. 234.

pp. 67–8   **One of Kernberg's patients commented after many failed love relationships**: Otto Kernberg quoted in Gabbard, *Psychodynamic Psychiatry in Clinical Practise*, p. 494.

pp. 68–9   **Kernberg found that by two or three years old:** Kernberg, 'Further Contributions to Treatment of Narcissistic Personalities', pp. 253–4.

p. 70   **'It regularly emerges that the admired individual …':** Kernberg, *Borderline Conditions and Pathological Narcissism*, p. 236.

p. 70   **Relationships for a narcissist are 'like squeezing a lemon and then dropping the remains':** ibid., p. 233.

p. 70   **'the image of a hungry, enraged, empty self …':** ibid., pp. 233–4.

p. 71   **Rather than take pleasure:** Gabbard, *Psychodynamic Psychiatry in Clinical Practise*, p. 508.

p. 71   **Her influence threads through many of the more recent contributions:** Helen Block Lewis, *Shame and Guilt in Neurosis*, International Universities Press, New York, 1971; Michael Lewis, *Shame: The Exposed Self*, The Free Press, New York, 1992; Francis Broucek, 'Shame and its Relationship to Early Narcissistic Developments', *International Journal of Psychoanalysis*, vol. 65, 1982, pp. 369–78; Francis Broucek, *Shame and the Self*, Guilford Press, New York, 1991; Andrew P. Morrison, *Shame: The Underside of Narcissism*, The Analytic Press, New York, 1989; Ronningstam, *Identifying and Understanding the Narcissistic Personality*.

p. 72   **Careful empirical work by psychologists like June Tangney:** June Price Tangney and Ronda L. Dearing, *Shame and Guilt*, The Guilford Press, New York, 2002.

p. 73   **'When we deal with self-esteem …':** Morris Rosenberg, *Society and Adolescent Self-image*, Princeton University Press, Princeton, 1965.

p. 73   **US psychiatrist Donald Nathanson draws attention:** Donald Nathanson, *Shame and Pride: Affect, Sex, and the Birth of the Self*, W. W. Norton & Co., New York, 1992.

p. 74   **Jessica Tracy from the University of British Columbia**: Jessica Tracy, Joey T. Cheng, Jason P. Martens, and Richard W. Robins, 'The Emotional Dynamics of Narcissism: Inflated by Pride, Deflated by Shame', in Campbell and Miller (eds), *The Handbook of Narcissism and Narcissistic Personality Disorder*, pp. 330–3.

Chapter Four: The Roots of Empathy

p. 75   'We did her a favour ...': Bruce Perry and Maia Szalavtiz, *Born For Love: Why Empathy is Essential—And Endangered*, William Morrow, New York, 2010, pp. 120–44.

p. 77   **Ryan would be one of those terrifying:** Baron-Cohen, *Zero Degrees of Empathy.*

pp. 77–8   **Simone Weil thought that if one had empathy:** Raimond Gaita, *A Common Humanity: Thinking about Love and Truth and Justice*, Text Publishing, Melbourne, 1999, p. 104. Gaita gives a lyrical description of Weill's words on perspective taking. His original and profound essays show empathy at every turn of the page.

p. 78   **'If a child feels no emotional attachment ...':** R. Karr-Morse and M. S. Wiley, *Ghosts From the Nursery: Tracing the Roots of Violence*, Atlantic Monthly Press, New York, 1997, p. 199.

p. 79   **On both sides of the Atlantic:** Sue Gerhardt, *Why Love Matters: How Affection Shapes a Baby's Brain*, Brunner-Routledge, New York, 2004; Sue Gerhardt, *The Selfish Society: How We All Forgot to Love One Another and Made Money Instead*, Simon & Schuster, London, 2010; Daniel Siegel and Mary Hartzell, *Parenting From the Inside Out: How a Deeper Understanding Can Help You Raise Children Who Thrive*, Penguin, New York, 2004; Daniel Siegel, *Mindsight: The New Science of Personal Transformation*, Bantam Books, New York, 2011, p. 80. I have also written extensively on attachment and its social and political importance, and draw on this work for this section. See Anne Manne, *Motherhood: How Should We Care for Our Children*, Allen & Unwin, Sydney, 2005, and 'Love and Money: The Family and the Free Market', *Quarterly Essay*, no. 29, Black Inc., Melbourne, 2008.

p. 79   **Anna Freud and Dorothy Burlingham:** Dorothy Burlingham and Anna Freud, *Young Children in Wartime London*, Allen & Unwin, London, 1942; Dorothy Burlingham and Anna Freud, *Infants Without Families*, Allen & Unwin, London, 1944.

p. 80   **Their behaviour was clearly the result:** Robert Karen, *Becoming Attached: First Relationships and How They Shape Our Capacity to Love*, Oxford University Press, Cambridge, 1994.

p. 81   **'None of them seemed to have ...':** John Bowlby, *Attachment and Loss, Vol. 1: Attachment*, Penguin, London, 1971; John Bowlby, *Attachment and Loss, Vol. 2: Separation: Anxiety and Anger*, Basic Books, New York, 1972; John Bowlby, *Attachment and Loss, Vol. 3: Loss: Sadness* and *Depression*, Penguin Books, New York, 1980; John Bowlby, *A Secure Base: Clinical Applications of Attachment Theory*, Routledge, London, 1988. See also account in Karen, *Becoming Attached.*

p. 81 **'Behind the mask of indifference ...':** Bowlby in Karen, *Becoming Attached*, p. 54.

p. 81 **'Feeling for their parents had died ...':** James Robertson and Joyce Robertson, *Separation and the Very Young*, Free Association Press Books, London, 1989, p. 15.

p. 81 **No longer fitting into the 'reciprocity of family life':** Description from Karen, *Becoming Attached*, p. 75.

p. 82 **From the inside, though:** Mary Ainsworth, quoted in ibid.

p. 84 **Later tests showed that the avoidant babies:** Kraus Grossman, 'Evolution and History of Attachment Research', in S. Goldberg, R. Muir and J. Kerr (eds), *Attachment Theory: Social, Developmental and Clinical Perspectives*, NJ Analytic Press, Hillsdale, 1995, pp. 111–3.

p. 84 **'Already by the age of twelve months ...':** Bowlby, *A Secure Base.*

p. 84 **It is now clear that it was *behaviour on reunion*:** Although the Strange Situation Assessment has been the source of some controversy, the most recent, comprehensive and sophisticated longitudinal study by the US National Institute of Child Health and Development validated the procedure.

p. 85 **Alan Sroufe, a psychologist in Minnesota:** See Karen, *Becoming Attached*; Alan Sroufe, 'Infant-Caregiver Attachment and Patterns of Adaptation in Preschool: The Roots of Maladaptation and Competence', in M. Perlmutter (ed), *Minnesota Symposium in Child Psychology*, Hillsdale, Erlbaum, vol. 16, 1983, pp. 41–81. Sroufe has now followed these children through to adulthood, in Alan Sroufe, Byron Egeland, Elizabeth Carlson and Andrew Collins, *The Development of the Human Person: The Minnesota Study of Risk and Adaptation from Birth to Adulthood*, The Guilford Press, 2009.

p. 86 **While secure attachment:** Karen, *Becoming Attached*, p. 184.

p. 87 **They 'either found a way ...':** ibid. See also M. Troy and Alan Sroufe, 'Victimisation Among Preschoolers: Role of Attachment Relationship History', *Journal of the American Academy of Child and Adolescent Psychiatry*, vol. 26, no. 2, March 1987, pp. 166–72.

p. 87 **'Whenever I see a teacher ...':** Karen, *Becoming Attached*, p. 187–90.

p. 88 **'seemed too preoccupied with their own needs ...':** ibid., p. 190.

p. 88 **Avoidant boys in whom aggression:** Some children are much more difficult than others. Depressed mothers and those rated by nurses as having a low interest in their baby before it was born, for example, were more likely to have anxiously attached children at one year. This finding—the relationship of attachment security to how babies are treated—was confirmed by a much later Dutch study by Dymphna van den Boom, 'The Influence of Temperamental and Mothering on Attachment and Exploration: An Experimental Manipulation of Sensitive Responsiveness among Lower-Class Mothers with Irritable Infants', *Child Development*, vol. 65, no. 5, 1994, pp. 1457–77. See also Dymphna Van den Boom 'Sensitivity and Attachment: Next Steps for Developmentalists', *Child Development*, vol. 68, no. 4, 1997. Supportive therapy can help. Mothers with babies assessed just after birth as having difficult, irritable temperaments, were given such therapy to help establish sensitive nurturing care. Sixty-eight per cent of those receiving therapeutic intervention established secure relationships, compared with only 28 per cent of a control group who received no help.

p. 89   **The model develops through what Daniel Stern:** Daniel Stern, *The Interpersonal World of the Infant: A View from Psychoanalysis and Developmental Psychology*, Basic Books, New York, 1985; Daniel Stern, *The Motherhood Constellation*, Basic Books, New York, 1995.

p. 90   **as Peter Fonagy puts it, of 'mentalising':** P. Fonagy, H. Steele, M. Steele, G. Moran and A. Higgett, 'The Capacity for Understanding Mental States: The Reflective Self in Parent and its Significance for Security of Attachment', *Infant Mental Health Journal*, vol. 13, 1991, pp. 200–17. See also P. Fonagy and P. Target, 'Attachment and Reflective Function: Their Role in Self-Organisation', *Development and Psychopathology*, vol. 9, 2001, pp. 679–700.

p. 91   **'cavorting beasties':** Karen, *Becoming Attached*, p. 349.

pp. 91–2   **'Gazing is a potent form of social communication ...':** Stern, *The Interpersonal World of the Infant*, p. 23.

p. 92   **The babies in Tronick's experiment:** ibid., p. 102.

pp. 92–3   **'It is clear that interpersonal communion ...':** ibid., pp. 151–2.

p. 95   **There is modest confirmation in the literature:** Simine Vazire and David C. Funder, 'Impulsivity and Self-Defeating Behaviour of Narcissists', *Personality and Social Psychology Review*, vol. 10, no. 2, 2006, pp. 154–65.

p. 96   **This may well affect his trust:** Bowlby, *A Secure Base*, p. 55.

p. 98   **They will blame themselves:** Children may go to many lengths, even blaming themselves for bad treatment, including abuse, to protect the parent in their mind. Better to maintain a relationship with a bad 'object' (parent/loved one) than have no relationship at all, as British psychoanalyst W. R. D. Fairbairn pointed out.

p. 99   **'The picture such a person ...':** Bowlby, *A Secure Base*, p. 56.

p. 100   **The 'love' 'leaves him empty handed':** Alice Miller, 'Pathological Forms of Self Esteem Regulation', in Morrison (ed), *Essential Papers on Narcissism*, p. 342; for children and problems with object relations, and showing narcissism by preschool, Karen L. Weise and Steven Tuber, 'The Self and Object Representations of Narcissistically Disturbed Children: An Empirical Investigation', *Psychoanalytic Psychology*, vol. 21, no. 2, 2004, pp. 244–58.

p. 100   **As preschoolers they are prone to histrionic:** see Phebe Cramer, 'A 20-year Longitudinal Study of the Contribution of Parenting Styles: Preschool Precursors of Narcissism', *Journal of Research in Personality*, vol. 45, no. 1, 2011, pp. 19–28; Weise and Tuber, 'The Self and Object Representations of Narcissistically Disturbed Children'.

pp. 101–2   **'receive high ratings on items ...':** National Institute of Child Health and Development (NICHD), 'Does Amount of Time Spent in Childcare Predict Socio-Emotional Adjustment During the Transition to Kindergarten', *Child Development*, vol. 74, no. 4, 2003, pp. 1478–500.

p. 102   **There would be plenty of at-home parents among:** Paul Tough, *How Children Succeed: Grit, Curiosity and the Hidden Power of Character*, Houghton, Mifflin & Harcourt, Boston, 2012. See also Madeline Devine, *The Price of Privilege: How Parental Pressure and Material Advantage are Creating a Generation of Disconnected and Unhappy Kids*, HarperCollins, New York, 2006.

p. 103   **'The emotional disconnection ...':** These are Paul Tough's words, summarising Kindlon's research. Tough, *How Children Succeed*.

p. 103   **One of the most important studies of parenting:** L. J. Otway and V. L. Vignoles, 'Narcissism and Childhood Recollections'.

pp. 103–4   **Erin Myer and Virgil Zeigler Hill:** Erin M. Myers and Virgil Zeigler-Hill, 'How Much do Narcissists Really Like Themselves? Using the Bogus Pipeline Procedure to Better Understand the Self-Esteem of Narcissists', *Journal of Research in Personality*, vol. 46, 2012, pp. 102–5.

p. 105   **Phebe Cramer from Williams College:** Cramer, 'A 20-year Longitudinal Study of the Contribution of Parenting Styles', pp. 19–28.

p. 105   **According to child developmentalist Jay Belsky:** Jay Belsky, 'Modern Evolutionary Theory and Patterns of Attachment', in J. Cassidy and P. R. Shaver, *Handbook of Attachment Theory, Research and Applications*, Guilford Press, New York, 1999, pp. 249–64.

pp. 105–6 **'... it might be highly adaptive for an avoidantly attached ...':** Sarah Blaffer Hrdy, *Mother Nature: Natural Selection and the Female of the Species*, Chatto & Windus, London, 1999, p. 525. She also quotes Belsky, ibid.

p. 106   **A new study published in April 2014:** Sophie Moullin, Jane Waldfogel and Elizabeth Washbrook, 'Baby Bonds: Parenting, Attachment and a Secure Base for Children', The Sutton Trust, UK, March 2014. For media reports see Graeme Paton, 'Four-in-10 Children "Missing out on Good Parenting"', *Telegraph*, 21 March 2014; Princeton University, Woodrow Wilson School of Public and International Affairs, 'Four in 10 Infants Lack Strong Parental Attachments', *Science Daily*, 27 March 2014.

p. 106   **Two other important studies by Sara Konrath:** Sarah Konrath, Edward O'Brien, and Courtney Hsing, 'Changes in Dispositional Empathy in American College Students Over Time: A Meta-Analysis', *Personality and Social Psychology Review*, vol. 15, no. 2, May 2011, pp. 180–98.

p. 106   **As Konrath suggests, those students showing:** Jean Twenge, *Generation Me*.

p. 107   **This mistrust, however, was much more pronounced among younger people:** Sarah Konrath, William J. Chopnik, Courtney K. Hsing and Edward O'Brien, 'Changes in Adult Attachment Styles in American College Students Over Time: A Meta-Analysis', *Personality and Social Psychology Review*, vol. 18, no. 2, 12 April 2014.

p. 107   **Konrath clearly thinks so:** Konrath notes that insecure attachments were less likely when a mother worked in the early years but had the father or other family members caring for the children. Benefits of parental or extended family care were also found in the NICHD study. Konrath recognises that returning to traditional family patterns, is often not possible, or desirable, so instead suggests a child friendly compromise of several families grouping together to support one another with child care and provide community—a 'village' during the childrearing years.

p. 107   **Decades ago, John Bowlby warned:** Bowlby, *A Secure Base*.

Chapter Five: Others Exist for Me

p. 112   **'"Had consented sex with Nate" …':** Anna Krien, *Night Games: Sex, Power and Sport*, Black Inc., Melbourne, 2013, p. 22–3.

p. 113   **Over 'the next two hours …':** Sarah Ferguson quoted in ibid., p. 42.

p. 114   **'How could she even begin to consent to that?':** ibid., pp. 40–1.

p. 115   **However, less than a year later:** ABC News, 'Chief of Army David Morrison Tells Troops to Respect Women or "Get Out"', *ABC News*, 14 June 2013; Simon Lauder, 'Army Email Scandal: Expert says Sexism is Deeply Ingrained in Defence Force', *ABC News*, 14 June 2013; Ian McPhedran, 'Civilian Universities Have Higher Rate of Sexual Harassment, Sex Attacks than the Australian Defence Force Academy', *News Limited*, 30 July 2013.

p. 115   **'Fucking Sluts! No Means Yes! Yes Means Anal!':** For sexual culture on campus see Nathan Harden, *Sex and God at Yale: Porn, Political Correctness, and a Good Education Gone Bad*, Thomas Dunne Books and St Martin's Press, New York, 2012; Gail Dines, *Pornland: How Porn has Hijacked our Sexuality*, Beacon Press, Boston, 2010; Peggy Reeves Sanday, *Fraternity Gang Rape: Sex, Brotherhood, and Privilege on Campus*, New York University Press, New York, 1990; Michael Kimmel, *Guyland: The Perilous World Where Boys Become Men*, HarperCollins, New York, 2008; Emily Friedman, 'Yale University Under Investigation for "Hostile Sexual Environment"', *ABC News (US)*, 1 April 2011.

pp. 116–7 **'In my immediate circle of friends …':** Jessica Bennett, 'The Title IX Complaint Against Yale', *The Daily Beast*, 4 February 2011.

p. 117   **'Treat me as a person …':** Gaita, *A Common Humanity*.

p. 119   **'Why "*my* job"?' Kimmel asked the panel:** Kimmel, *Guyland*, p. 59.

p. 119   **While women often struggle:** ibid., p. 60.

p. 120   **'Sometimes, at other schools …':** ibid., p. 231.

p. 122   **Young men, brought up on such images:** ibid., p. 175.

pp. 122–3 **'The men who make pornography …':** ibid., p. 186.

p. 123   **Performance artist Tim Cayler admitted:** ibid., p. 179.

p. 123   **The young men interviewed:** ibid., p. 182.

pp. 123–4 **'Each time I happened …':** ibid., p. 187.

p. 125   **One of the men complained:** ibid., p. 182.

p. 125   **A Yale undergraduate interviewed:** ibid., p. 218.

p. 125   **Consider these remarks:** ibid., p. 218.

pp. 125–6 **'Sometimes I can't believe what I've done …':** ibid., pp. 218–9.

p. 126   **As Kimmel says:** ibid., p. 220.

p. 127   **In a seminal article in 2002:** Roy Baumeister, K. R. Catanese and H. M. Wallace, 'Conquest by Force: A Narcissistic Reactance Theory of Rape and Sexual Coercion', *Review of General Psychology*, vol. 6, 2002. See also Kimberly A. Lonsway and Louise F. Fitzgerald, 'Attitudinal Antecedents of Rape Myth Acceptance: A Theoretical and Empirical Re-examination', *Journal of Personality and Social Psychology*, vol. 68, no. 4, 1995, pp. 704–11; Brad J. Bushman, Angelica M. Bonacci, Roy F. Baumeister, Mirjam van Dijk, 'Narcissism, Sexual Refusal, and Aggression: Testing a Narcissistic Reactance Model of Sexual Coercion', *Journal of Personality and Social Psychology*, vol. 84, no. 5, 2003, pp. 1027–40; Kathryn M. Ryan, 'Further Evidence for a Cognitive Component of Rape', *Aggression and Violent Behavior*, vol. 9, 2004, pp. 579–604; Dennis E. Reidy, Amos Zeichner, Josh D. Foster and Marc A. Martinez, 'Effects of Narcissistic Entitlement and Exploitativeness on Human Physical Aggression', *Personality and Individual Differences*, vol. 44, 2008, pp. 865–75.

pp. 127–8 **The same pattern is shown:** Jeff Benedict, *Public Heroes, Private Felons: Athletes and Crimes against Women*, Northeastern University Press, Boston, 1997. See also Jeff Benedict, *Athletes and Acquaintance Rape*, Thousand Oaks, Sage Publishing, 1998.

p. 128   **Indeed 'defenders of star athletes …':** Baumeister, Catanese and Wallace, 'Conquest by Force', p. 124.

p. 128   **Their daydreams consist of:** R. Raskin and J. Novacek, 'Narcissism and the Use of Fantasy', *Journal of Clinical Psychology*, vol. 47, 1991, pp. 490–9; R. Raskin, J. Novacek and R. Hogan, 'Narcissism, Self-esteem, and Defensive Self-enhancement', *Journal of Personality*, vol. 59, 1991, pp. 19–38; R. Raskin, J. Novacek and R. Hogan, 'Narcissistic Self-esteem Management', *Journal of Personality and Social Psychology*, vol. 60, 1991, pp. 911–8.

p. 128   **One study shows:** Baumeister, Catanese and Wallace, 'Conquest by Force', p. 104, quoting a study by K. E. Dean and N. M. Malamuth, 'Characteristics of Men who Aggress Sexually and of Men who Imagine Aggressing: Risk and Moderating Variables', *Journal of Personality and Social Psychology*, vol. 72, 1997, pp. 449–55.

p. 128   **Narcissists are also more likely:** ibid., p. 97.

p. 130   **Others ask to kiss the victim:** These three examples taken from David Champion, *Narcissism and Entitlement: Sexual Aggression and the College Male*, LFP Scholarly Publishing, New York, 2002, p. 55.

p. 130   **Diana Scully's study:** Baumeister, Cantenese and Wallace, 'Conquest by Force', p. 110.

p. 130   **One man claimed:** D. Scully and J. Marolla, 'Convicted Rapists' Vocabulary of Motive: Excuses and Justifications', *Social Problems*, vol. 31, 1984, pp. 530–44.

p. 130   **Instead, even when they had used a weapon:** Baumeister, Cantenese and Wallace, 'Conquest by Force', summarising Scully's points.

p. 131   **Sexually aggressive men:** ibid., p. 111.

p. 131   **'Sexually coercive men ...':** ibid., p. 112.

p. 132   **This was exactly what they found:** Bushman, Bonacci, Baumeister and van Dijk, 'Narcissism, Sexual Refusal, and Aggression', pp. 1027–40 (especially p. 1027, 1034).

p. 132   **They simply tune out:** Baumeister, Cantenese and Wallace, 'Conquest by Force', p. 120.

p. 133   **'Rapists showed the highest levels ...':** Baumeister, Cantenese and Wallace, 'Conquest by Force', p. 122.

p. 134   **Narcissistic injury can be a 'triggering factor':** Champion, *Narcissism and Entitlement*.

Chapter Six: It's Not about the Bike

p. 137   **Linda stayed true:** Lance Armstrong, *It's Not about the Bike: My Journey Back to Life*, Allen & Unwin, Sydney, 2002 (Kindle edition).

p. 138   **His mother was his:** ibid.

p. 138   **'I was the guy who did weird sports ...':** ibid.

p. 138   **Already a self-made man:** ibid.

p. 139   **In his acceptance speech for his seventh victory:** Lance Armstrong's acceptance speech for the 2005 Tour de France, quoted in David Walsh, *Seven Deadly Sins: My Pursuit of Lance Armstrong*, Simon & Schuster, London, 2013 (Kindle edition). See also Joseph Burgo, 'How Aggressive Narcissism Explains Lance Armstrong', *Atlantic*, 28 January 2013.

p. 139   **He had become a 'Citizen Saint':** Daniel Coyle, *Lance Armstrong's War: One Man's Battle against Fate, Fame, Love, Death, Scandal, and a Few Other Rivals on the Road to the Tour de France*, HarperCollins, New York, 2009 (Kindle edition).

p. 140   **'In the beginning we had this brand …':** David Walsh, *From Lance to Landis: Inside the American Doping Controversy at the Tour de France*, Ballantine Books, New York, 2007, p. 166.

p. 140   **It *is* possible, said the Lance Armstrong story:** Spiegel Online, 'The Fraud Part I: Lance Armstrong's Long Fall', *Spiegel Online*, 15 January 2013.

p. 141   **As one commentator quipped:** ibid.

p. 144   **For a world-class athlete:** Quoted in Tyler Hamilton and Daniel Coyle, *The Secret Race: Inside the Hidden World of the Tour de France*, Bantam Books, New York, 2012, p. 50.

pp. 144–5 **'the race would start …':** ibid., pp. 30–1.

pp. 145–6 **'set an empty transfusion bag on a …':** ibid., p. 123.

p. 146   **'I felt good …':** ibid., p. 128.

p. 147   **Armstrong's notorious appetite, even while married:** Thomas Flynn, 'Dope on Wheels: Speed Read of "Wheelmen" About Lance Armstrong', *The Daily Beast*, 16 October 2013.

p. 148   **He might begin by seeming charming and charismatic:** Coyle, *Lance Armstrong's War*.

p. 148   **Once they stopped serving the interest of the self:** Hamilton and Coyle, *The Secret Race*, p. 151.

p. 148   **'Kevin thinks he's gonna get paid' …:** ibid., p. 132.

p. 148   **He assumed that everyone else:** ibid., p. 151.

p. 149   **When he saw British rider David Millar:** David Millar, *Racing through the Dark*, Simon & Schuster, New York, 2011, p. 125.

pp. 151–2 **At a Colorado restaurant, a rage-filled Armstrong created a scene:** Hamilton and Coyle, *The Secret Race*, p. 259.

p. 152   **He said to Oprah that in a telephone conversation:** Telegraph, 'Lance Armstrong Tells Oprah Winfrey: "I Called Betsy Andreu a Crazy Bitch, but I Never Called Her Fat"', *Telegraph*, 27 January 2013.

p. 153   **'I had started with nothing …':** Quoted in Burgo, 'How Aggressive Narcissism Explains Lance Armstrong'. Burgo quotes from Armstrong, *It's Not about the Bike* (my emphasis).

p. 154   **'He would shoot me for saying this …':** Quoted in Walsh, *From Lance to Landis*, p. 100.

p. 154   **'If you interrupted Lance …':** Hamilton and Coyle, *The Secret Race*, p. 111.

p. 154   **While other team members celebrated:** ibid., p. 118.

p. 155   **He said of the Armstrongs:** Armstrong, *It's Not about the Bike*.

p. 156   **She hoarded them all:** ibid.

p. 157   **'My mother and I became very open ...':** ibid. (my emphasis).

p. 158   **'That night I told my mother ...':** ibid.

p. 159   **Crawford apologised for disciplining Lance:** Quoted in Coyle, *Lance Armstrong's War.*

p. 161   **David Walsh, the journalist who has done most to expose the doping scandals:** Walsh, *From Lance to Landis*, p. 35. See also Geoffrey Wheatcroft, 'The Tour De Farce', *New York Times*, 9 November 2012.

p. 162   **There are, he said:** Christopher Lasch, 'The Corruption of Sports', *New York Review of Books*, 28 April 1977, p. 100, 105.

p. 162   **Surely nothing can be further from the spirit of play:** Coyle, *Lance Armstrong's War.*

p. 162   **There can be no sense of play:** ibid.

p. 162   **Nor for those like former Tour winner Marco Pantani:** Matt Rendell, *The Death of Marco Pantani*, Phoenix Publishing, London, 2004. See also Matt Rendell, 'The Long Lonely Road to Oblivion', *Guardian*, 7 March 2004.

p. 163   **Armstrong alleged in late 2013:** Matt Lawton, 'Cycling Chiefs Helped Me to Cheat! Disgraced Star's Explosive New Drug Claim Rocks Sport', *Mail Online*, 17 November 2013.

Chapter Seven: The Goddess of the Market

p. 168   **More specifically, the power of a contemptibly evil idea:** Ayn Rand, *The Voice of Reason: Essays in Objectivist Thought by Ayn Rand*, edited by Leonard Piekoff, Meridan, Penguin, New York, 1990.

p. 168   **'Altruism is a moral theory ...':** ibid., p. 151.

p. 168   **Whatever was good for them:** Rand repeats a common misquote of Charles Erwin Wilson, former president of General Motors and then Secretary of Defence. In a Senate inquiry, during a furore over the stock he owned, he was asked if he would make a decision as Secretary of Defence against General Motors' interests. He said yes, but qualified it with how he couldn't conceive of it happening, 'because for years I thought what was good for our country was good for General Motors, and vice versa'. This was then often misquoted as 'What's good for General Motors is good for the country'.

p. 169   **In Jennifer Burns' biography of Rand:** Jennifer Burns, *Goddess of the Market: Ayn Rand and the American Right*, Oxford University Press, New York, 2009.

p. 170 **Rand's narcissism was on display:** Gary Weiss, *Ayn Rand Nation: The Hidden Struggle for America's Soul*, St Martin's Press, New York, 2012.

p. 174 **This, as one commentator puts it:** Robert Manne and David McKnight (eds), *Goodbye to All That*, Black Inc., Melbourne, 2010, p. 15.

p. 176 **Sociologist Richard Sennett, in his landmark study:** Richard Sennett, *The Corrosion of Character: The Personal Consequences of Work in the New Capitalism*, W. W. Norton & Co., New York, 1998, p. 51. See also Richard Sennett, *Respect: The Formation of Character in an Age of Inequality*, Allen Lane, London, 2003. The quote from the *New York Times* writer comes from a collection, New York Times (author), *Downsizing America*, Three Rivers Press, 1996, pp. 7–8.

p. 176 **As a *New York Times* writer put it:** Quoted in Sennett, *The Corrosion of Character*, p. 97.

pp. 176–7 **At one end was a highly paid:** Helen Trinca and Catherine Fox, *Better than Sex: How a Whole Generation Became Hooked on Work*, Random House, Sydney, 2004.

p. 177 **At the other were those affected by the 'Brazilianisation':** Ulrich Beck, *The Brave New World of Work*, Polity Press, Cambridge, 2000.

p. 177 **There was a shift not merely in economic activity:** Zygmunt Bauman, 'On the Post-Modern Deployment of Sex', in his *Postmodernity and Its Discontents*, p. 146.

p. 177 **On the eve of the GFC:** Stephen Lacey, 'This Whopping Life', *Sydney Morning Herald*, 8–9 March 2003. See also Clive Hamilton, *Growth Fetish*, Allen & Unwin, Sydney, 2003.

p. 180 **By 2008 more than a third of Americans:** Weiss, *Ayn Rand Nation*.

p. 180 **'The basis of regulation is armed force ...':** Bill Goldstein, 'Word for Word/"Greenspan Shrugged": When Greed Was a Virtue And Regulation the Enemy', *New York Times*, 21 July 2002.

p. 182 **In 1963, in pro-business America, Greenspan warned darkly:** ibid. (my emphasis).

pp. 182–3 **In the face of rising concern:** Charles R. Morris, *The Two Trillion Dollar Meltdown: Easy Money, High Rollers and the Great Credit Crash*, Black Inc., Melbourne, 2009, p. 54.

p. 183 **As Morris says sharply:** ibid., p. 55.

p. 183 **Because bank loans seemed 'insured':** ibid., pp. 68–9; Manne and McKnight (eds), *Goodbye to All That*, pp. 22–3.

p. 183 **'Put up $1 billion ...':** Morris, *The Two Trillion Dollar Meltdown*, p. 61.

290

p. 184   **Greenspan's fellow Federal Reserve governor:** ibid., p. 69.

p. 184   **'The industry's underbelly ...':** According to Yale University's Robert Shiller, ibid., p. 69.

p. 184   **'The global financial system ...':** Quoted in Morris, *The Two Trillion Dollar Meltdown*, p. 63.

p. 185   **Deregulation prompted the greatest real estate boom:** Weiss, *Ayn Rand Nation*.

p. 185   **Greenspan—who had earlier written:** Quoted in ibid.

p. 185   **He then gave a little lecture to the congressman:** Quoted in ibid.

p. 186   **In the *Financial Times*:** Quoted in ibid.

p. 186   **'So the meltdown of the world ...':** ibid.

p. 188   **But in the neoliberal era:** Tomas Chamorro-Premuzic, 'The Dark Side of Executive Narcissism: How CEOs Destroy Companies' Reputation and Employee Morale', *Huffington Post*, 2 January 2014.

p. 188   **And the top 1 per cent took almost one-quarter:** Julia Baird, 'Rich People Couldn't Care Less', *Sydney Morning Herald*, 12 October 2013.

p. 188   **President Obama, in his 2011 and 2013 addresses:** Paul Krugman, 'The Undeserving Rich', *New York Times*, 19 January 2014.

p. 190   **John Thain, CEO of Merrill Lynch, certainly didn't sit on his hands:** Louise Story, 'Chief Struggles to Revive Merrill Lynch', *New York Times*, 11 July 2008.

p. 190   **As the *Huffington Post* reported:** Chamorro-Premuzic, 'The Dark Side of Executive Narcissism'.

p. 191   **'The leaders who work most effectively ...':** Peter Drucker, quoted in ibid.

Chapter Eight: Because I'm Worth It!

p. 195   **There has been a movement from the delayed gratification of the industrial era:** Bauman, 'On the Post-Modern Deployment of Sex', p. 146.

p. 195   **In the era of affluenza:** Term coined by Robert Frank.

p. 196   **'A house may be large or small ...':** Karl Marx, 'Wage Labour and Capital', *Neue Rheinische Zeitung*, 5–8 and 11 April 1849 (delivered 1847).

p. 198   **There are more than a thousand sites in Australia:** Lacey, 'This Whopping Life'. See also Hamilton, *Growth Fetish*.

p. 198   **The TV star endorsing the product range, Patrick Dempsey:** Peter Moss, *There Are Alternatives: Markets and Democratic*

Experimentalism in Early Childhood Education and Care, working paper no. 54, Bernard van Leer Foundation and the Bertelsmann Stiftung, The Hague, 27 August 2009.

p. 200   **New work from Californian psychologist Paul Piff:** P. Piff, 'Wealth and the Inflated Self: Class, Entitlement, and Narcissism', *Personality and Social Psychology Bulletin* (in press); P. Piff, D. M. Stancato, S. Côté, R. Mendoza-Denton and D. Keltner, 'Higher Social Class Predicts Increased Unethical Behavior', *Proceedings of the National Academy of Sciences*, vol. 109, no. 11, 13 March 2012, pp. 4086–91; M. W. Kraus, P. Piff, R. Mendoza-Denton, M. L. Rheinschmidt and D. Keltner, 'Social Class, Solipsism, and Contextualism: How the Rich are Different from the Poor', *Psychological Review*, vol. 119, no. 3, 2012, pp. 546–72; L. R. Saslow, R. Willer, M. Feinberg, P. K. Piff, K. Clark, D. Keltner and S. Saturn, 'My Brother's Keeper? Compassion Predicts Generosity More Among Less Religious Individuals', *Social Psychological and Personality Science*, vol. 4, no. 1, January 2013, pp. 31–38; P. K. Piff, M. W. Kraus, S. Côté, B. H. Cheng, D. Keltner, 'Having Less, Giving More: The Influence of Social Class on Prosocial Behaviour', *Journal of Personality and Social Psychology*, vol. 99, no. 5, November 2010, pp. 771–84.

p. 201   **They primed participants with status and wealth statements:** Maia Szalavitz, 'Wealthy Selfies: How Being Rich Increases Narcissism', *Time Magazine*, 20 August 2013.

p. 202   **Tellingly, his entitled attitude paid dividends:** ibid.

p. 203   **Piff says: 'The more severe inequality becomes …':** ibid.

p. 204   **He recognised that he had been rewarded by a market system:** Warren Buffett, 'My Philanthropic Pledge', <www.givingpledge.org> (accessed 8 May 2014).

p. 205   **'There's this idea that the more you have, the less entitled and more grateful you feel …':** Szalavitz, 'Wealthy Selfies'.

p. 205   **In 2011, the wealthiest Americans:** Ken Stern, 'Why The Rich Don't Give to Charity: The Wealthiest Americans Donate 1.3 Percent of Their Income; The Poorest, 3.2 Percent. What's Up With That?', *Atlantic*, 20 March 2013.

p. 206   **'We're not suggesting rich people are bad at all …':** Szalavitz, 'Wealthy Selfies'.

p. 206   **'… They are more likely to exhibit characteristics …':** Ken Stern, 'Why the Rich Don't Give to Charity'. Jean Twenge praised Piff's study because he used such a wide range of experimental methods in reaching his findings.

pp. 206–7   **'moves beyond the myth of its practitioners ...':** Ginia Belafante, 'In "The Devil Wears Prada", It's Not Couture, It's Business (With Accessories)', *New York Times*, 18 June 2006.

p. 207   **Tom Wolfe, in his 1976 essay 'The Me Decade':** Tom Wolfe, 'The Me Decade: The Third Great Awakening', *New York Magazine*, 23 August 1976.

p. 208   **Constantine Sedikides, a leading scholar in narcissism at the University of Southampton:** Constantine Sedikides, Sylwia Cisek and Claire M. Hart, 'Narcissism and Brand Name Consumerism', in Campbell and Miller, *The Handbook of Narcissism and Narcissistic Personality Disorder*, pp. 382–92.

p. 210   **There is more:** ibid.

p. 210   **As Yi-Fi Tuan has remarked:** Yi-Fi Tuan, 'The Significance of the Artifact', *Geographical Review*, vol. 70, 1980, pp. 462–72, quoted in Sedikides, Cisek and Hart, 'Narcissism and Brand Name Consumerism', p. 386.

p. 210   **When people agreed with such items:** Sedikides, Cisek and Hart, 'Narcissism and Brand Name Consumerism', p. 386.

pp. 212–3   **'the first and most noteworthy ...':** Carolyn Pulfrey and Fabrizio Butera, 'Why Neo-liberal Values of Self-Enhancement Lead to Cheating in Higher Education: A Motivational Account', *Psychological Science*, vol. 24, no. 11, 2013, p. 2159.

p. 213   **In a single paragraph, Wolfe captures the myopic self-absorption:** It was specifically an Erhard Seminars Training (EST) program, which ran weekend-long workshops with additional evening sessions. They were known for the aggressive, cajoling and bullying tactics of the life coaches and for sessions that went on for hours, with few bathroom breaks. People often responded to being shouted at and browbeaten by having a religious conversion-type experience.

p. 215   **'In the Howard years Australia became a much meaner ...':** Karl Mathiesen, 'We Got the PM We Voted for, Says Brown', *New Matilda*, 13 December 2013.

Chapter Nine: The Care Deficit

p. 218   **'There are these two young fish ...':** David Foster Wallace, 'This Is Water: Some Thoughts, Delivered on a Significant Occasion, about Living a Compassionate Life', commencement address to Kenyon College, Ohio, United States, 21 May 2005.

p. 223   **Sandal suggests that outsourcing some things 'is to demean them ...':** Michael Sandal, *What Money Can't Buy: The Moral Limits of Markets*, Penguin, London, 2012, p. 10.

p. 224   **Just like a bull's semen, colostrum, the highly nutritious substance:** Julie Stephens, *Confronting Postmaternal Thinking: Feminism, Memory and Care*, Columbia University Press, New York, 2011, p. 159.

p. 224   **'Duck into the ladies room at a conference ...':** ibid., p. 135.

p. 227   **Others cheered her on:** Amy Chua, *Battle Hymn of the Tiger Mother*, Penguin, New York, 2011. Chua said in an interview that she wrote the book to get attention, in competition with her husband Jed, who had recently penned a crime novel that was a bestseller in the United Kingdom. If she wanted attention, she certainly got it.

p. 229   **Right about the same time, there was a headline in the *Australian*:** Jonathon Leake, 'Pushy Parents Damage Rich Kids, Research Finds', *Australian*, 10 November 2013.

pp. 231–2 **When these children go off the rails:** Suniya Luthar, 'Poor Little Rich Kids', *Psychology Today*, 5 November 2013.

p. 233   **More cheating occurs too:** Quoted in ibid.

p. 233   **'is a way of transferring the cult of efficiency ...':** Arlie Russell Hochschild, *The Time Bind: When Work Becomes Home and Home Becomes Work*, Henry Holt & Company, New York, 1997, p. 50.

p. 234   **'the truth is these parents or children ...':** Chrystia Freeland, 'Poor Little Rich Kids', *Reuters*, 9 May 2013.

p. 236   **As Ulrich Beck writes in *The Brave New World of Work*:** Friedrich Nietzsche, quoted in Beck, *The Brave New World of Work*, p. 61.

p. 238   **The women's movement's long-overdue struggle:** Barbara Pocock, *The Work/Life Collision: What Work is Doing to Australians and What to do About it*, Federation Press, Annandale, 2003.

p. 238   **As Hochschild notes, for an increasing number of women too:** Hochschild, *The Time Bind*, p. 197.

p. 238   **In the new capitalism:** Richard Sennett makes this point; 'exclusive reliance' is his phrase.

p. 238   **According to historians Linda Gordon and Nancy Fraser:** Nancy Fraser and Linda Gordon, 'A Genealogy of *Dependency*: Tracing a Keyword of the U. S. Welfare State', *Signs*, vol. 19, no. 2, 1994, pp 309–36; Eva Fuda Kittay and Ellen K. Feder, *The Subject of Care: Feminist Perspectives on Dependency*, Rowan & Littlefield, Lanham, p. 26.

p. 242   **As psychiatrist John Bowlby once said:** As quoted in Sennett, *The Corrosion of Character*, p. 97.

Chapter Ten: Narcissism and the Commons

p. 246   **In the same year the CSIRO confirmed Australia was getting hotter:** Zoe Leviston, Jennifer Price, Sarah Malkin and Rod McCrea, *Fourth Annual Survey of Australian Attitudes to Climate Change: Interim Report*, CSIRO, Perth, January 2014.

p. 246   **'Why,' asks social theorist Ulrich Beck:** Ulrich Beck, 'Climate for Change, or How to Create a Green Modernity?', *Theory, Culture and Society*, vol. 27, no. 2–3, 2010, pp. 254–66.

p. 246   **Hannah Arendt once said about another catastrophe:** Hannah Arendt, *Men in Dark Times*, Harcourt Brace & Company, Orlando, 1968.

p. 248   **In his *States of Denial*:** Stanley Cohen, *States of Denial: Knowing about Atrocities and Suffering*, Polity Press, Cambridge, 2001, p. 50. He is quoting from Saul Bellow, *Mr Sammler's Planet*, Widenfield & Nicholson, London, 1970, p. 81.

p. 250   **In her arresting book:** Kari Norgaard, *Living in Denial: Climate Change, Emotions and Everyday Life*, The MIT Press, Cambridge, 2011.

p. 253   **Sociologists Riley Dunlap and Aaron McCright:** Aaron McCright and Riley E. Dunlap, 'Cool Dudes: The Denial of Climate Change among Conservative White Males in the United States', *Global Environmental Change*, vol. 21, no. 4, October 2011, pp. 1163–72.

p. 253   **Myanna Lahsen, an anthropologist:** Myanna Lahsen, 'Experiences of Modernity in the Greenhouse: A Cultural Analysis of a Physicist "Trio" Supporting the Backlash Against Global Warming', *Global Environmental Change*, vol. 18, 2008, pp. 204–19.

p. 255   **'desired presentation of self can be characterised …':** ibid.

p. 257   **The Cool Dudes' denialism:** Dan M. Kahan, 'Culture and Identity-Protective Cognition: Explaining the White Male Effect in Risk Perception', *Journal of Empirical Legal Studies*, vol. 4, no. 3, 2007.

p. 258   **In an extraordinarily important contribution:** W. Keith Campbell, Carrie Pierce Bush, Amy B. Brunell and Jeremy Shelton, 'Understanding the Social Costs of Narcissism: The Case of the Tragedy of the Commons', *Personality and Social Psychology Bulletin*, vol. 31, 2005, pp. 1358ff.

p. 259   **Garrett Hardin's 1968 essay:** Garrett Hardin, 'The Tragedy of the Commons', *Science*, vol. 162, no. 3859, 13 December 1968, pp. 1243–8.

p. 262   **The big new idea to avert the consequences:** Clive Hamilton, *Earth Masters: Playing God with the Climate*, Allen & Unwin, Sydney, 2013.

p. 263   **'buy things we don't need with money ...':** Clive Hamilton, 'Till Debt Us Do Part: Where Will the Credit Binge End for the Many Thousands of Australians who now Live in Permanent and Growing Debt?', *Four Corners*, 24 May 2004.

p. 264   **Kasser has consistently found:** Tim Kasser, *The High Price of Materialism*, MIT Press, Cambridge, 2003; Tim Kasser and D. Kanner, *Psychology and Consumer Culture: The Struggle for a Good Life in a Materialistic World*, American Psychological Association, 2013.

p. 264   **In Australia, Shaun Saunders and Don Munro found:** Shaun Saunders and Don Munroe, 'The Construction and Validation of a Consumer Orientation Questionnaire (SCOI) designed to measure Fromm's (1955) "Marketing Character" in Australia', *Social Behaviour and Personality*, vol. 28, no. 3, 2000, pp. 215–40; Shaun Saunders and Don Munroe, 'Maslow's Hierarchy of Needs and its Relationship with Psychological Health and Materialism', *South Pacific Journal of Psychology*, vol. 10, 1998, pp. 15–25.

p. 265   **'When family environments poorly satisfy ...':** Kennon M. Sheldon, Charles P. Nichols and Tim Kasser, 'Americans Recommend Smaller Ecological Footprints when reminded of Intrinsic American Values of Self—Expression, Family and Generosity', *Ecopsychology*, vol. 3, no. 2, June 2011. See also Taciano L. Milfont, Isabel Richter, Chris G. Sibley, Marc S. Wilson and Ronald Fischer, 'Environmental Consequences of the Desire to Dominate and Be Superior', *Personality and Social Psychology Bulletin*, vol. 39, no. 9, September 2013, pp. 1127–38.

p. 265   **Kasser also found that the more:** Sheldon, Nichols and Kasser, 'Americans Recommend Smaller Ecological Footprints when reminded of Intrinsic American Values of Self—Expression, Family and Generosity'.

Index